I0818373

PASSPORT PHOTO SERVICE

PASSPORT PHOTO SERVICE

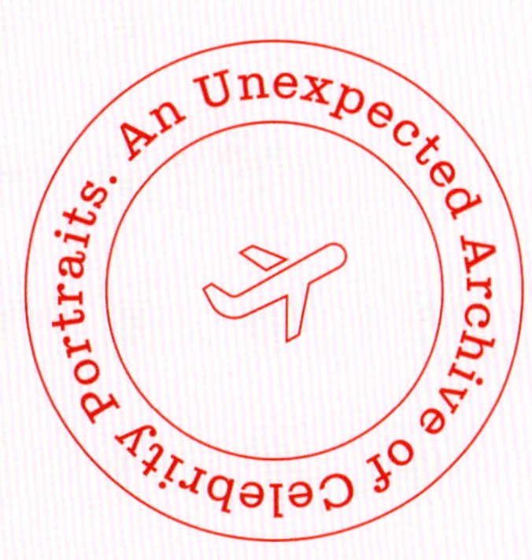

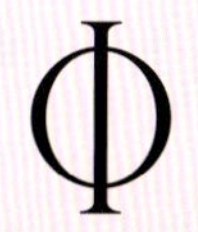

PHILIP SHARKEY

For Michael
6 November 1955 – 23 September 1985

CONTENTS

INTRODUCTION

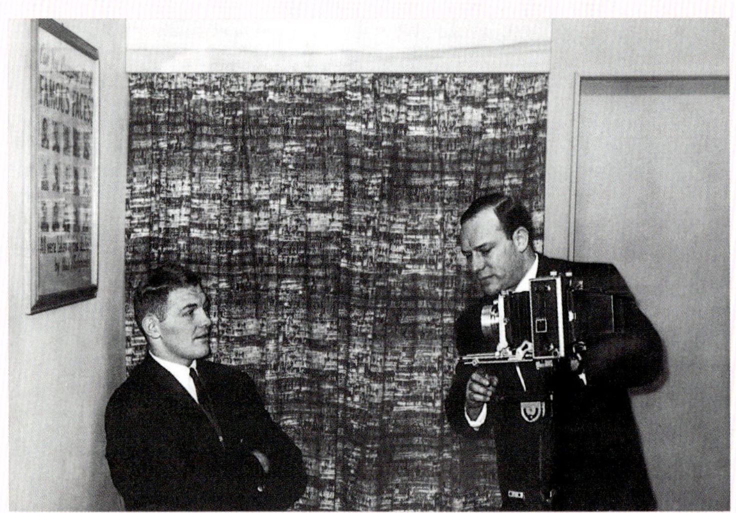

OXFORD ST. OPP. SELFRIDGES 1953–2019

PHILIP SHARKEY

No. 6

'Muhammad Ali, Joan Collins, Mick Jagger, Arnold Schwarzenegger – I don't believe you've photographed all these famous people!' I heard statements like this many times while I was working in the photography studio that my family ran for sixty-six years on Oxford Street, London. One ordinary Saturday in 1987, a customer was scrutinizing the three large frames full of celebrity passport photos that hung on the wall. Tutting and shaking his head, he – like other customers before him – expressed his disbelief that they had all come to us. A lady in her early sixties, dressed casually and sporting a large pair of glasses, replied, 'Well, everybody needs a passport, so they have to have somewhere to go to be photographed.' After the gentleman had left, Ava Gardner looked up at me with a smile. 'I don't think I convinced him,' she said.

Passport Photo Service was where people in London went to be photographed for their travel documents, visas and green cards from 1953 until 2019, and some of them just happened to be famous. From the day Errol Flynn kicked open our door, placed his hands on his hips, puffed out his chest and announced to all, 'Yep, it's me!', a steady stream of worldwide travellers made their way up the flight of stairs to be snapped by us.

My father, David Sharkey, came up with the idea for a quick and easy photography service when he got talking to an angry American in Wolfe's Coffee Shop in London's West End. The American was complaining, 'This lousy town, it's so backward! I need to fly back to the States, and I can't get my passport photo developed until tomorrow.' Dave realized that the man was right – there was no place in the city that could provide such fast service.

A professional boxer who grew up in London's East End, Dave got his start in photography capturing images of events all over the city, juggling that with his boxing career. An injury in the form of a badly cut eye in 1950, as well as the recognition that there would be a more rewarding future for him in photography, encouraged him to end his time in the ring. After a few years snapping tourists at the seaside and in Trafalgar Square, Dave – who had always had an ambition to have his own Mayfair studio, and was now encouraged by the spark of inspiration from the angry American – set up Express Photos in 1953 on Oxford Street. In 1957, the year I was born, he moved the business to our longest home, 449 Oxford Street, where the renamed Passport Photo Service would exist until 2019, originally on the first floor and later upstairs. It was a building with an interesting past; the second-floor space had been the workshop of the Arts and Crafts textile designer William Morris from 1877 to 1919, and, although it retained the original skylights, none of his famous wallpaper survived. We were directly opposite the luxury department store Selfridges, and being close to Grosvenor Square meant that we were less than a minute's walk from the US, Canadian and Japanese embassies. 'READY IN 10 MINUTES' became our slogan before anyone else in the city was able to provide such a quick turnaround.

The studio was a family affair. In 1955 Dave met and married Ann, a professional dancer who, at twenty-two, was already a veteran of the London Palladium and other major variety venues in the UK. Giving up her career on the stage, Ann became the receptionist, and her younger brother, my uncle Peter, joined the business soon afterwards. Only fifteen years old when he started, Peter retired more than fifty years later at the age of sixty-six. He was an integral part of the studio's success, and his natural skill in design and invention enabled him to hand-build the technical equipment, such as enlargers, on which the business relied. Whenever we moved premises, he would configure the design of the new studio to ensure that we operated as efficiently as possible, even tackling most of the electrical work. He also designed the iconic photo wallets that contained the prints we produced.

Since we were not on the ground floor and immediately visible to shoppers, one of the most effective ways to advertise was our 'sandwich board' men. The two longest-serving of these were Arthur and Henry, who walked up and down Oxford Street in all weathers from the 1950s until the late 1970s. Arthur had been in the merchant navy and was always dressed in a shirt and tie. Henry stood out much more, with his long, unkempt beard, straggly hair and ripped, ragged clothes. (We only found out that 'Henry' was actually 'James' when, after he retired, my father started to pay him a pension and soon thereafter received

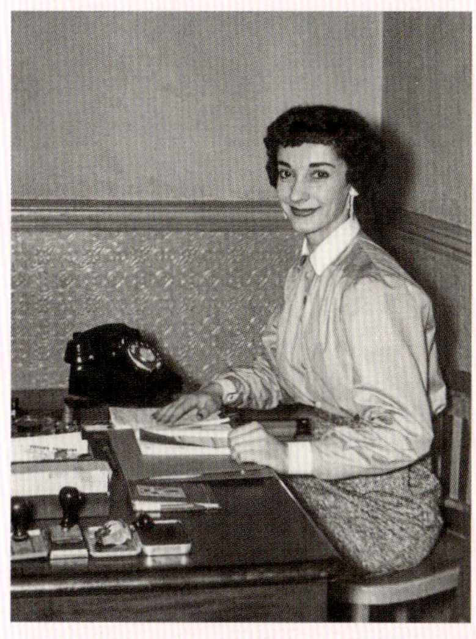

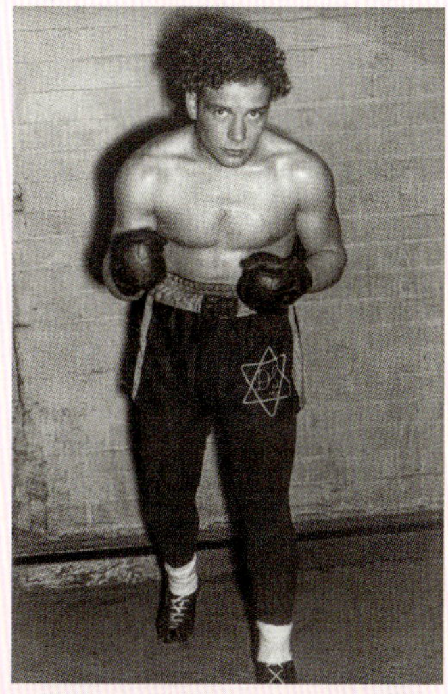

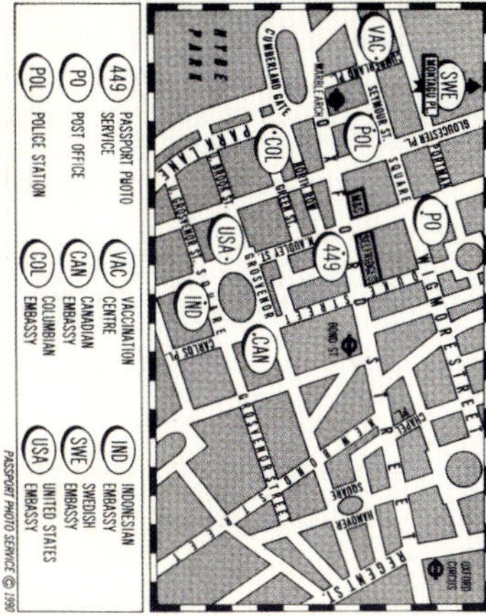

ANN GILBERT (top left)
Receptionist at 309 Oxford Street, 1955.

DAVE SHARKEY (top right)
Professional boxer, 1947.

PASSPORT PHOTO SERVICE
Photo wallet (bottom) with embassy locations, 1990.

No. 9

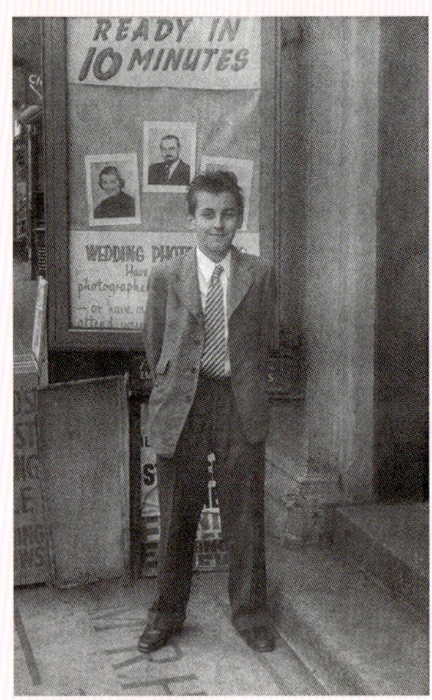

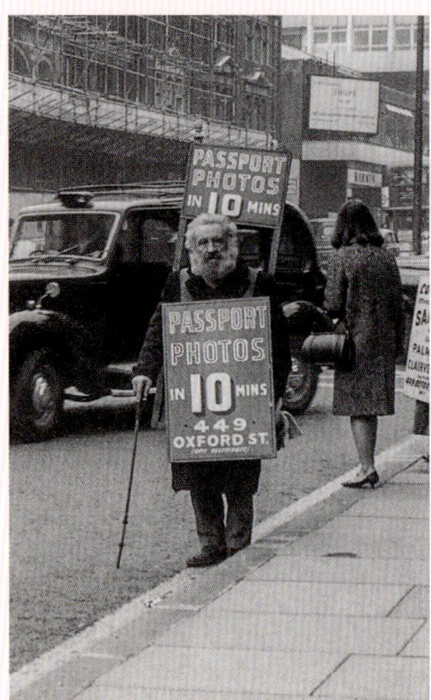

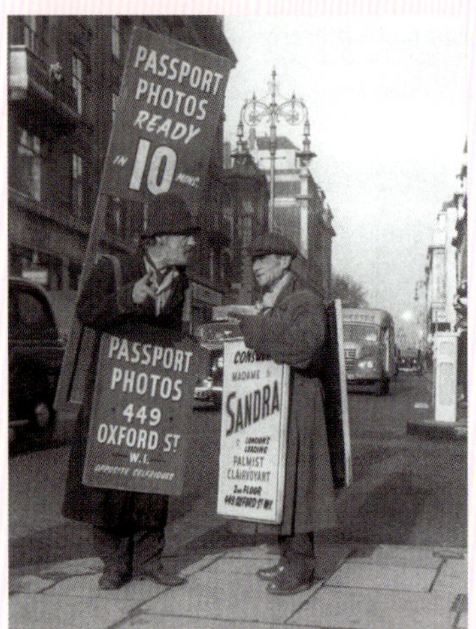

PETER GILBERT (top left) Outside 309 Oxford St., 1956.

JAMES (AKA HENRY) (top right), the sandwich board man on Oxford St., late 1950s.

'THE MEETING' (bottom) Sandwich board men, 1950s.

a letter from the government stating that they could not honour a state pension for 'James' if we were also giving him one.) With the help of Arthur and Henry, Passport Photo Service's business grew steadily and customers – both famous and unknown – kept coming through the doors.

I started working at the studio in 1973, when I was sixteen, and our ten-minute promise was still setting us apart from the countless other photo services in the city, even if the technology we relied on to make it happen had changed. We originally used card negatives, or emulsion-covered cards, which we would develop by hand in the darkroom. We would develop, fix, wash and dry the negative, then place it on the enlarger to print and repeat the process until we were finally ready to cut the prints by hand to the required size – all in ten minutes. In 1977 card negatives became obsolete, and we bought a Kodak Versamat machine that developed large 5 × 4 inch (12.7 × 10 cm) film negatives in five minutes. By 1981 we had acquired a Kodak Veribrom machine that developed completed prints in five minutes, so there was no more making up dishes of chemicals in the morning, and the whole process was much less labour-intensive.

Every country had its own specifications and rules regarding passport and visa photos. Possibly the most particular was Canada, where the prints had to have the photo studio's name and address stamped on the back, as well as the date the photograph was taken, and there had to be a strip underneath the photo for the applicant to sign their name. After assassinating Martin Luther King Jr in 1968, James Earl Ray had fled the United States on a forged Canadian passport, so Canada devised these rules to make its passports harder to fake.

For the Dutch passport, the sitter had to be shown in three-quarters profile, with the left ear clearly visible. US green card visas required the opposite: a three-quarters profile with the right ear visible, the photograph exactly 1½ in (3.8 cm) square. US passports were larger than those of other countries because the photos were originally 2½ in (6.4 cm) square, and that meant they were easier to pickpocket. First thing most mornings we had a queue of frustrated American customers in emergency situations and in need of new passports.

Indonesian passport photos had to have a red background, Malaysian blue. Brazil's had to measure 2 × 3 in (5 × 7.5 cm). The head of their passport section at the Brazilian embassy was a lady who hated 'hippies' and thought long hair made men look degenerate. She asked us to make sure that long hair was behind the customers' ears and tucked into their shirt so it did not show in the photo. She also supplied us with a tie for men to wear so that all their citizens looked smart and respectable.

By the late 1990s we had started using what is by today's standards a fairly basic digital camera, which was connected to its own printer. The quality was not as good as our 5 × 4 in (12.5 × 10 cm) negatives, but customers were now able to choose the final image. With the advent of e-passports in 2006, a result of the 9/11 terrorist attacks in the United States in 2001, each subject now had to face the camera straight on with no smile or glasses, and much creativity was lost as global travel documents became standardized.

In 2014 we moved to a new studio at the rear of our building, with a new address: 39 North Row. We had never missed a day of trading, not even when the IRA bombed Selfridges in December 1974, and the new location did not affect our business too significantly. In fact, we were more visible to people coming from Grosvenor Square. But by early 2018 many of the embassies had left the neighbourhood, and the US embassy's move that year to its new site at Nine Elms, across the Thames, was the final nail in the coffin. In June 2019, Passport Photo Service finally closed its doors.

Since 1953 we had photographed countless people for their passport photos, including more than 800 celebrities, so many that we often ran out of space in our big frames of famous faces. That sometimes got us into trouble. Once we took down the portrait of an actor who had been on our wall for some time to make room for better-known celebs. A few days later, of course, she waltzed into the studio for her new passport photo and noticed immediately, announcing, 'Oh, I do love seeing who you've added since I was last here!' The others ran for the darkroom and hid, leaving me to stutter that I must have forgotten to put her back when we had moved things around.

I'm sure there were plenty of celebs we didn't recognize, and some who 'got away'. One customer told me she had brought in the singer Marvin Gaye in the 1970s, when she worked for a record company and he had been living in Belgium. He was apparently in a sorry state, having lost both his passport and his ID. When she went to the American embassy with him, the only way he could convince the officials of his identity was to sing for them. The legendary model Twiggy came in with her daughter, and although she was friendly, I thought it best not to ask her for her photograph since she had been snapped so often. I did ask Rod Stewart, though, when he came in with his girlfriend. 'I'm not working today, thanks,' was his reply. Fair enough. As is bound to happen with a sixty-plus-year-old business, some negatives seem to have been lost along the way. My father told me he photographed Gary Cooper and Julie Andrews, among others, but I've never been able to find those prints.

Our dedicated following was mainly thanks to one thing: location. Being a brisk walk from the American embassy meant that most people could just march right in. Repeat celebrity customers would become friends, coming by even when they didn't need a photograph and holding court with those waiting for their prints. John McDonald, the well-known sports announcer, and 'background artist' Michael Leader came by often. Leader was always happy to remind us and other customers that he was the storm trooper who famously bangs his head on the beam in the first *Star Wars* film. We also got lucky with the consistency of our staff over the decades; alongside Peter, other long-serving photographers were Bridie Bonas, Ivo Carmo, Piotr Gorka, Graeme Humphrey and Stephen Oakes-Monger.

But our promise of speed – of developing photographs in less than ten minutes, guaranteed – as well as our discretion didn't hurt. Over the years we had requests from newspapers, such as the *Sun*, the *Daily Mirror* and the *Daily Express*, to publish our celebrity photographs, and we always refused. In all my years working, I had to sign only three non-disclosure agreements as people just trusted us. For one of these, we had to go miles out of the city at eight o'clock sharp to snap an Oscar-winning actor under a veil of secrecy. I sent one of our photographers, Piotr, who got stuck for eight hours waiting for her. We had to charge her overtime, and the bill ended up being £892. Afterwards, we found out she had an appointment at the US embassy the next morning. Well, I was always at the studio by 7.15 a.m. If she had just popped by before her appointment, as many others did, she would have only had to pay £8.50!

It wasn't until the studio closed that I thought about telling Passport Photo Service's story, since independent family businesses like ours are becoming less common, not just on Oxford Street, but throughout London. One thing is for sure: whoever we photographed, famous or not, we treated them all with the same care and respect. In that moment, when the flash goes off, your passport photo becomes a great leveller.

It has been a hard task to select the more than three hundred images that feature in this book, which are organized loosely alphabetically. We could easily have chosen another five hundred people who are just as interesting and remarkable. I hope you enjoy our story, a story that is not only about the changing faces that came through our doors – some of them famous – but also about the changing face of London and of a family business.

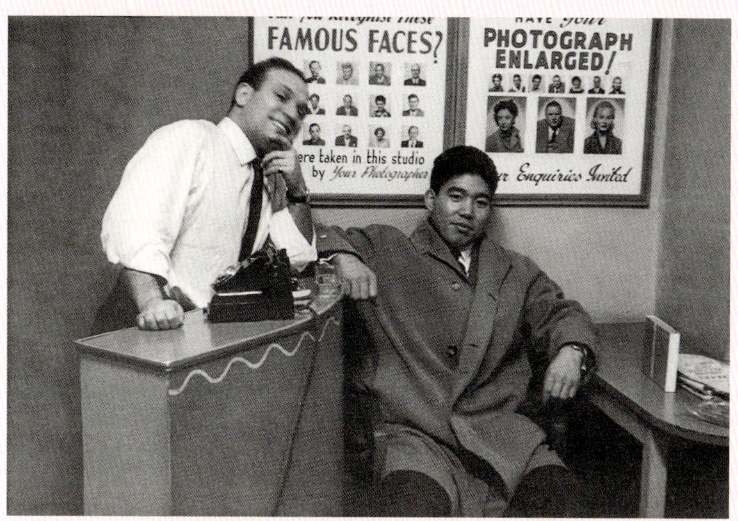

PASSPORT PHOTOS

READY IN TEN MINUTES

DOCUMENTS PHOTO-COPIED INSTANTLY

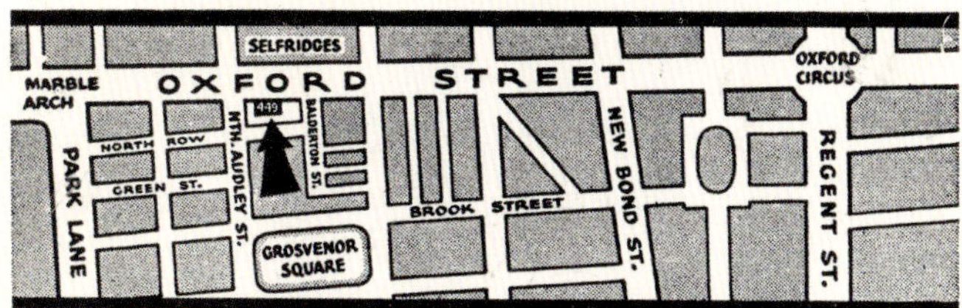

PASSPORT PHOTO SERVICE

449 OXFORD STREET, LONDON, W.1

Telephone : 01-629 8540

DAVE SHARKEY (top) with customer, 1962.

MAP CARD (bottom) from the 1960s.

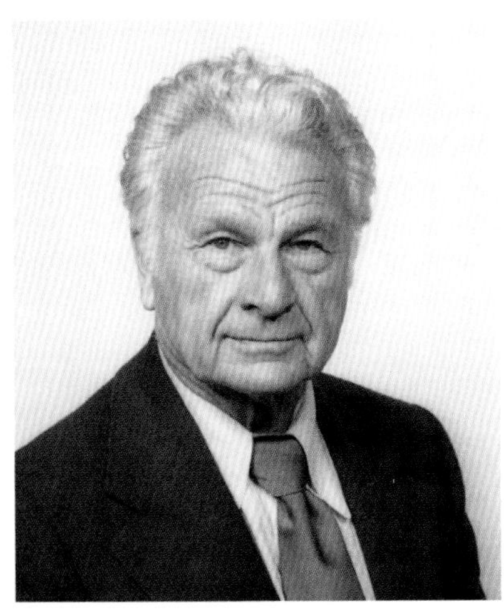

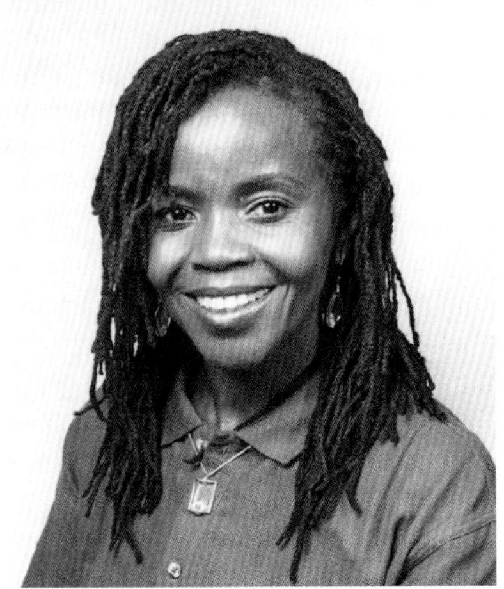

EDDIE ALBERT
Actor, 5 June 1980

P. P. ARNOLD
Singer, 18 June 1987

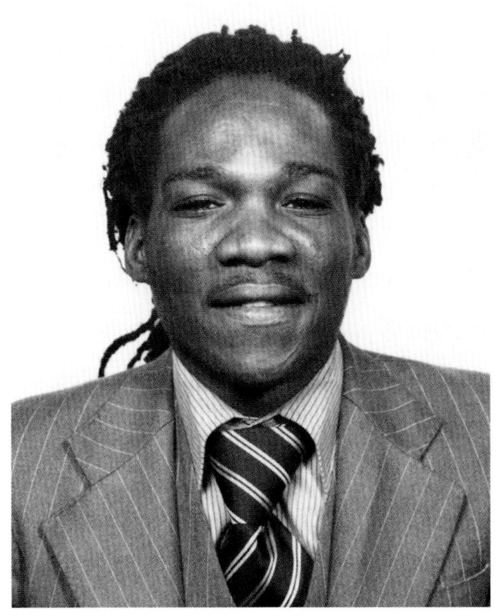

DR ALIMANTADO

Singer, 7 April 1978

Early one morning Dr Alimantado came bounding up the stairs of the studio to be photographed for his US visa. He seemed rather surprised that I recognized him. He was a favourite singer among punk bands such as The Clash and the Sex Pistols and became so popular that his name was spray-painted over practically every wall in London at the time, along with such slogans as 'DOC ALIMANTADO SAY FREE SOUTH AFRICA'.

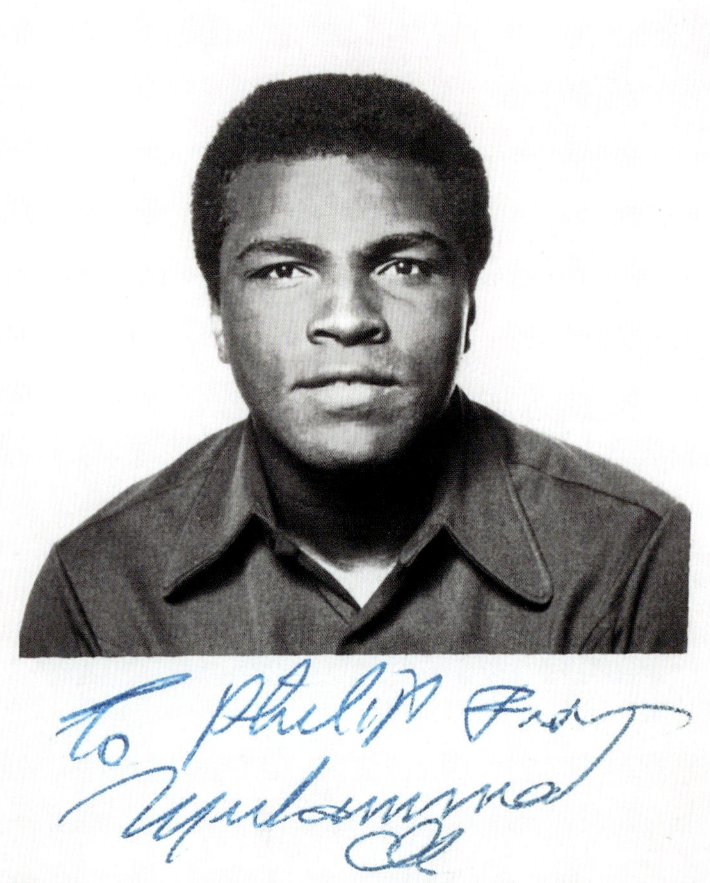

No. 18

MUHAMMAD ALI

Boxer, 11 June 1974

On his way to Zaire (now the Democratic Republic of the Congo) for his upcoming 'Rumble in the Jungle' fight with arch-rival George Foreman, Muhammad Ali forgot to pack his passport. Presumably he was so famous that passport control in the United States just waved him through. However, when he landed at Heathrow to catch his connecting flight, the London authorities spotted his mistake, and he was taken straight to the US embassy. He then walked the short distance to our studio, where my father was waiting to photograph him. My father had been a professional boxer, and Ali, after asking him about his career, told him, 'All those fights, and you're almost as pretty as me!' He was with his entourage, which included his business manager and friend, Gene Kilroy, whom my father also snapped. After he had his picture taken, Ali asked him to make multiple prints, which he proceeded to sign for all the waiting customers and even, I believe, the staff back at the embassy and anybody else walking down North Audley Street. On seeing the framed pictures of past celebrity customers hanging on our wall, he exclaimed loudly, 'Take that down and just have one big photo of me ... I AM THE GREATEST.'

No. 19

WOODY ALLEN

Actor/Director, 21 April 1980

Woody Allen came into the studio around the time his movie *Stardust Memories* was released. He might even have been in London to promote it. When customers who are so recognizable look a bit cheesed off at having to dash from the embassy to have their picture taken and then rush back, I always think it best to leave them be. So we had only the briefest interaction. When it came time to pay, he didn't seem to understand the value of UK currency and just thrust some notes at me, which I carefully picked out, giving him a rough conversion rate. He didn't seem too bothered by that.

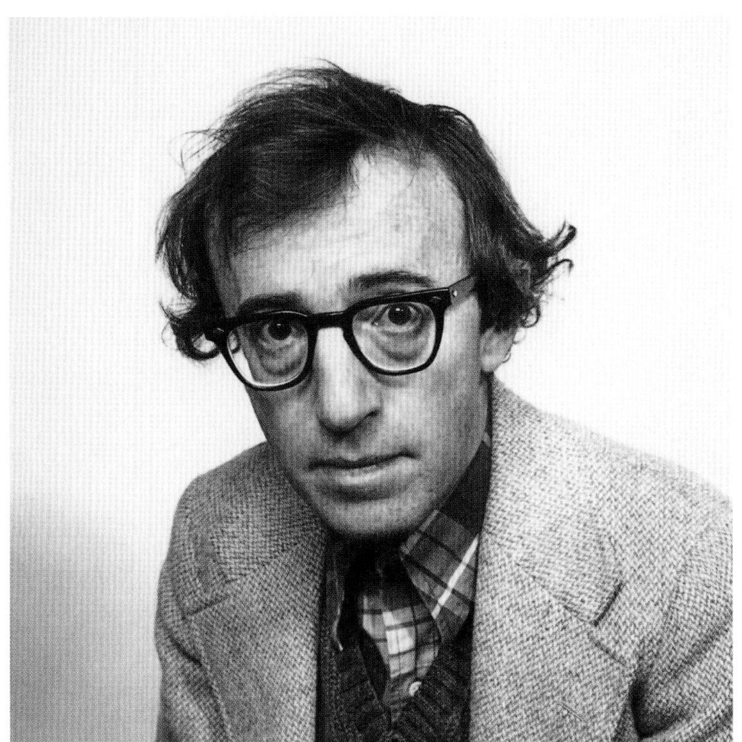

No. 21

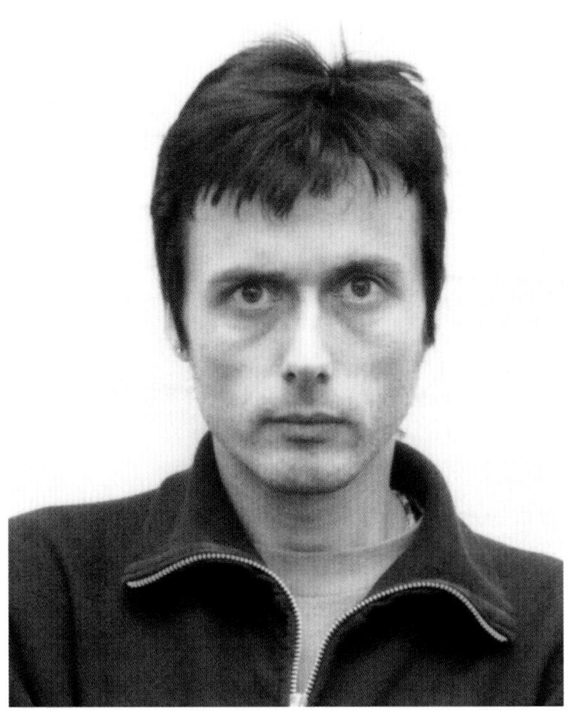

BRETT ANDERSON

Musician, 20 March 1999

I went to photograph Brett Anderson and his band Suede at their rehearsal studio right before they released their chart-topping album *Head Music* that May. It was a Saturday, so I took my daughter Juliet, who was nearly two years old and still in the early stages of walking. We were waiting for the band to finish when the soundproofed door opened and the noise was so loud it knocked Juliet not quite off her feet, but enough for her to stagger a few steps back. Even as a toddler, she thought it was hilarious.

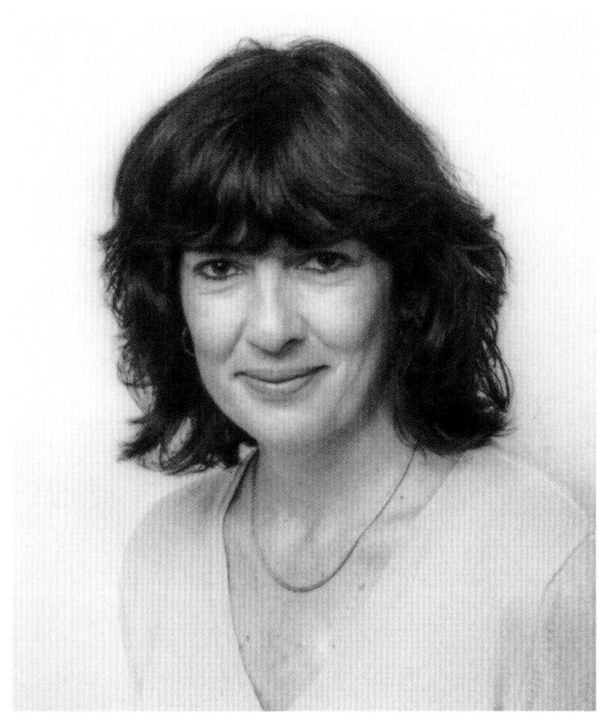

CHRISTIANE AMANPOUR

Journalist, 15 October 2002

The studio was fortunate enough to photograph journalists from all the major news outlets, including ABC, NBC, CNN, BBC and CBC. We provided a service whereby they were able to phone and order more prints for visas, passports or accreditations as needed, so that they could report from around the world at the drop of a hat. Someone who very often needed multiple prints was Christiane Amanpour, whom we photographed for both CNN and ABC from 1998 onwards.

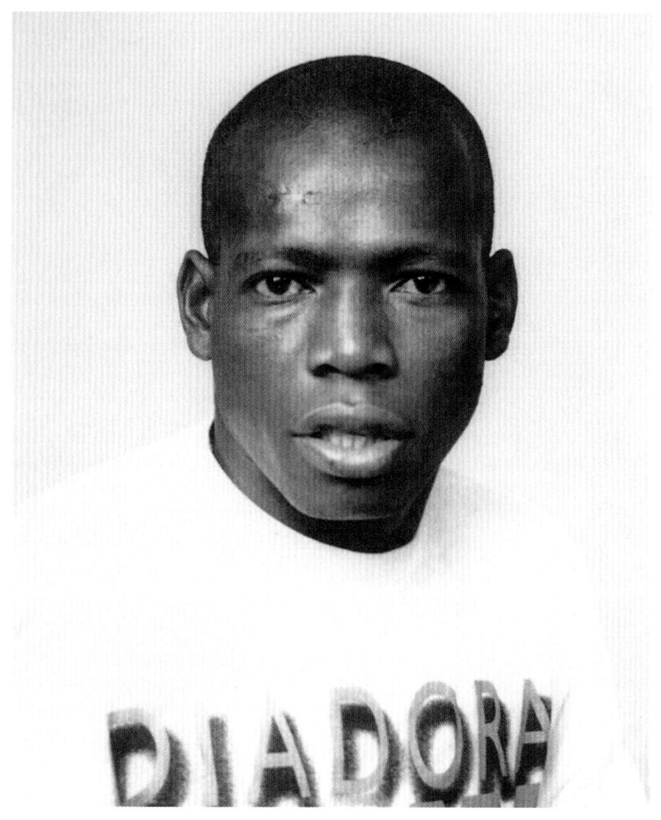

FAUSTINO ASPRILLA

Footballer, 25 July 1996

Another customer who unceremoniously thrust a fistful of cash at me was the Colombian footballer Faustino Asprilla. He had just arrived in England to play for Newcastle United and spoke very little English, so when it was time to pay, he dug in his pocket and produced a large wad of £50 notes. Sadly, but rather unsurprisingly, I discovered he filed for bankruptcy in 2007.

No. 24

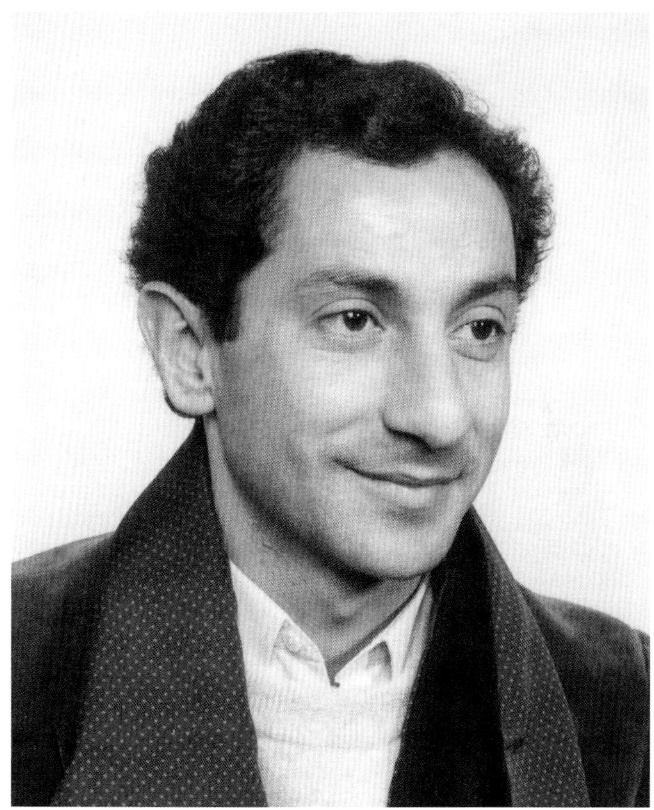

OSSIE ARDILES

Footballer, 9 January 1986

Back in 1986, smoking was allowed in shops and various other places, and our studio was no exception. Ossie Ardiles was a midfield footballer renowned for his work rate and speed, so I was quite surprised to see him smoke two cigarettes within the ten minutes it took to develop his photos.

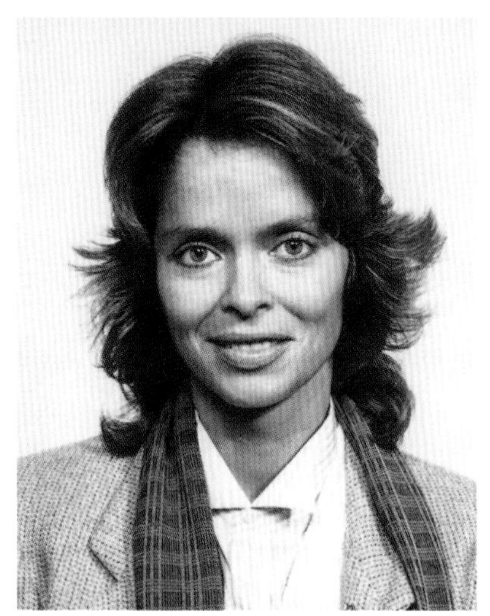

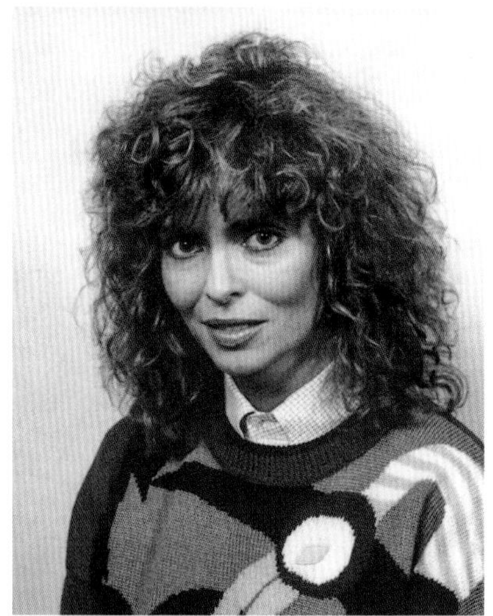

BARBARA BACH
Actor, 4 June 1982 and
10 November 1986

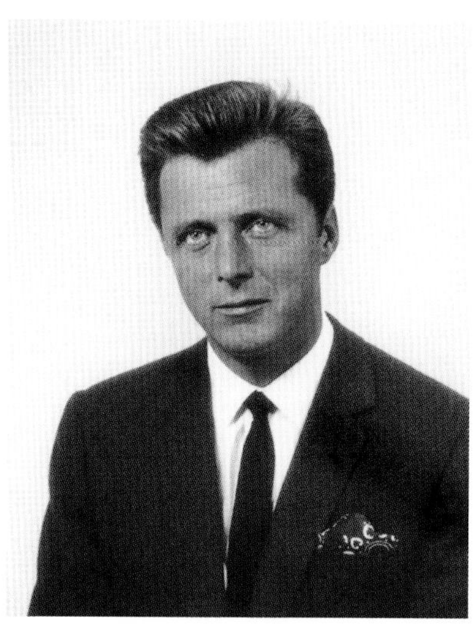

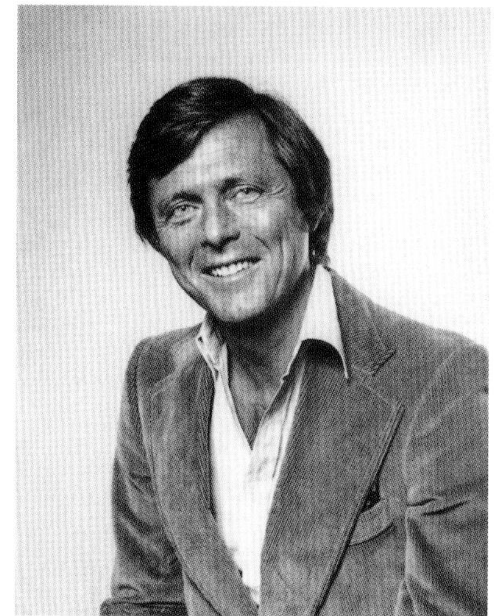

EDD BYRNES
Actor, 31 May 1966 and
2 June 1976

No. 27

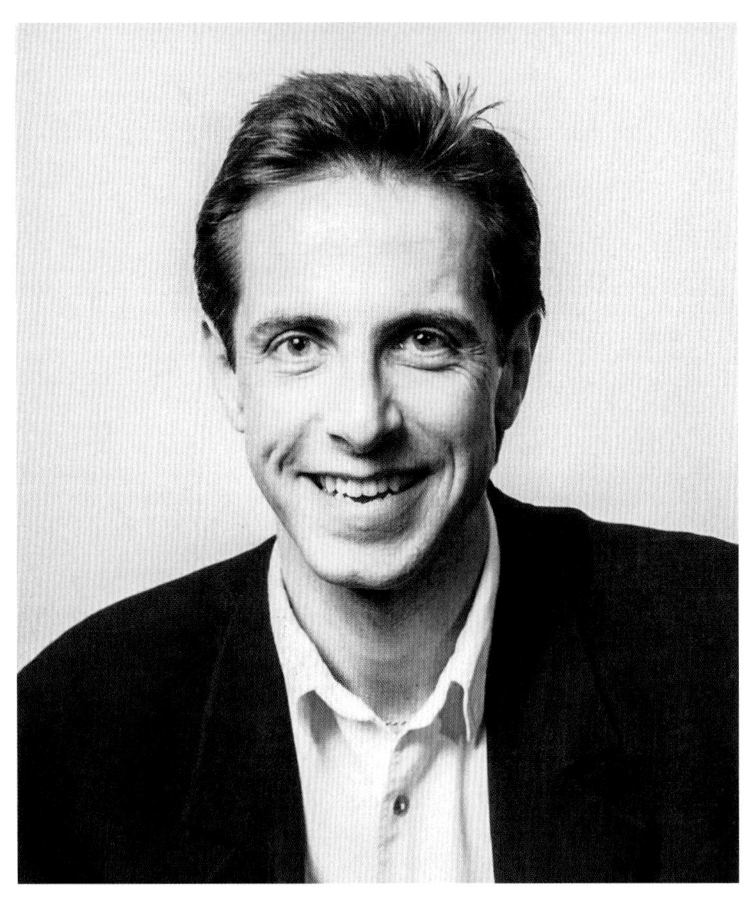

CLIVE BARKER
Writer/Director, 26 October 1990

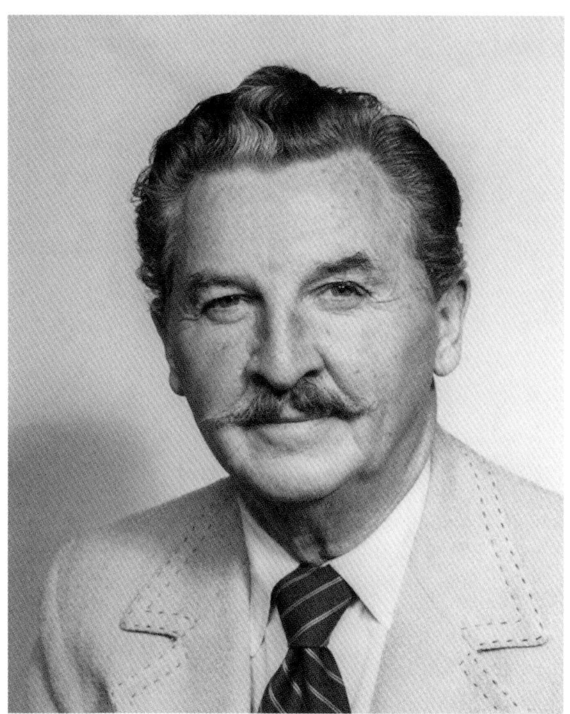

EDDIE BRACKEN

Actor, 30 August 1979

Eddie Bracken is surely the only actor to have appeared in movies with two men who would become President of the United States: Ronald Reagan in *The Girl from Jones Beach* in 1949 and *Home Alone 2: Lost in New York* in 1992 with Donald Trump.

No. 29

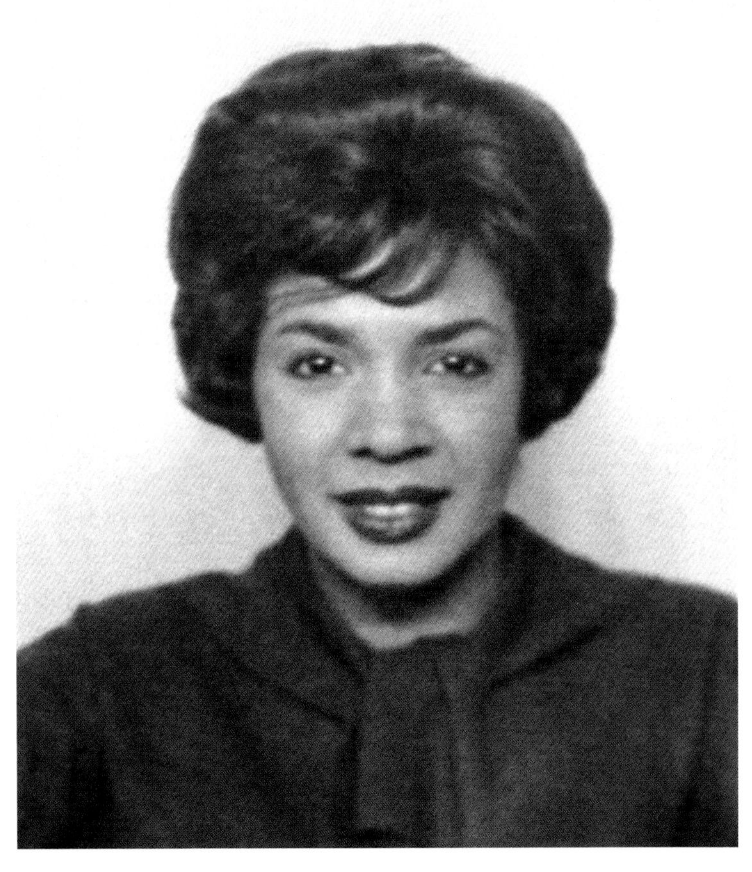

SHIRLEY BASSEY
Singer, 17 October 1960

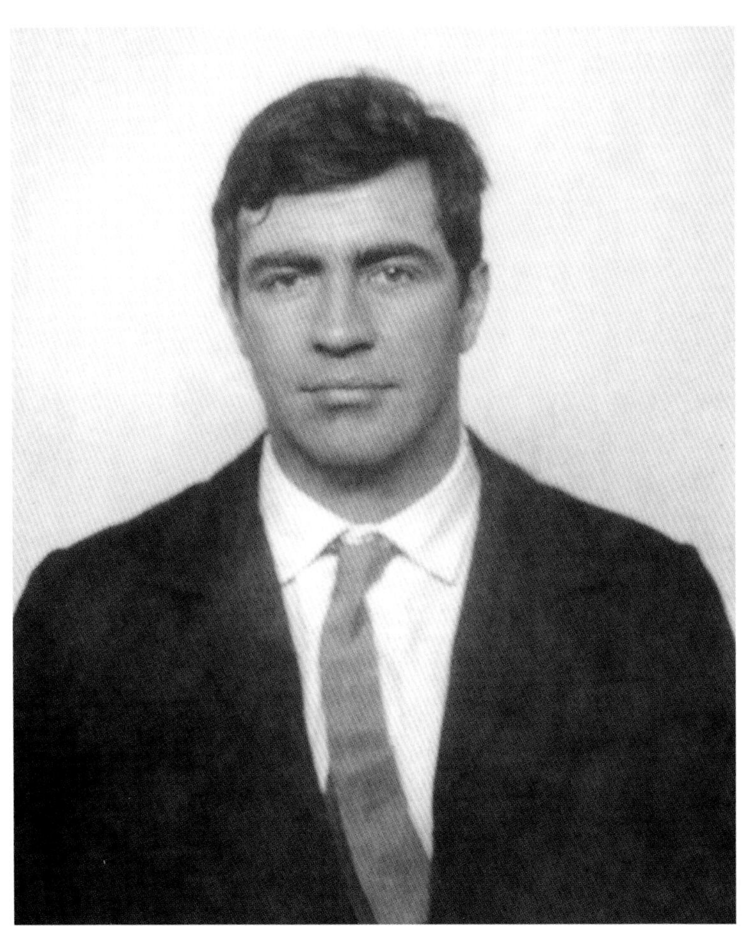

ALAN BATES
Actor, 31 January 1964

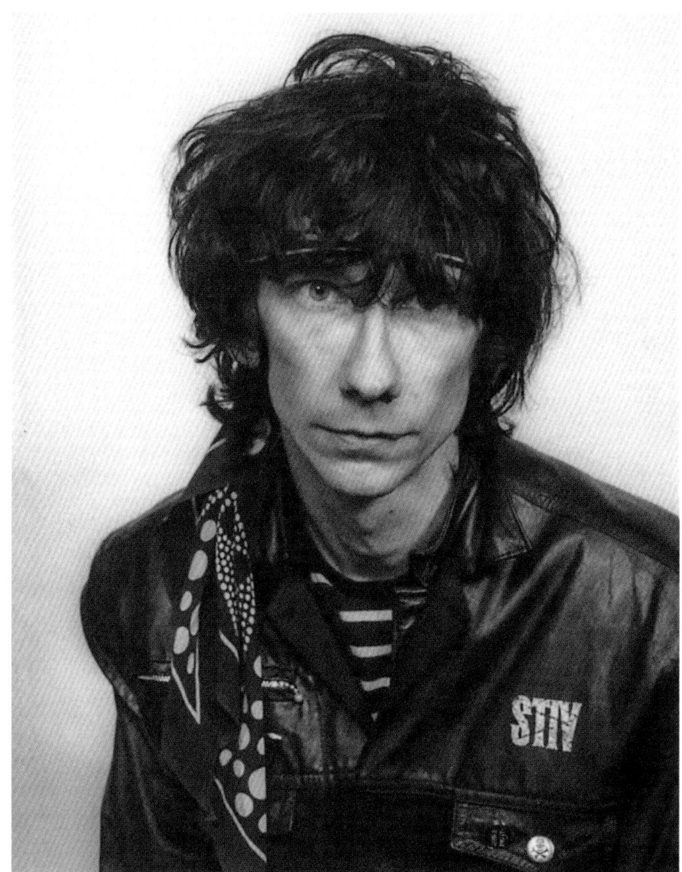

STIV BATORS

Musician, 25 October 1982

How did I know it was punk legend Stiv Bators? I only had to look at his leather jacket. He was living in London and had recently formed a supergroup with Brian James of The Damned, called Lords of the New Church. He died tragically young in 1990 after being knocked off his motorbike in Paris.

No. 32

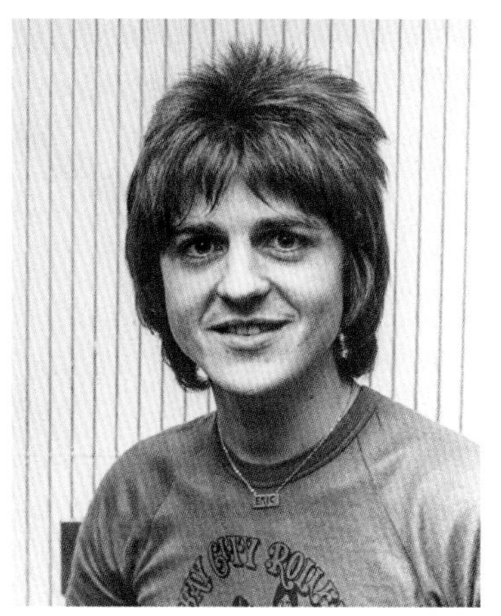

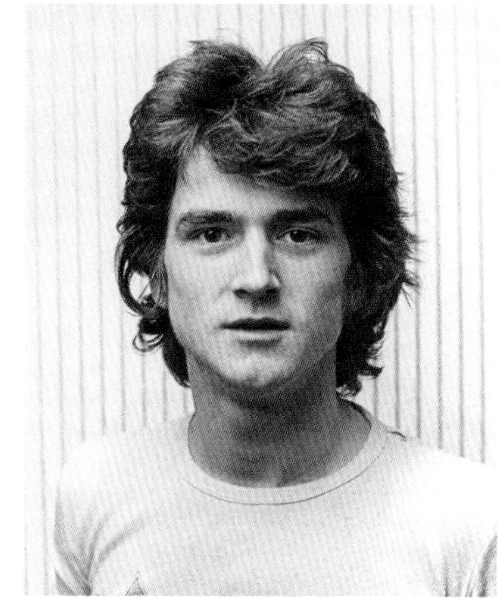

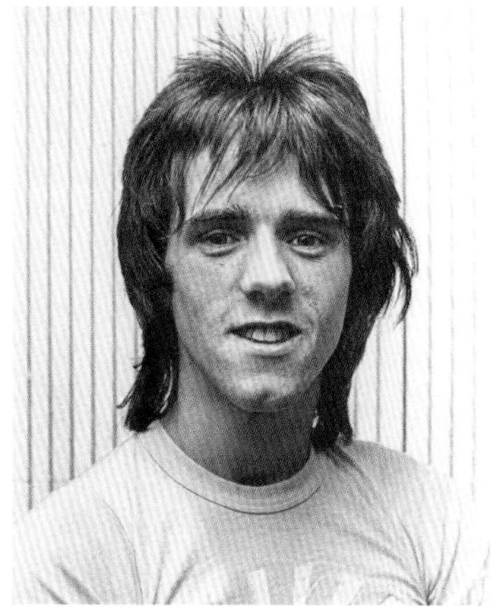

BAY CITY ROLLERS

ERIC FAULKNER
Musician, 13 January 1976

LES MCKEOWN
Musician, 13 January 1976

STUART 'WOODY' WOOD
Musician, 13 January 1976

Peter photographed the Bay City Rollers at the height of their popularity. 'Make it a fucking good one,' advised lead singer Les McKeown.

No. 33

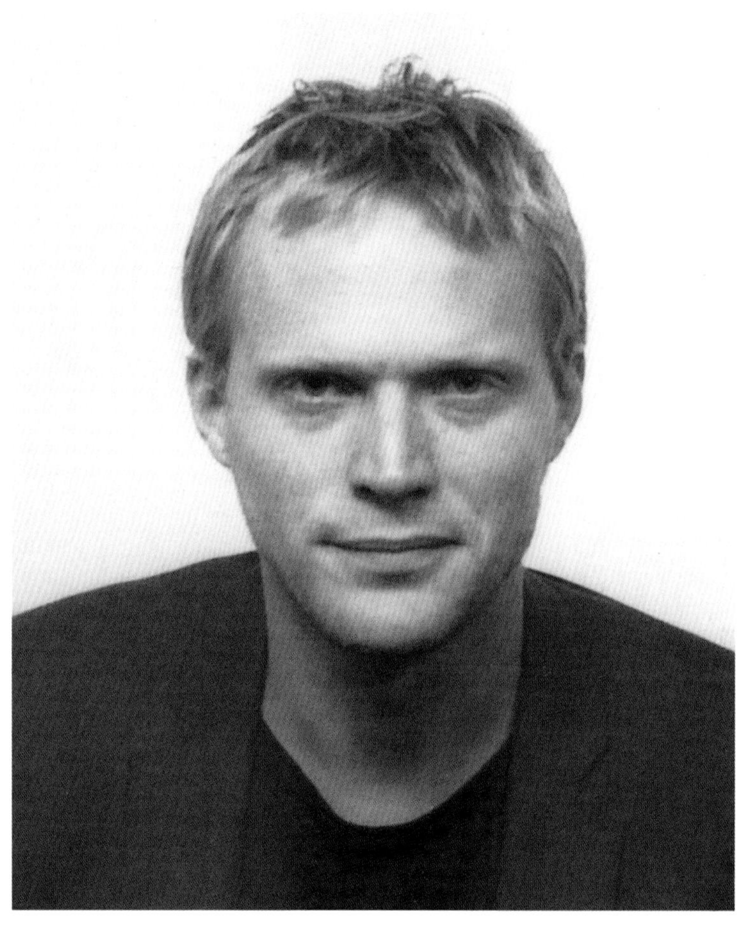

PAUL BETTANY
Actor, 15 June 2004

No. 34

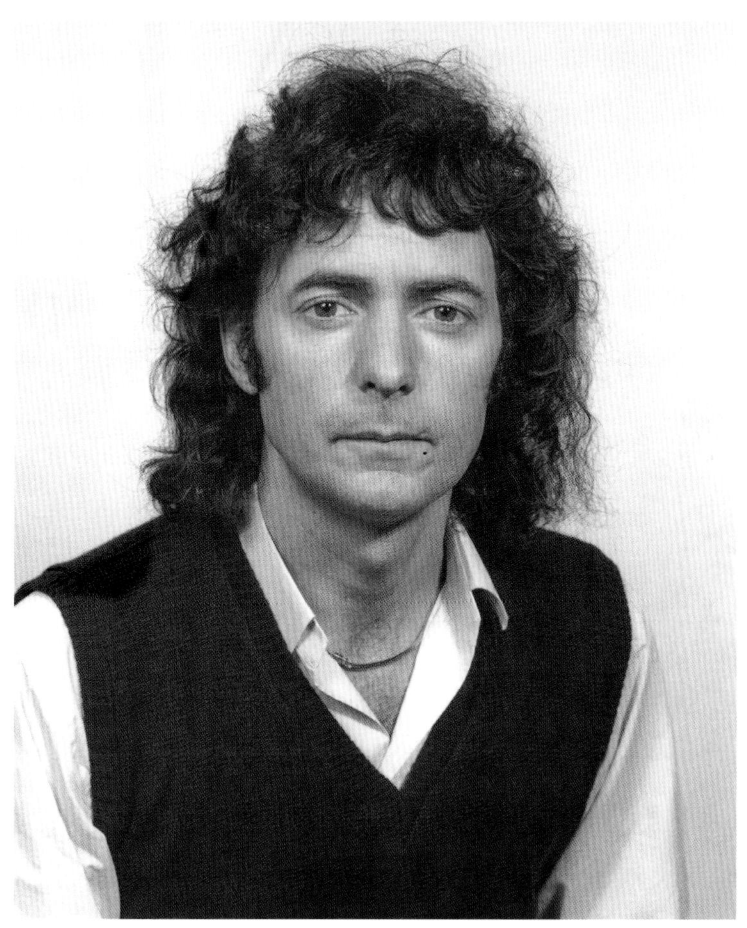

RITCHIE BLACKMORE
Musician, 26 September 1983

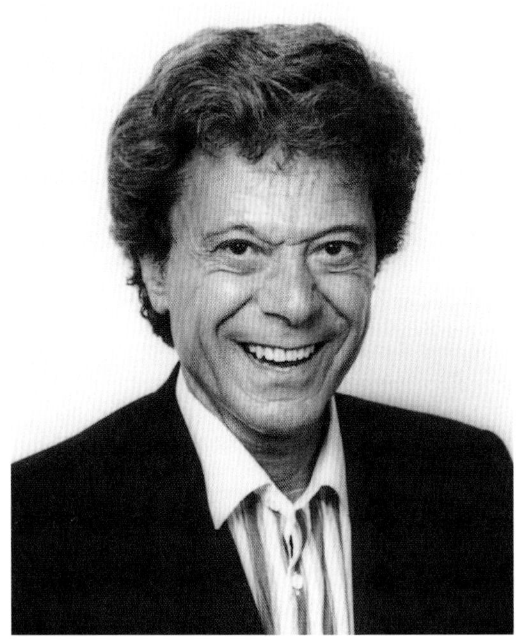

LIONEL BLAIR

Entertainer, 9 July 1992

A lesser-known fact about Lionel Blair is that he was a dual British and Canadian citizen, so he had to renew his Canadian passport every five years, making him quite a regular visitor to the studio. He was always as charming and friendly as he appeared in *Name That Tune* or *Give Us a Clue*. He once popped over to Selfridges during the ten minutes it took to develop his pictures, returning about an hour later with a parking ticket in his hand. He joked, 'I just can't help myself chatting with everyone who says hello, and then I always run over time with my parking.' He was a lovely man who obviously enjoyed being in front of the camera.

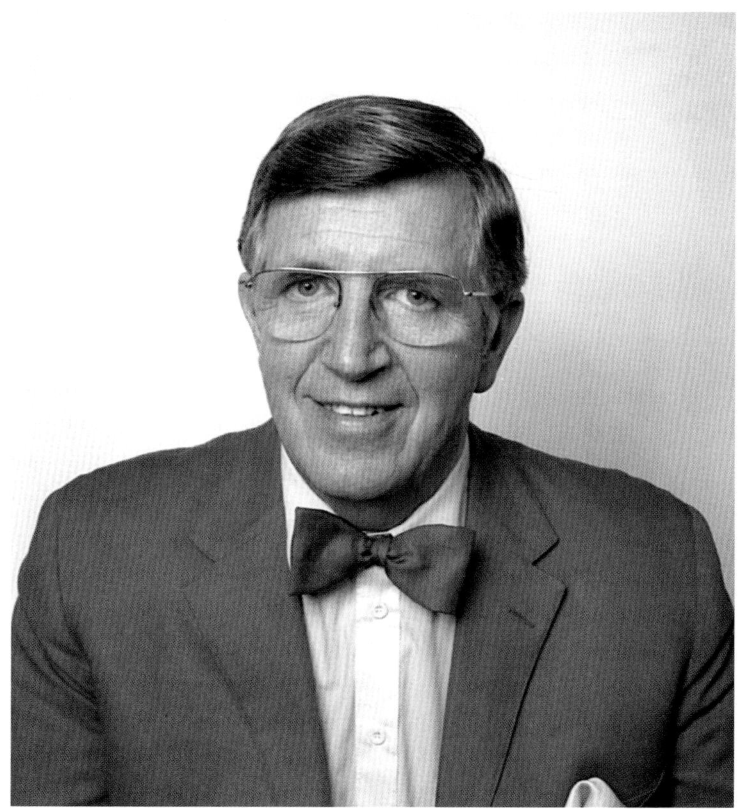

BRUCE BOA

Actor, 27 February 1990

'You know me,' this jovial man said to me upon entering the studio. 'I'm the American guy who orders the Waldorf salad in *Fawlty Towers*.' Bruce Boa and his family became regulars at the studio thanks to his successful acting career in the UK. Although he was actually Canadian, he often played the token American in British films and television shows.

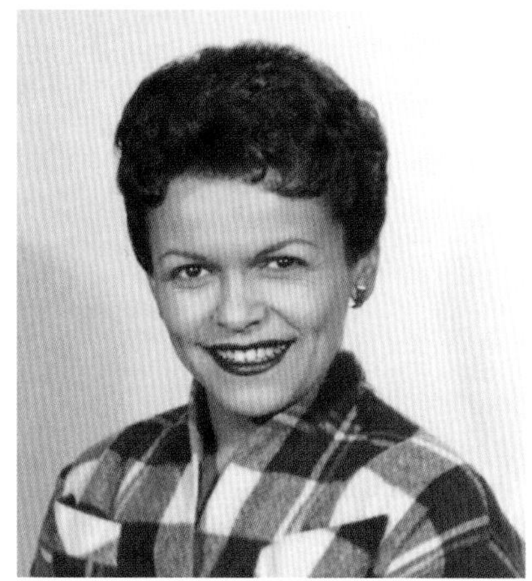

CONNIE BOOTH
Actor, 29 December 1975

EVE BOSWELL
Singer, 1950s

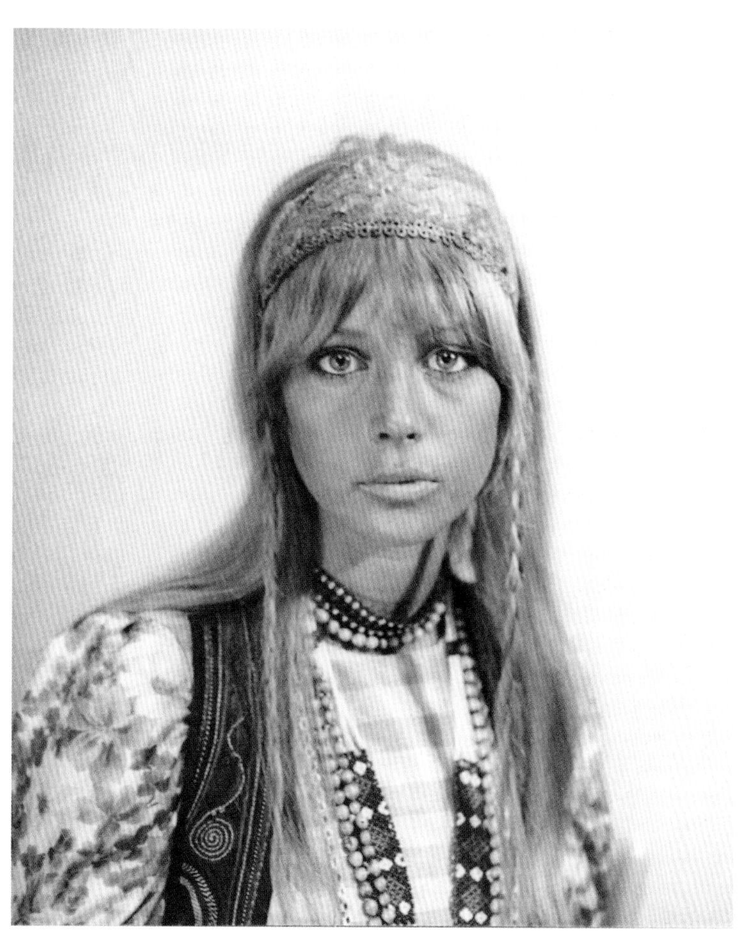

PATTIE BOYD
Model, 1960s

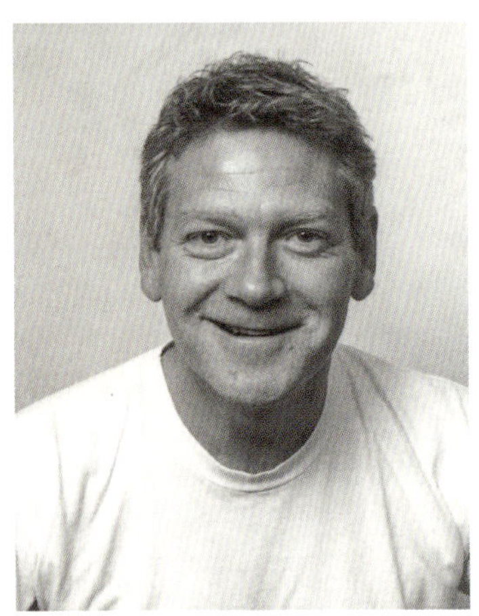

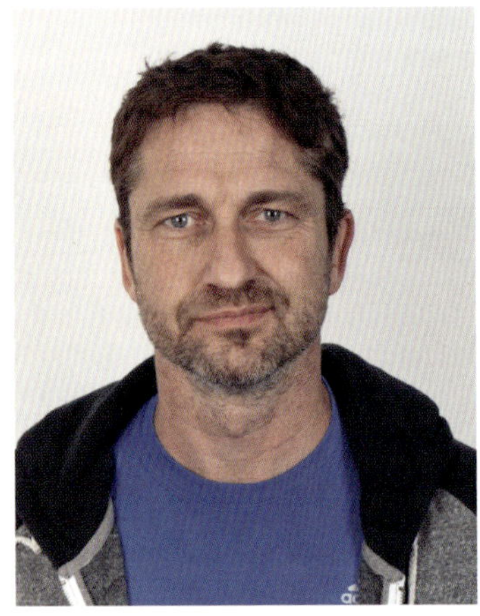

KENNETH BRANAGH
Actor/Director, 9 September 2004

GERARD BUTLER
Actor, 8 June 2015

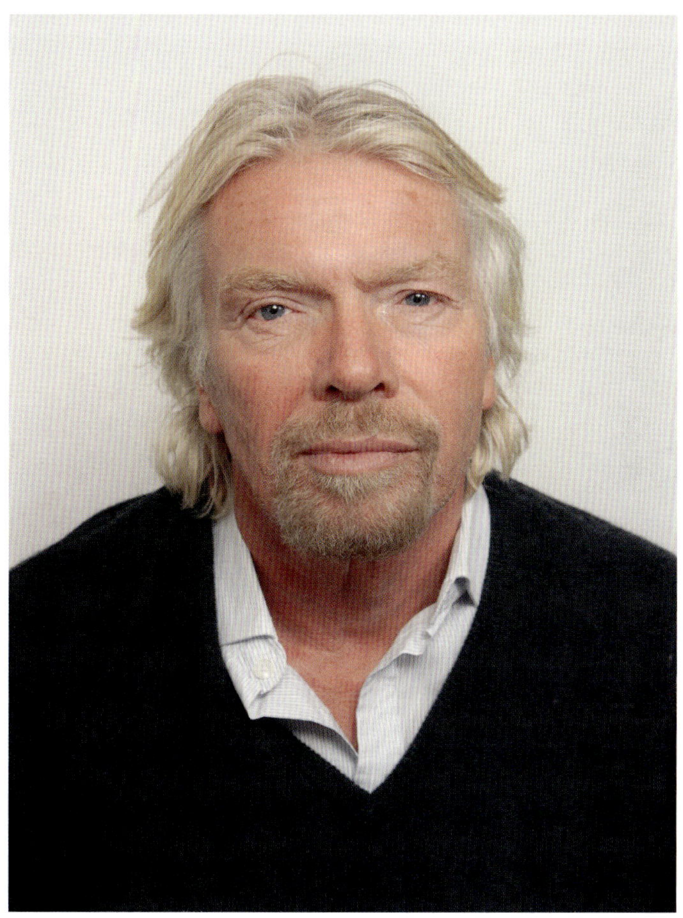

RICHARD BRANSON

Entrepreneur, 21 April 2011

Like us, Richard Branson had his first premises on Oxford Street, selling records above a shoe shop. He might have branched out, but we preferred to stay where we were!

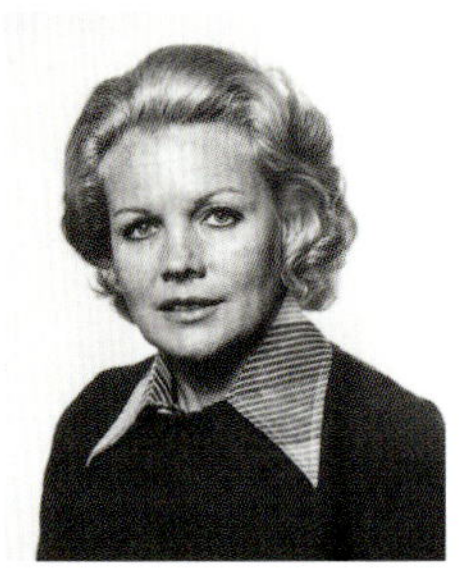

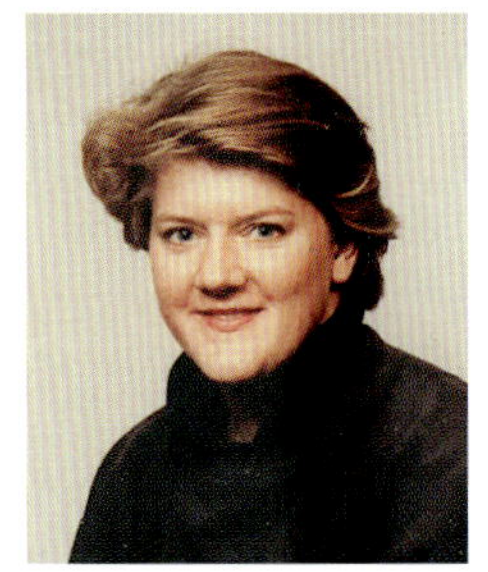

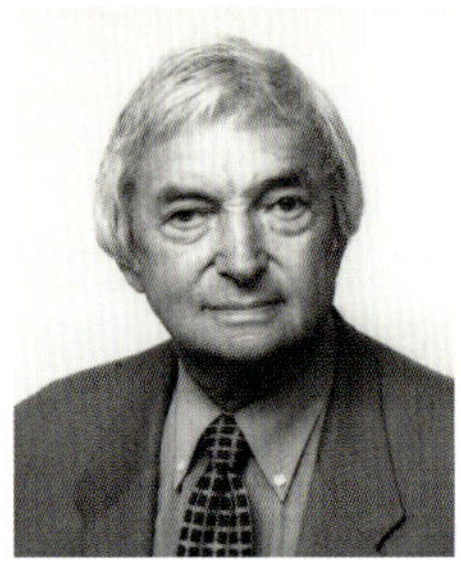

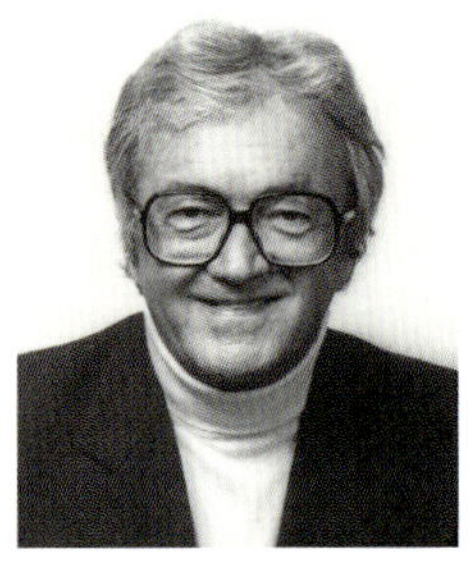

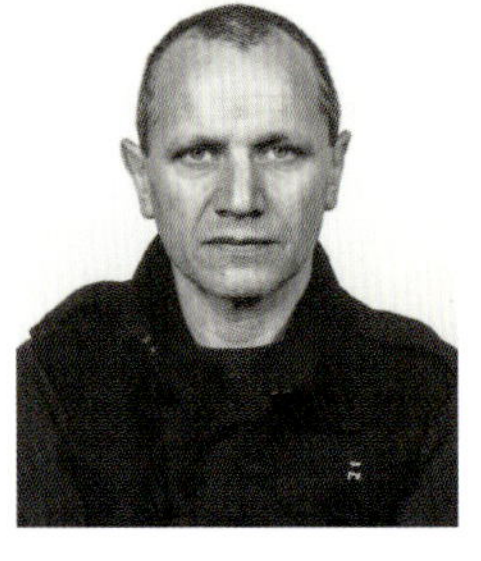

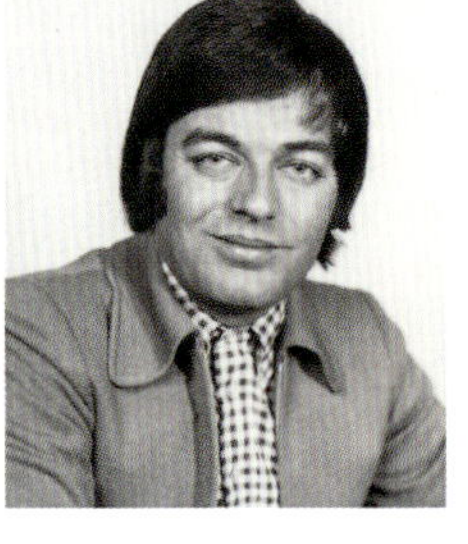

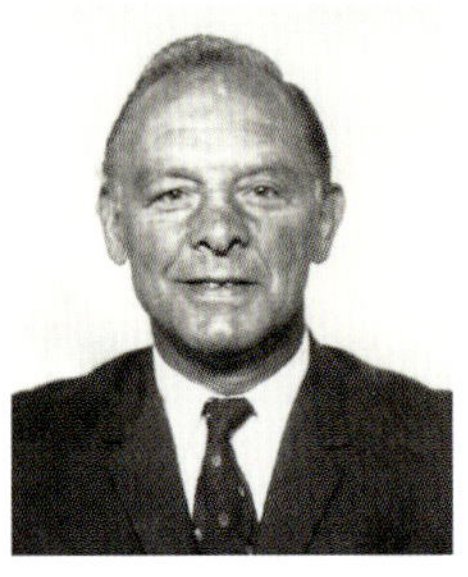

CARROLL BAKER
Actor, 20 March 1985

STEVEN BERKOFF
Actor, 7 February 1984

CLARE BALDING
Broadcaster, 7 June 1995

RICHIE BENAUD
Cricketer, 14 May 2001

TONY BLACKBURN
Radio DJ, 21 May 1969

LESLIE BRICUSSE
Composer, 30 August 1996

JACK 'KID' BERG
Boxer, 19 July 1963

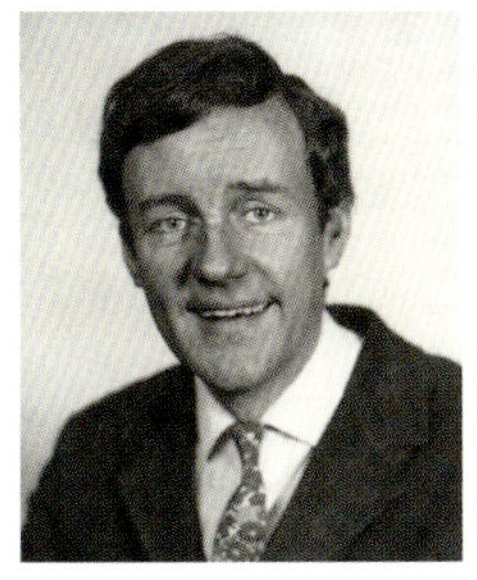

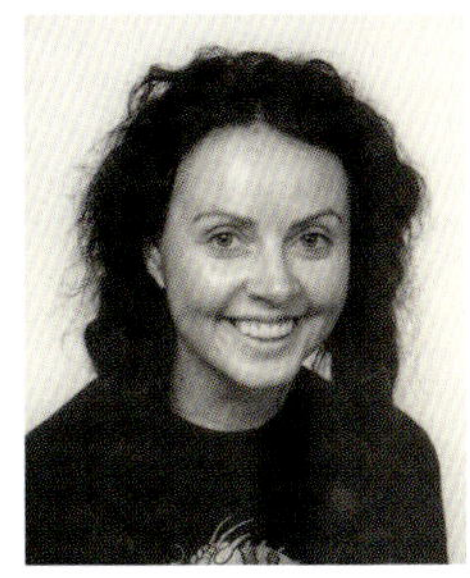

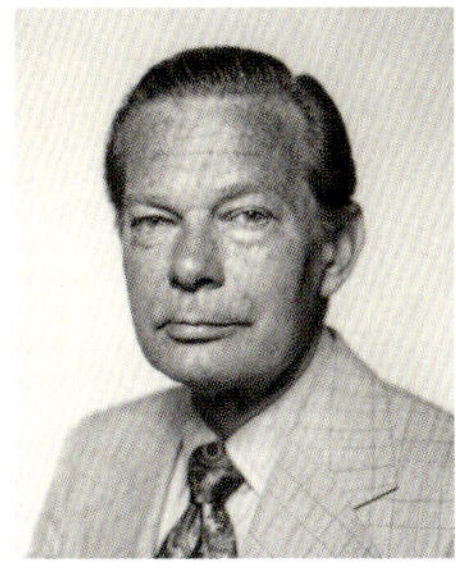

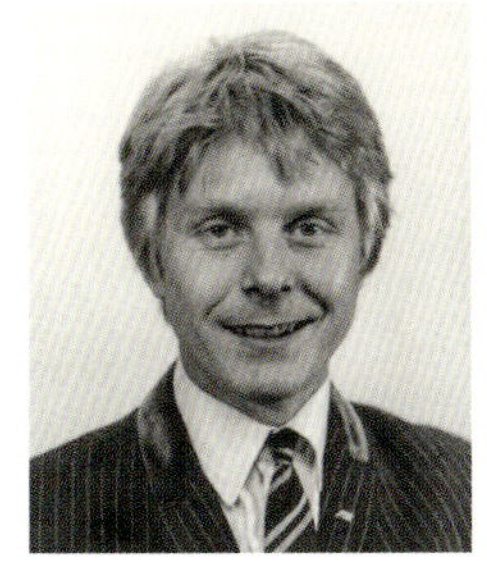

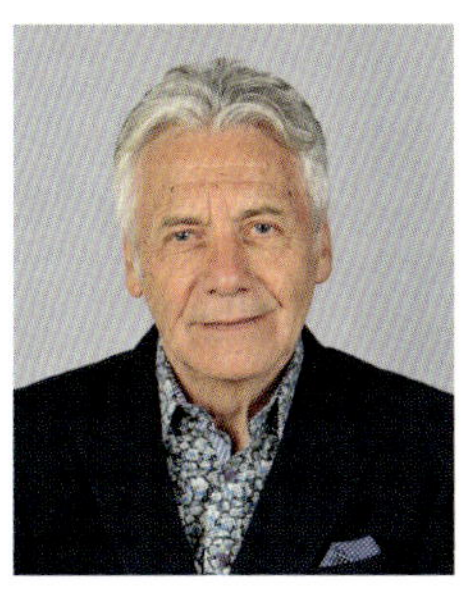

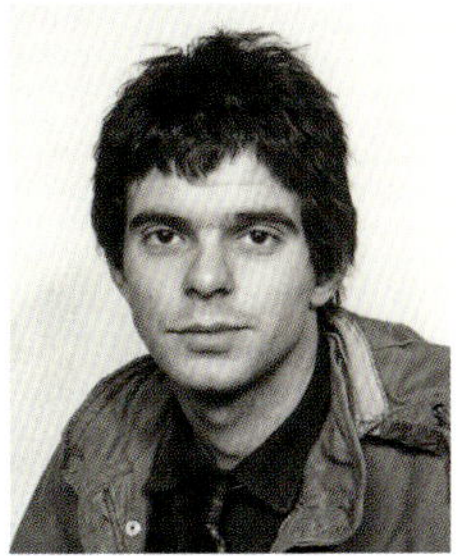

DAVID BRINKLEY
Journalist, 1974

JEFF BANKS
Fashion designer, 21 June 2018

RICHARD BRIERS
Actor, 4 March 1966

JOE BROWN
Musician, 14 May 1964

SARAH BRIGHTMAN
Singer, 23 January 2001

JJ BURNEL
Musician, 22 January 1980

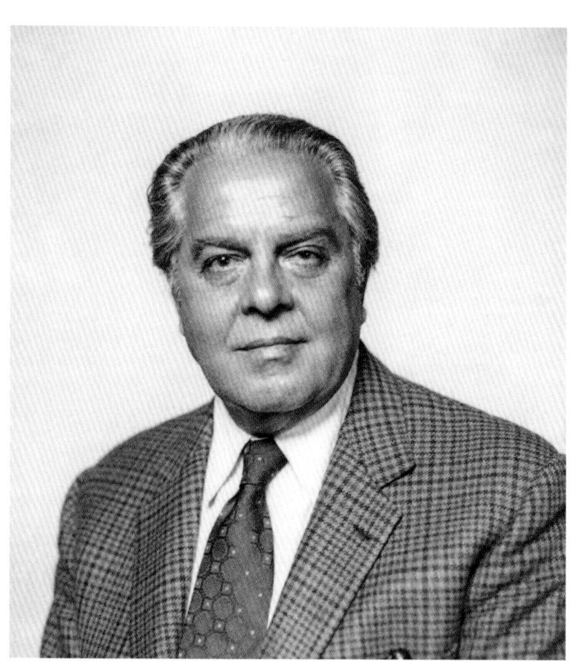

ALBERT R. 'CUBBY' BROCCOLI
Producer, 1970s

No. 44

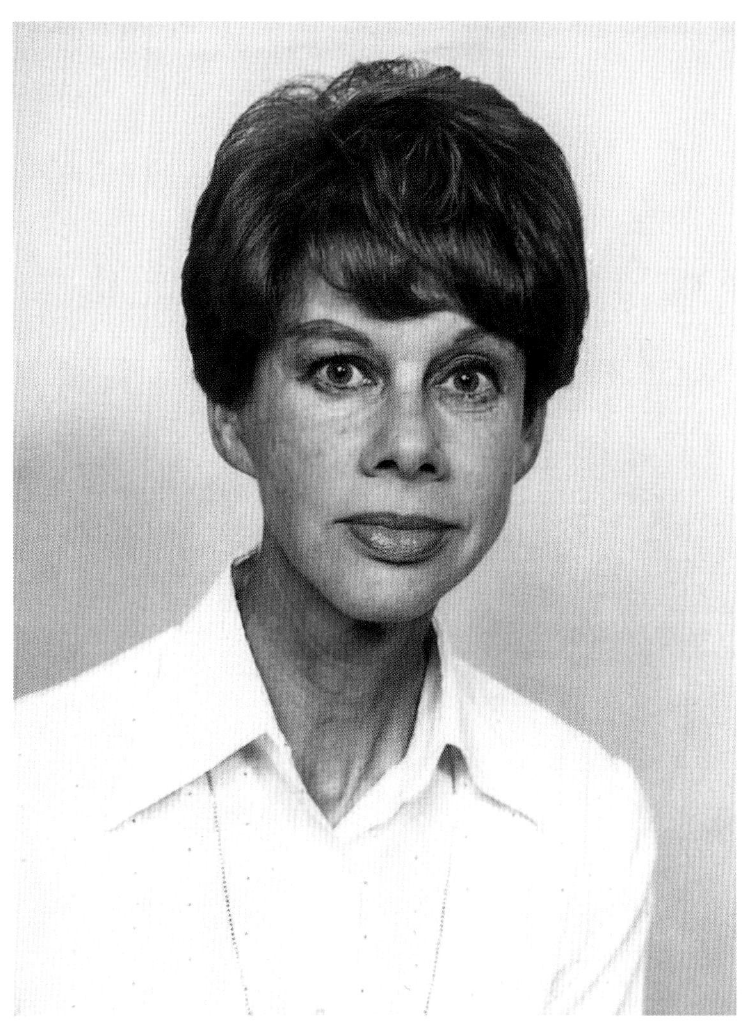

ANITA BROOKNER
Writer, 25 July 1980

No. 45

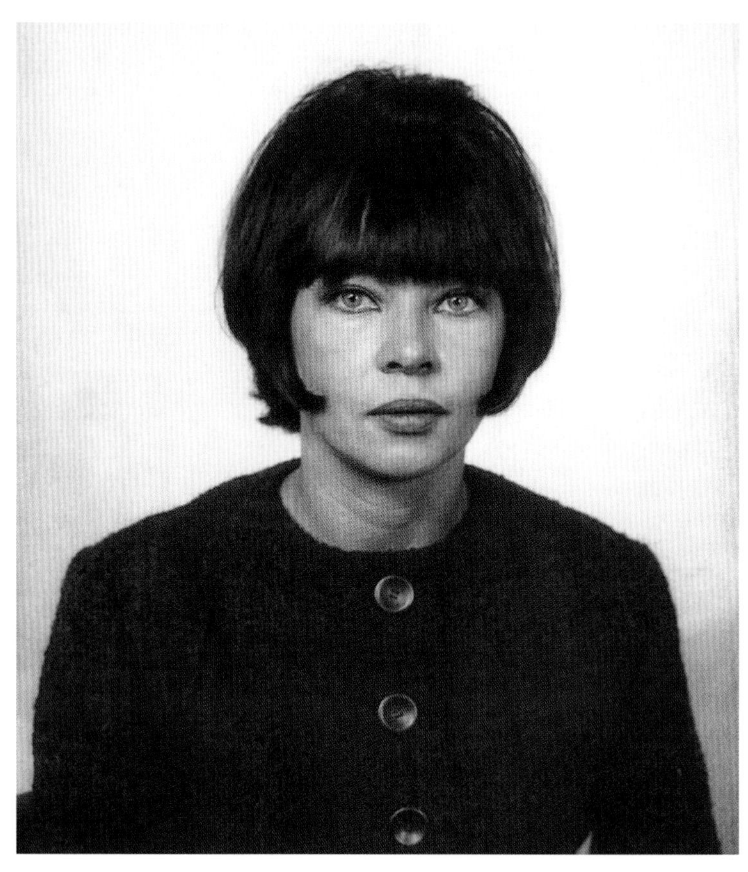

LESLIE CARON
Actor/Dancer, 1960s

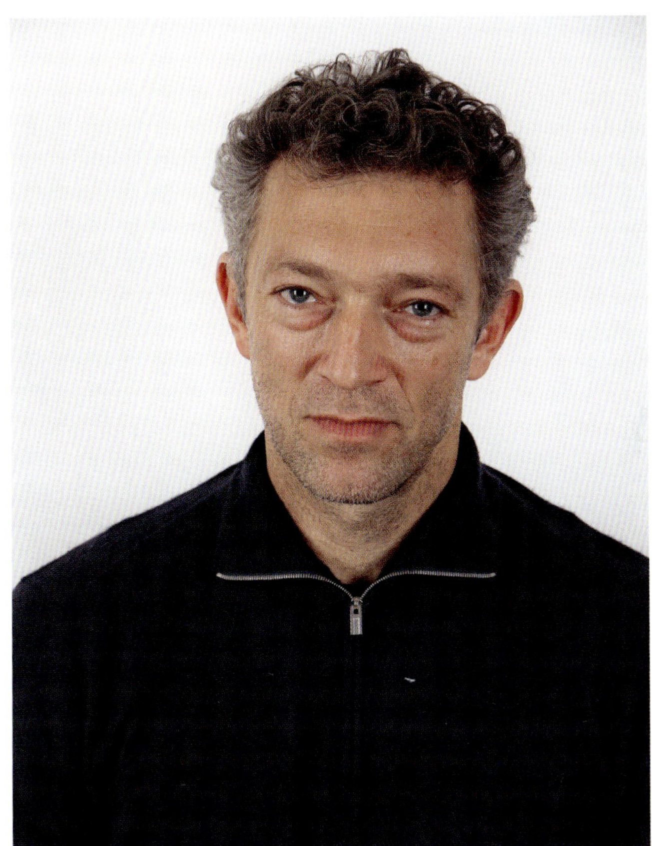

VINCENT CASSEL

Actor, 10 October 2015

Vincent Cassel debonairly checked himself in the mirror before Ivo snapped him and, noticing Ivo's accent, asked him where he was from. When Ivo explained he was from Setúbal, a little town near Lisbon, Cassel switched to fluent Portuguese and said he knew it very well and loved to holiday there. In a personal moment, they agreed that Ivo's hometown is a beautiful place and talked of Lisbon and all the beaches nearby.

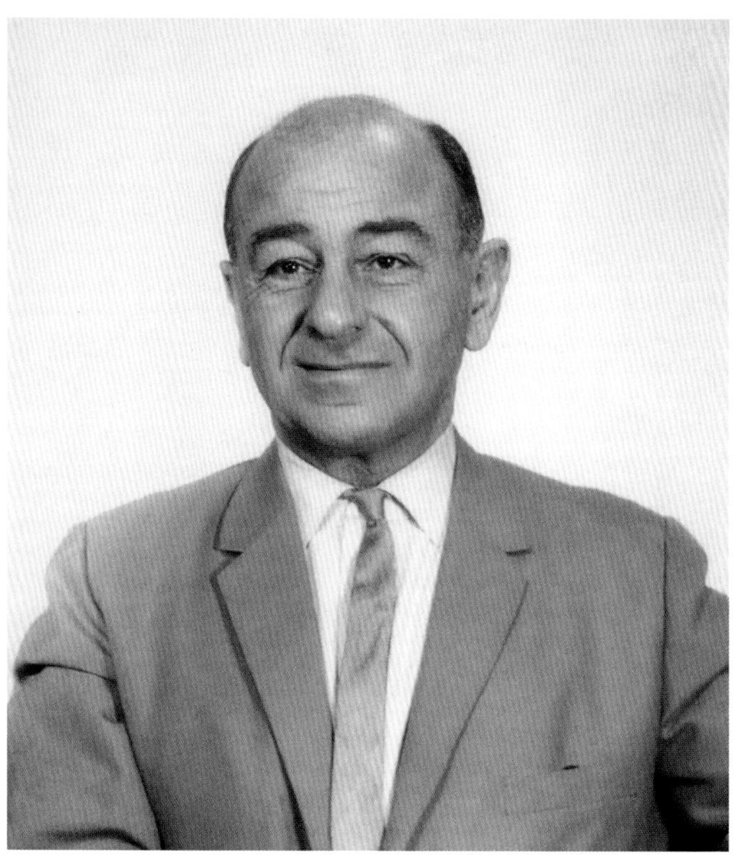

No. 48

SHURA CHERKASSKY

Pianist, 11 May 1965

One of my parents' favourite performers, the famed virtuoso pianist Shura Cherkassky came in for his photograph by strange coincidence on the same day as Lena Horne, another musical icon they loved. (Ms Horne had just finished a month-long engagement singing at the London Palladium. My parents had gone to see her perform during that run, so I'm sure they must have congratulated her on the show, and she seems happy judging by her smiling photo; see p.117.) Mr Cherkassky returned in 1972, and he and my father became quite friendly; the pianist even sent him a postcard thanking him for the photographs. My parents travelled to New York to hear him play at Carnegie Hall some years later.

No. 49

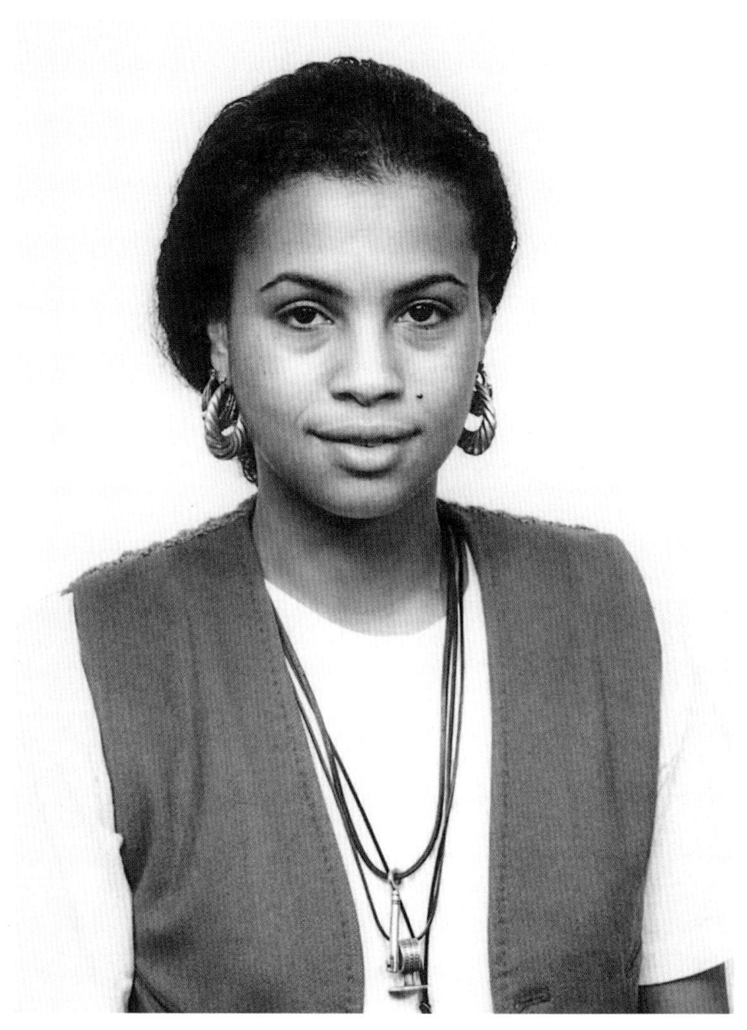

NENEH CHERRY
Singer, 5 November 1993

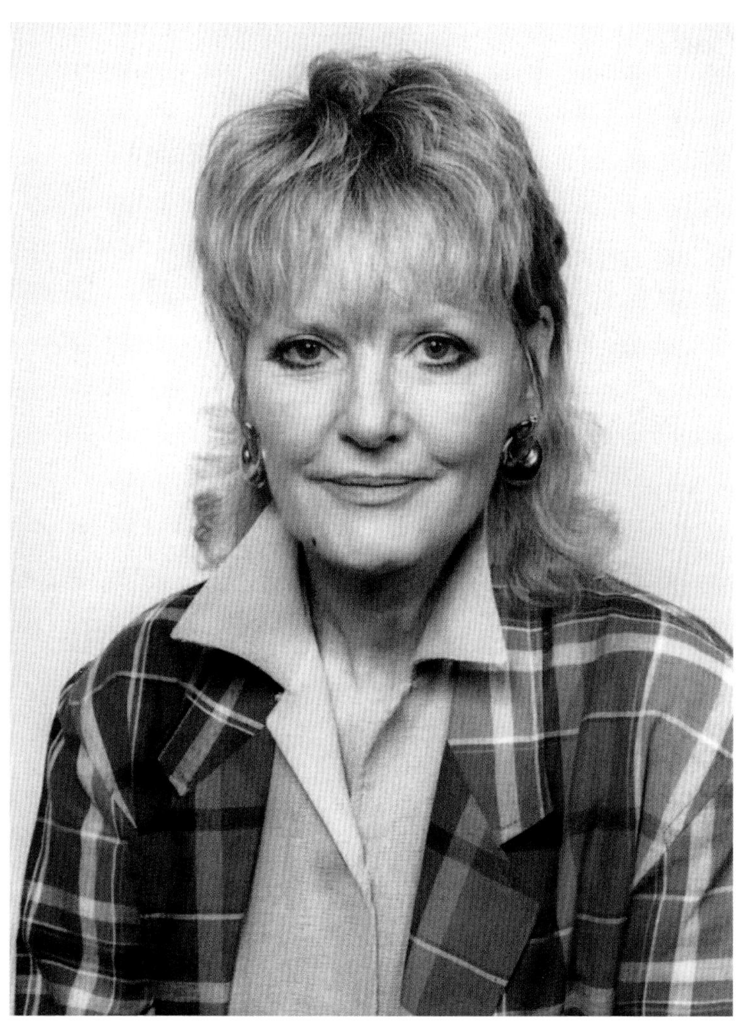

PETULA CLARK
Singer, 13 May 1986

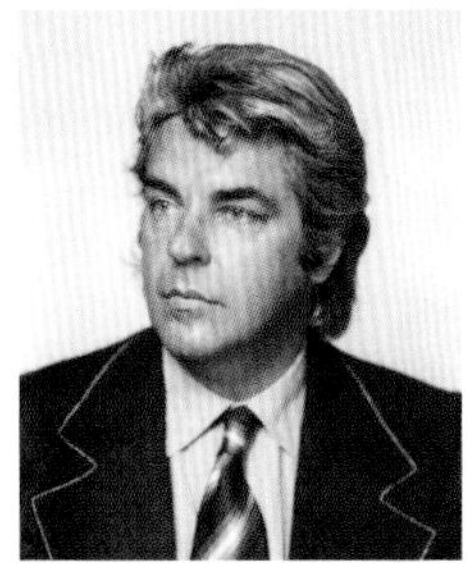

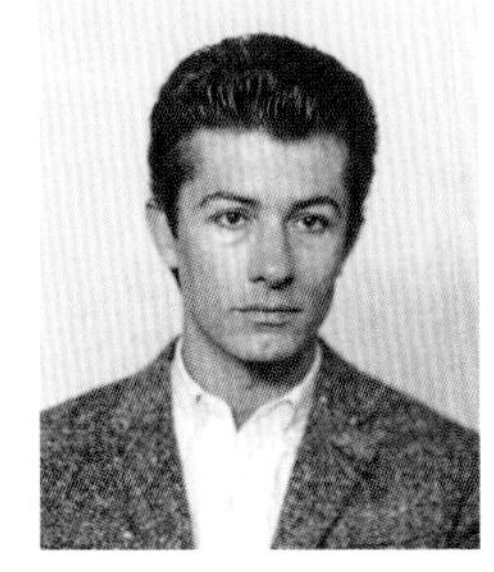

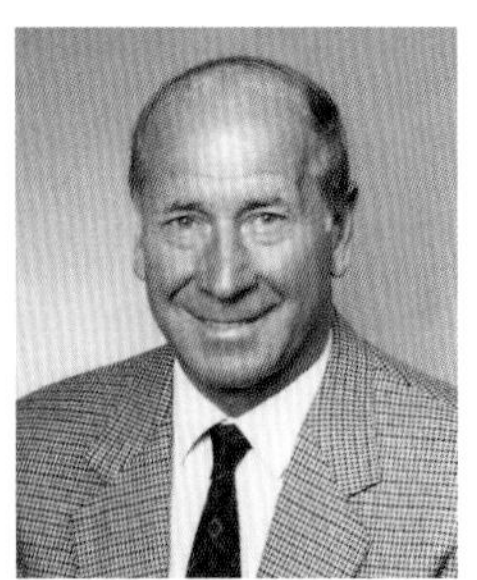

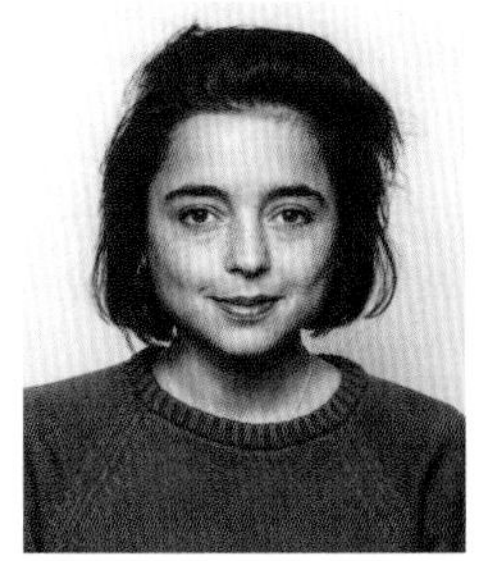

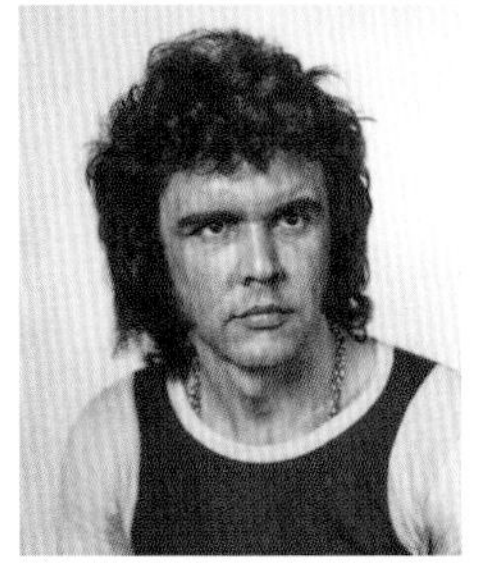

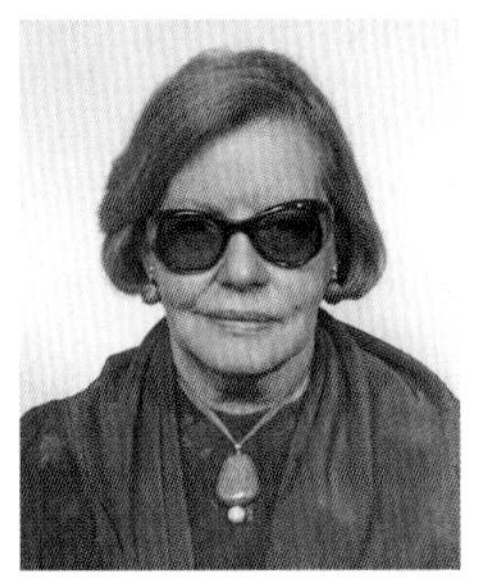

ROBERT CARRIER
Chef, 8 April 1981

BOBBY CHARLTON
Footballer, 19 May 1989

CHARLOTTE COLEMAN
Actor, 15 October 1990

DAVE CLARK
Musician, 5 January 1972

GEORGE CHAKIRIS
Actor, 27 December 1962

FLEUR COWLES
Editor, 18 March 1983

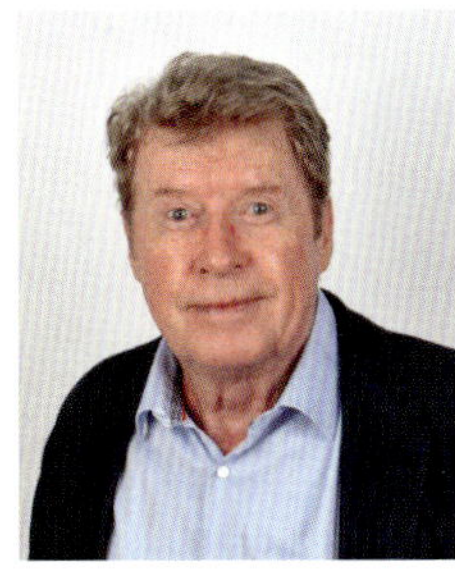
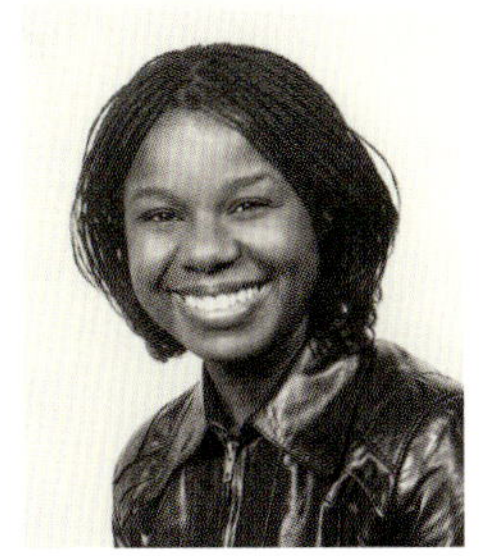
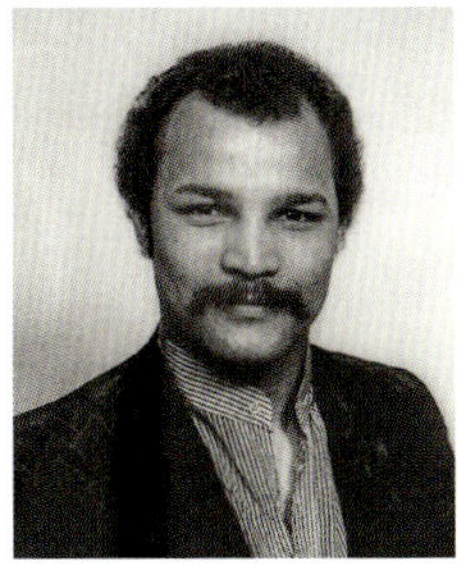
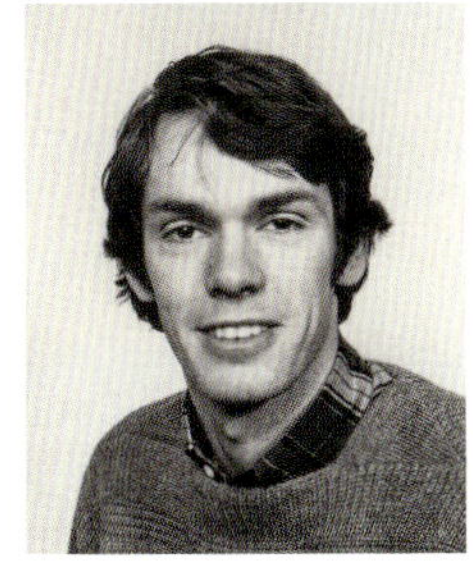
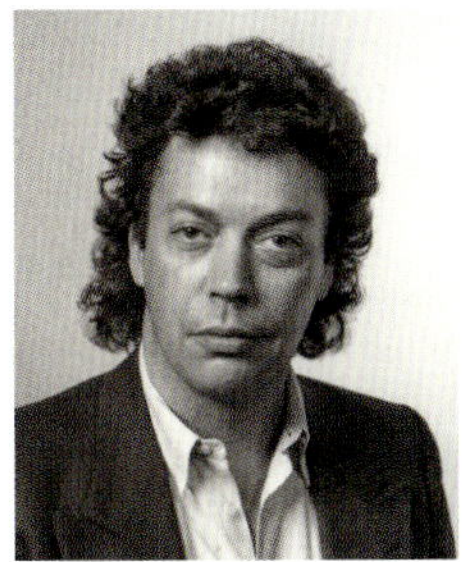
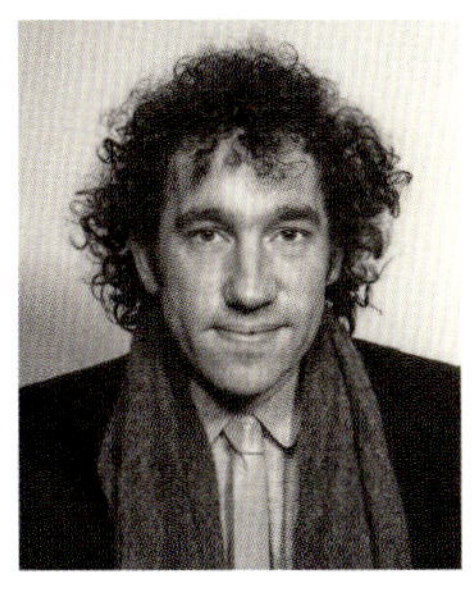
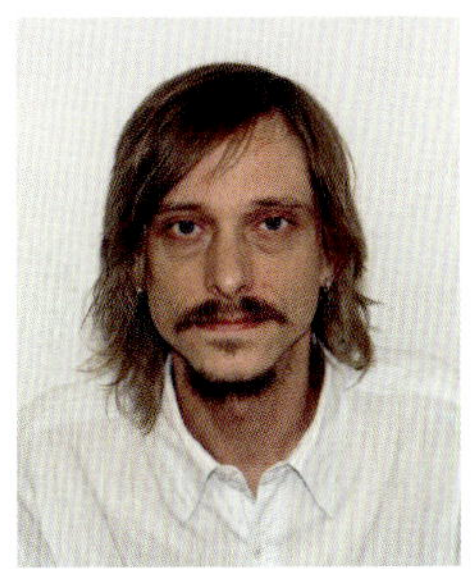

MICHAEL CRAWFORD
Actor, 8 September 2017

JOHN CONTEH
Boxer, 25 March 1981

SIMON CALLOW
Actor, 27 November 1979

RANDY CRAWFORD
Singer, 9 July 1981

JOHN CURRY
Figure skater, 17 April 1978

TIM CURRY
Actor, 31 August 1984

MACKENZIE CROOK
Actor, 27 August 2008

ERIC CLAPTON

Musician, 2 February 2001

When I first photographed Eric Clapton, I was standing in the corridor of the Royal Albert Hall watching him chat with his old Blind Faith bandmate Steve Winwood (see p.250). Both had been idols of mine for years, and I had to stop myself from snapping away, remembering that I was just there to take photos for their visas. I photographed the whole touring party that day, not just the musicians but even the roadies and caterers. Twenty years later, in May 2021, I photographed Clapton at his home/office in southwest London. 'Just to remind you that you're not allowed to smile on your passport photo these days,' I said. 'That suits me, I'm a miserable sod most of the time,' he replied with a stifled chuckle. Through his long-time road manager John 'Collie' Collins, Clapton kindly invited me to watch his concert later that week.

No. 54

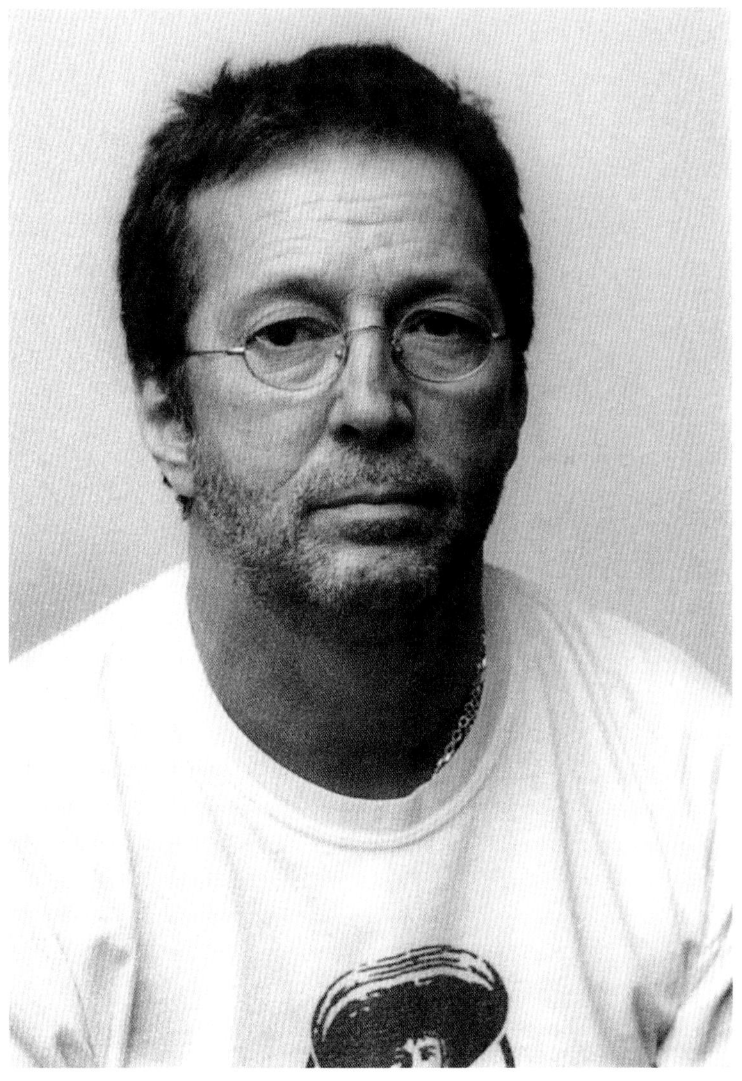

No. 55

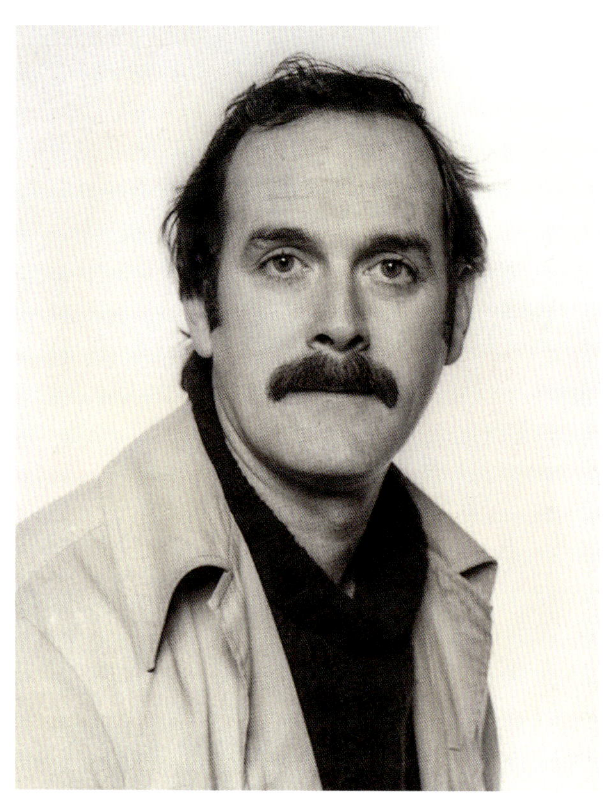

JOHN CLEESE
Actor, 11 May 1977

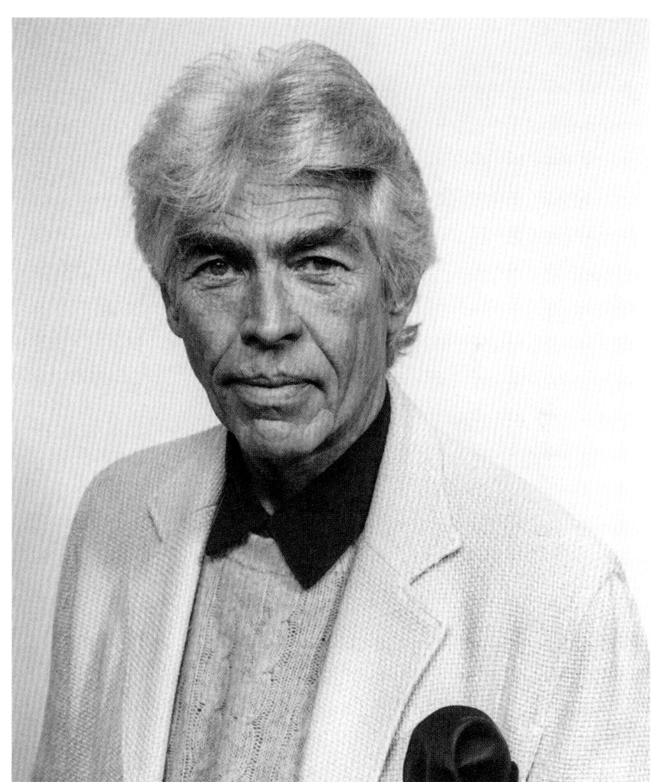

JAMES COBURN

Actor, 17 June 1981

Along with the politician Clement Freud and boxer John Conteh (both of whom we also photographed at the studio; see Conteh on p.53), James Coburn was pictured on the cover of Paul McCartney and Wings' album *Band on the Run* (1973). When Bridie snapped him, he asked whether he should strike a serious or smiling pose. Although he was famous for playing tough guy roles, he happily sat on the banister leading into the waiting area, smoking a large cigar and chatting breezily to the other customers while waiting for his photos to be printed.

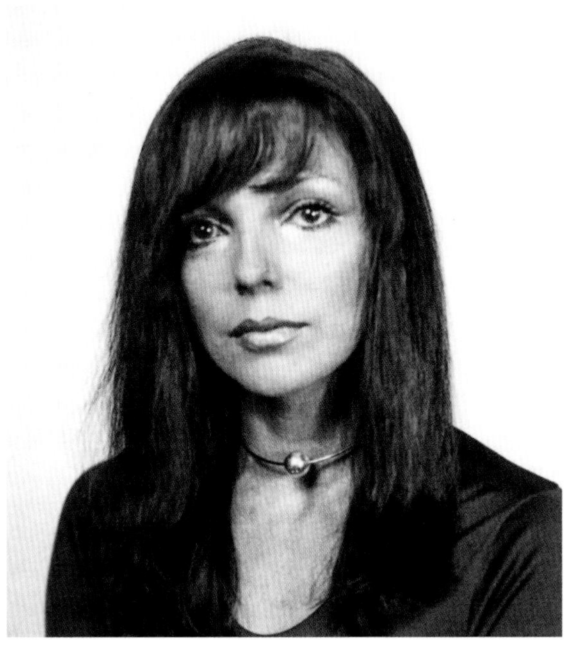

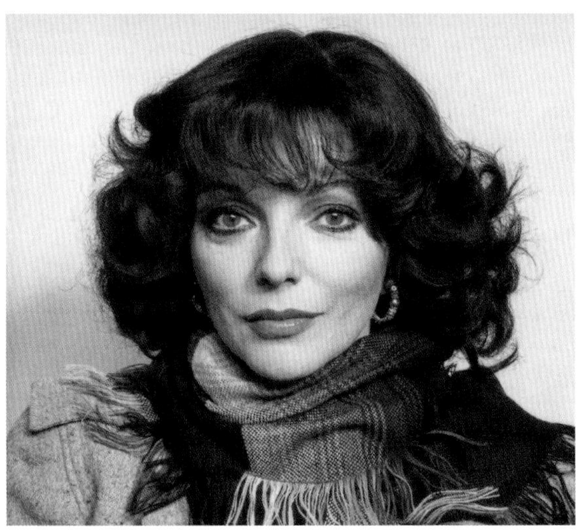

No. 58

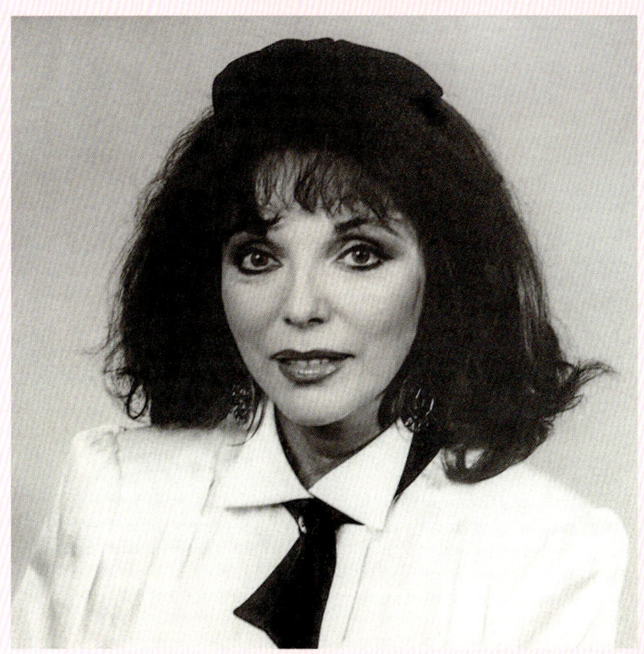

JOAN COLLINS

Actor, 13 July 1971, 31 October 1979 and 5 July 1988

When Joan Collins walked into the studio to be photographed for a third time in July 1988, she was at the peak of her fame. She had been in a few times before with her children, but *Dynasty* was now a huge television series. The customers who were waiting sat open-mouthed as she said to us, 'Darlings, how are you? It is so nice to see you all again,' before telling the stunned onlookers, 'I never go anywhere else for my passport photos.' Thank you, Ms Collins, for the great PR. Perhaps unsurprisingly, she knew exactly how she wanted to be posed: on a very slight angle to the left.

No. 59

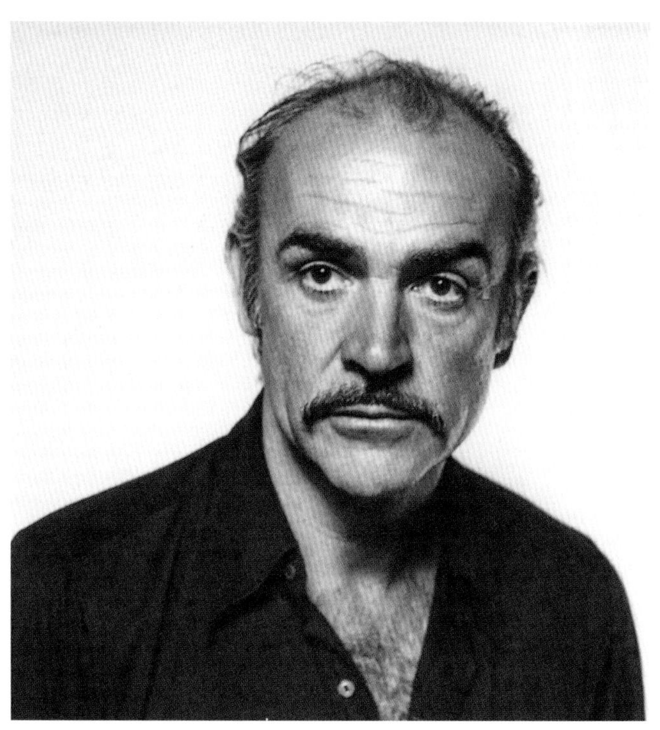

SEAN CONNERY
Actor, 14 September 1977
and 15 May 1989

No. 60

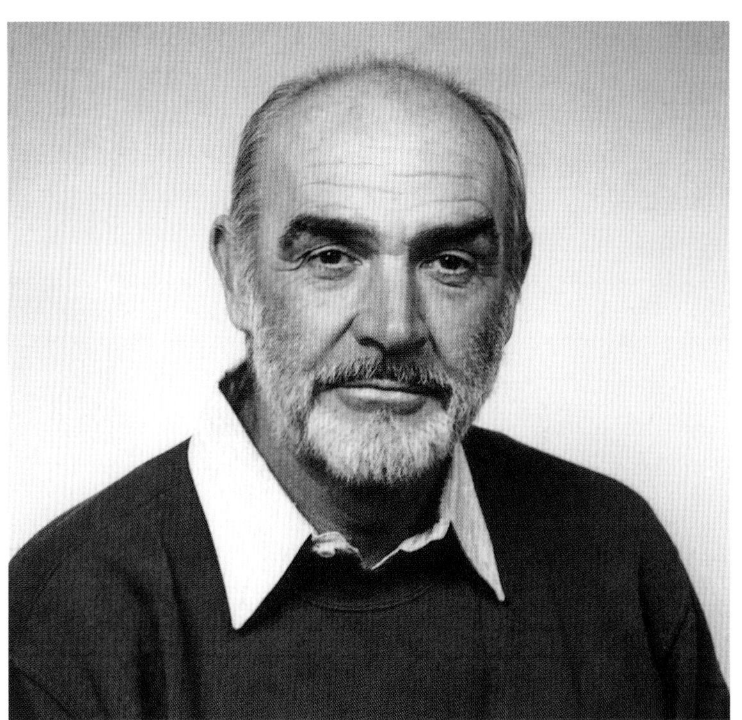

No. 61

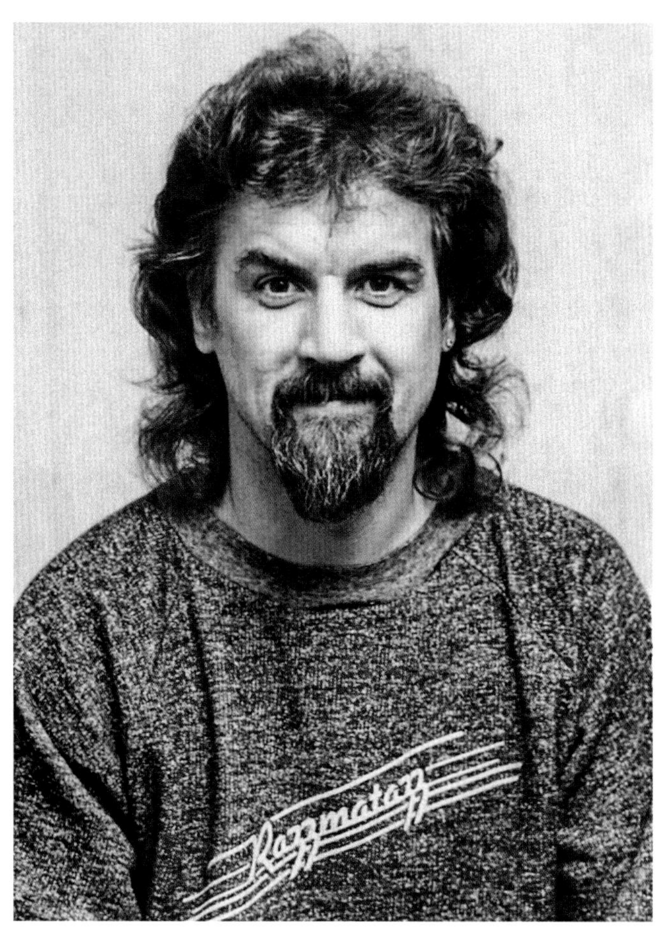

BILLY CONNOLLY
Actor, 1980s

No. 62

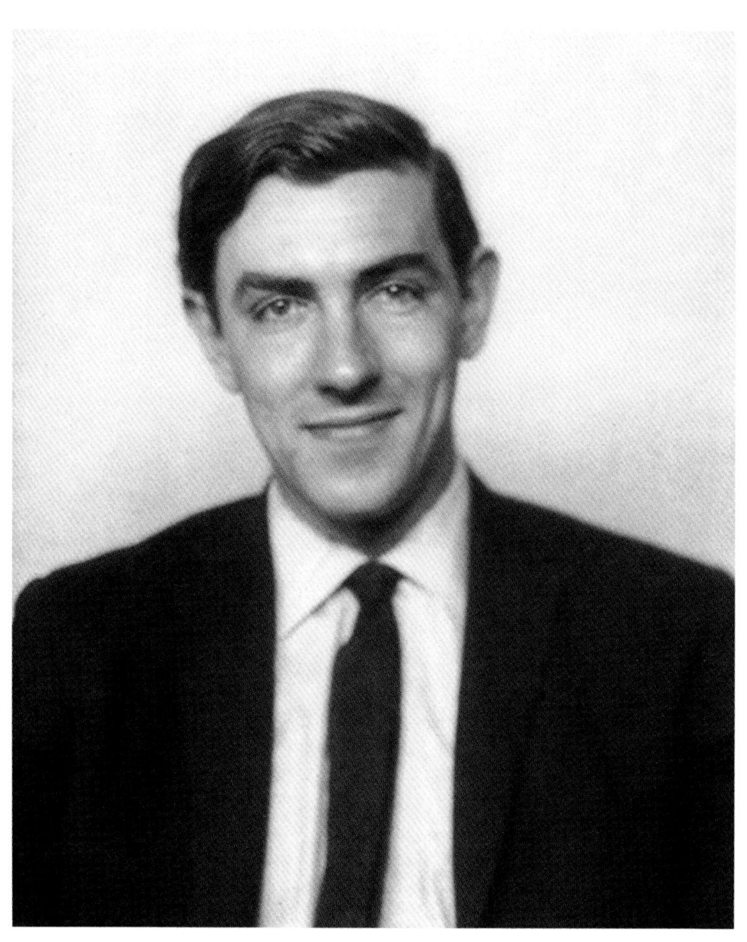

PETER COOK
Actor/Comedian, 12 June 1962

No. 63

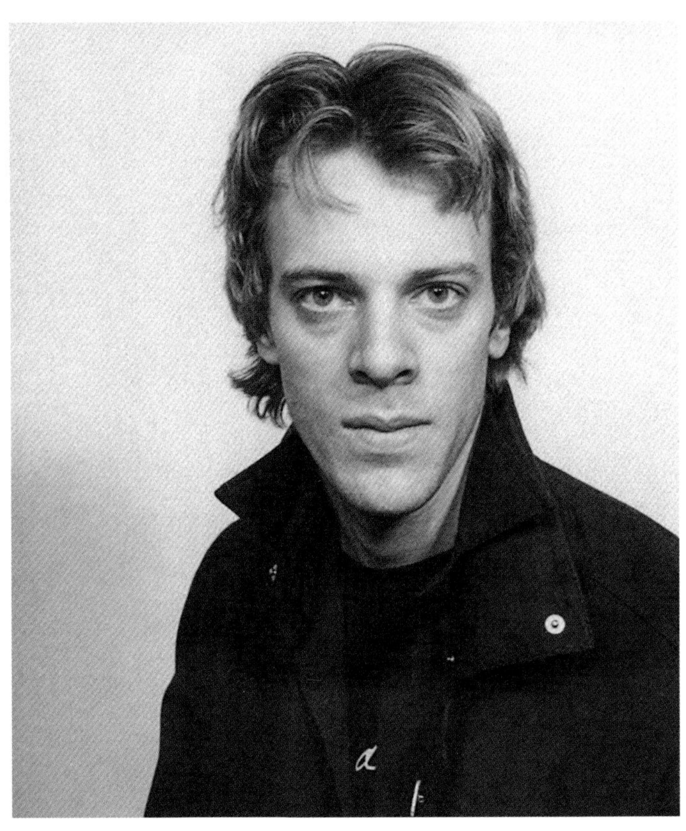

STEWART COPELAND
Musician, 15 January 1980

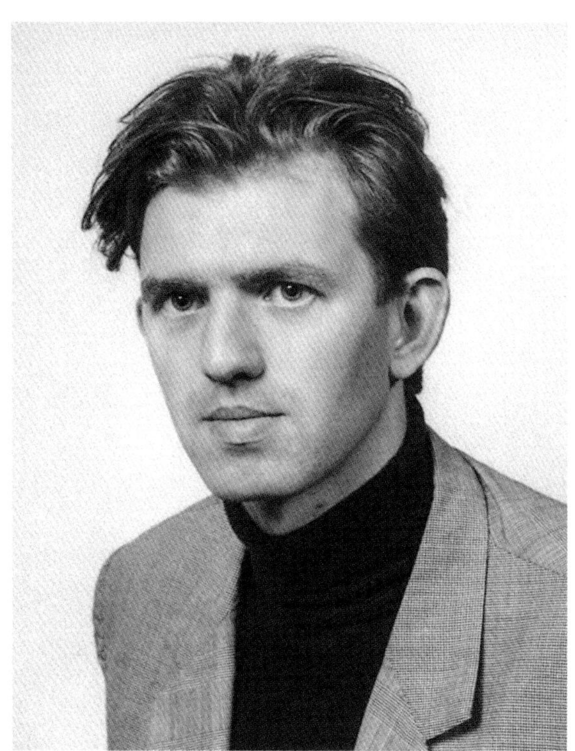

ANTON CORBIJN
Photographer/Director, 2 March 1987

No. 65

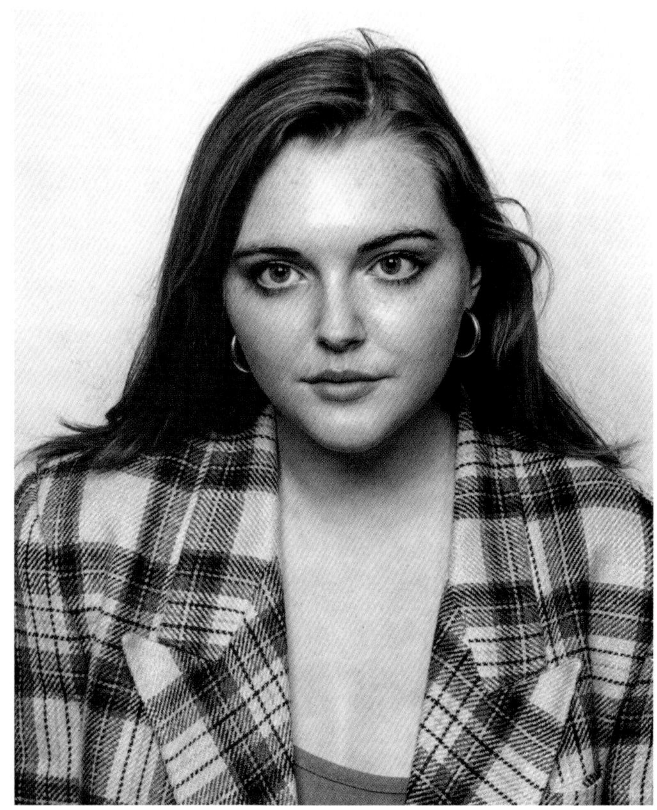

SOPHIE DAHL

Model/Writer, 1990s

This one turned out to be a family affair. Not only had we photographed Sophie Dahl's mother and siblings, but also, I discovered, we had snapped her paternal grandfather, the comic actor Stanley Holloway (see p.119). Her maternal grandfather, however, the great children's author Roald Dahl, never made it onto our walls.

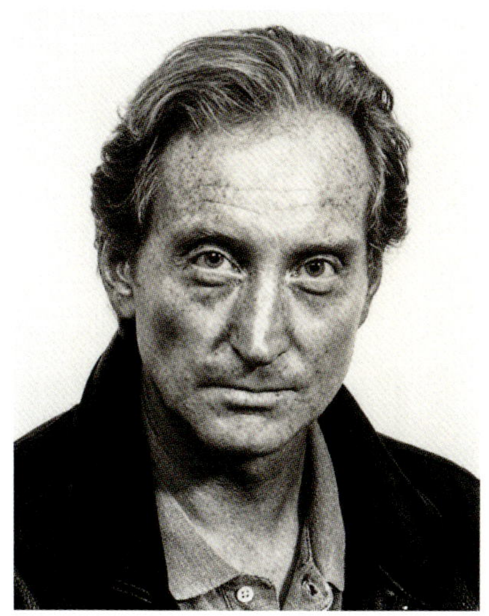

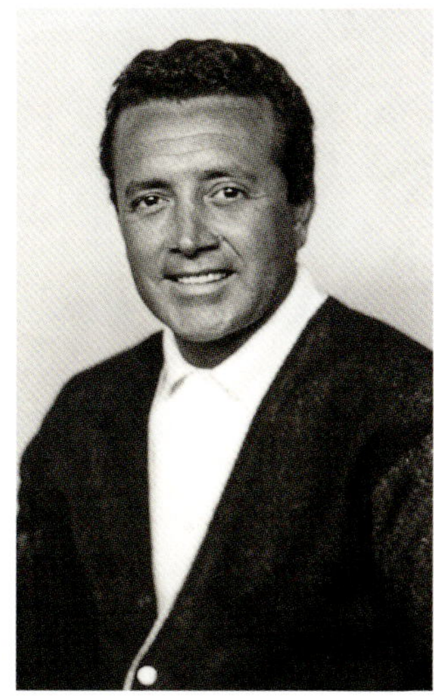

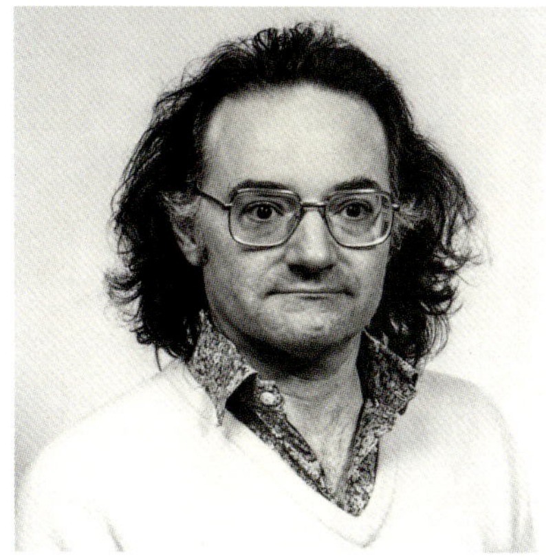

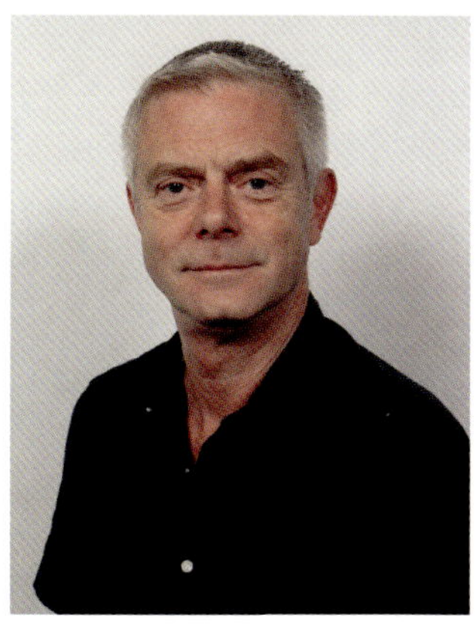

CHARLES DANCE
Actor, 26 July 1993

CARL DAVIS
Composer, 21 April 1993

VIC DAMONE
Singer, 11 August 1961

STEPHEN DALDRY
Director, 2 June 2013

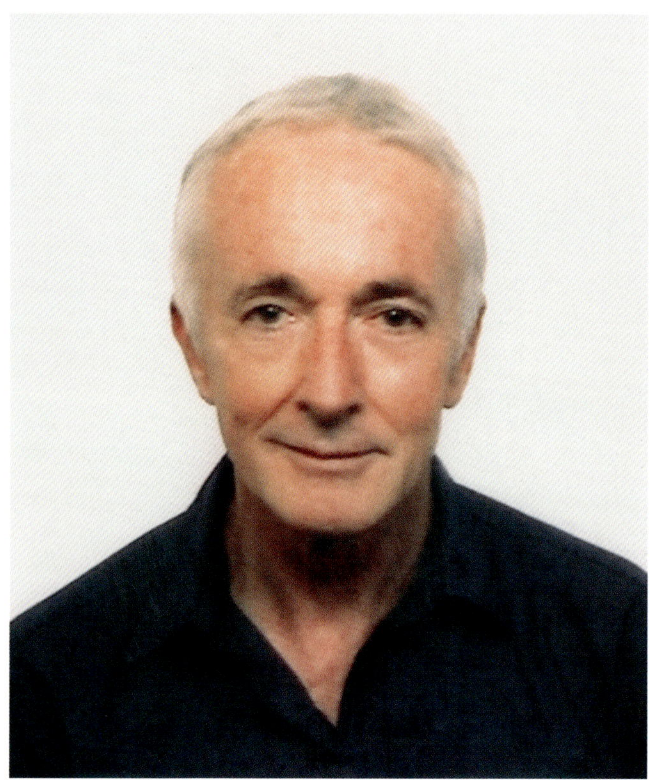

ANTHONY DANIELS

Actor, 3 February 2010

'You may not recognize me, but I am the only actor to have appeared in every *Star Wars* film,' Anthony Daniels said with a smile. Well, he did have to tell us, because he didn't come to the studio dressed as C-3PO! An actor and a mime, he was a friendly, interesting guy who became a regular customer.

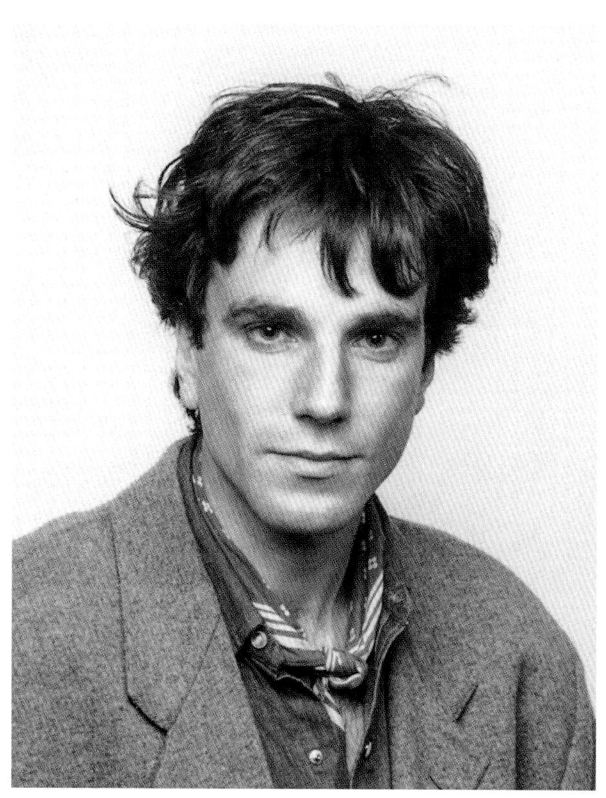

DANIEL DAY-LEWIS
Actor, 19 May 1987

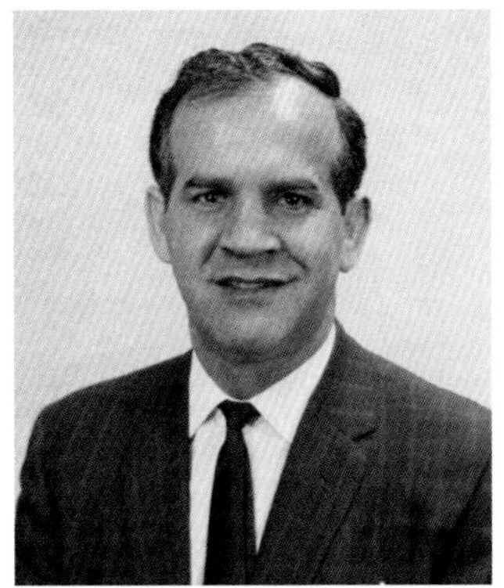

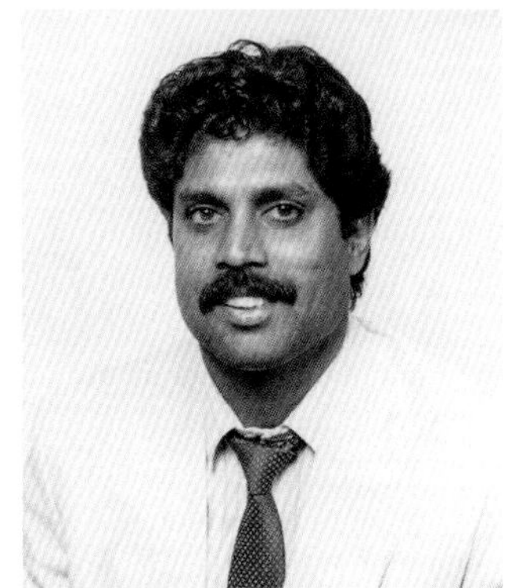

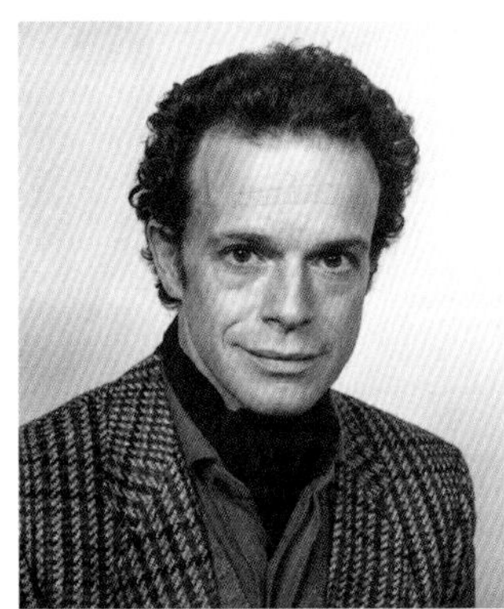

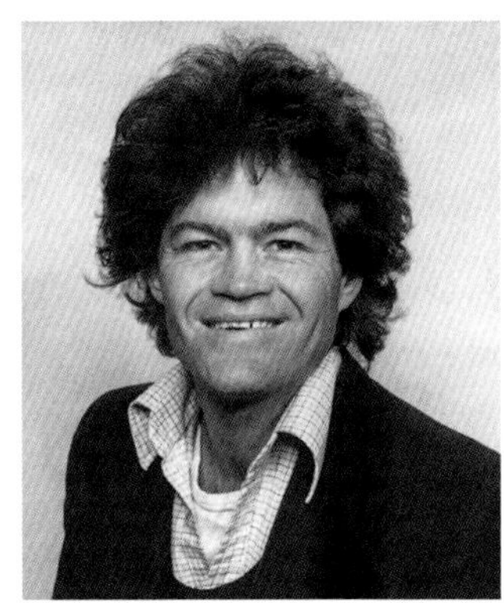

MICKEY DUFF
Boxer, 9 January 1967

ANTHONY DOWELL
Ballet dancer, 2 December 1980

KAPIL DEV
Cricketer, 16 July 1985

MICKY DOLENZ
Musician, 16 October 1978

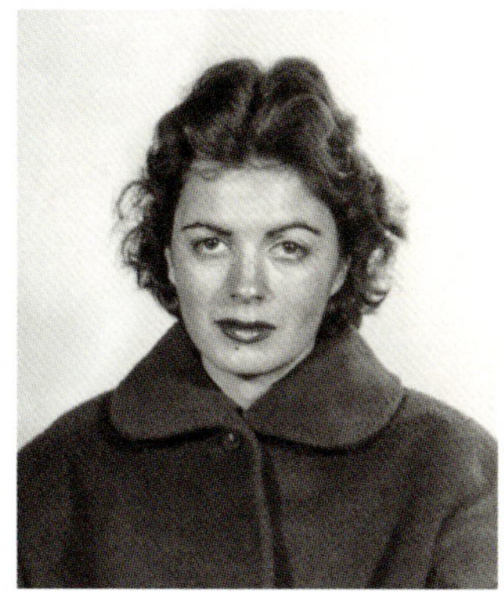

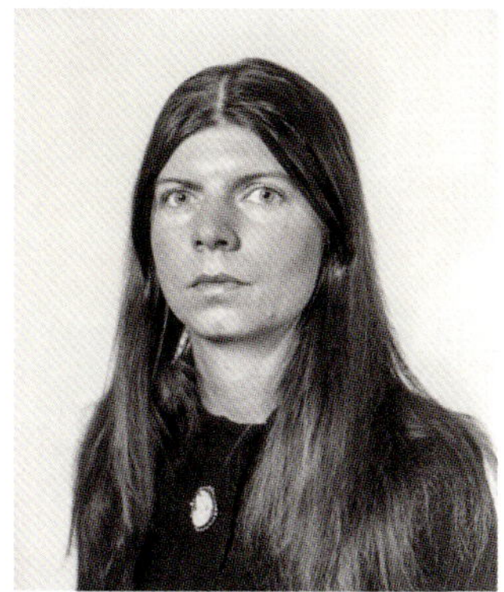

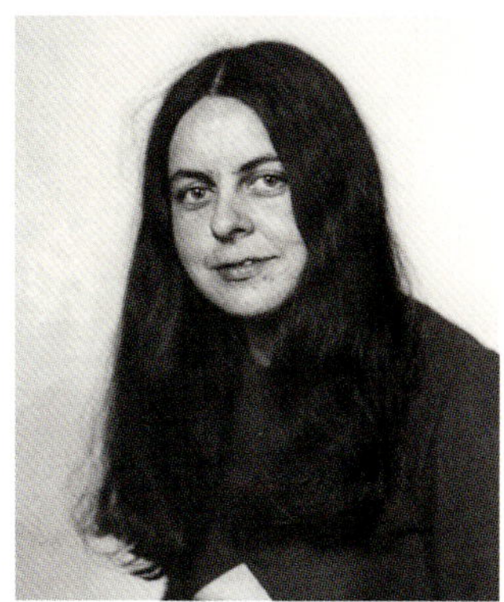

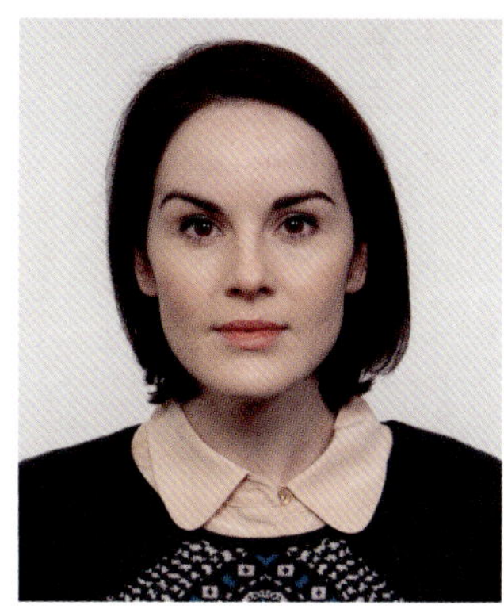

FAITH DOMERGUE
Actor, 1950s

BERNADETTE DEVLIN MCALISKEY
Politician, 1970s

MARGARET DRABBLE
Writer, 27 January 1972

MICHELLE DOCKERY
Actor, 21 November 2012

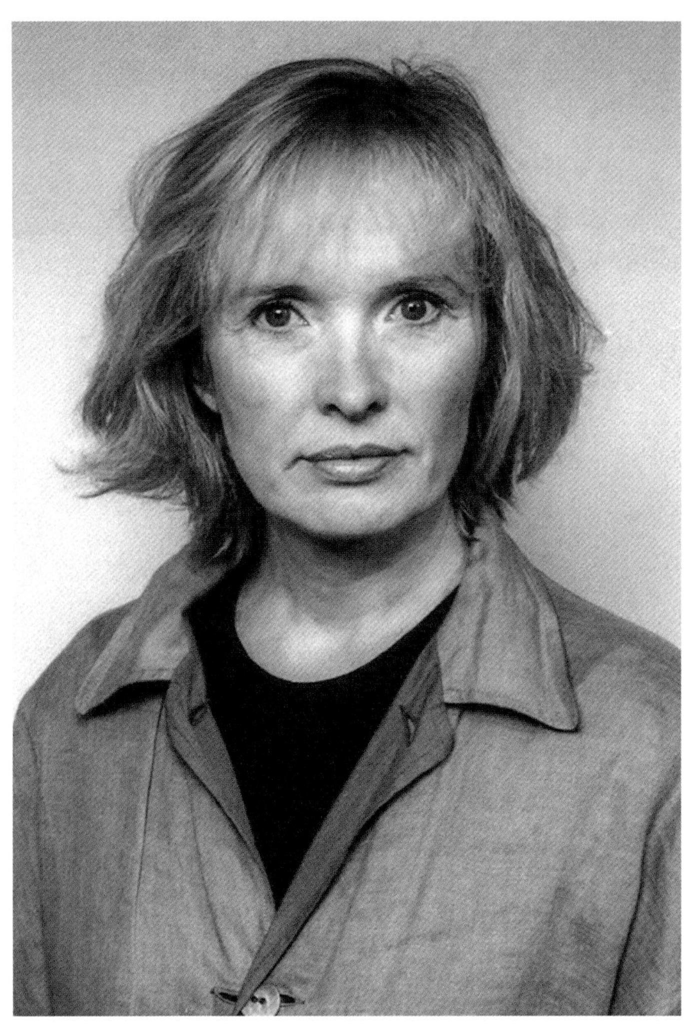

LINDSAY DUNCAN
Actor, 13 May 1998

No. 72

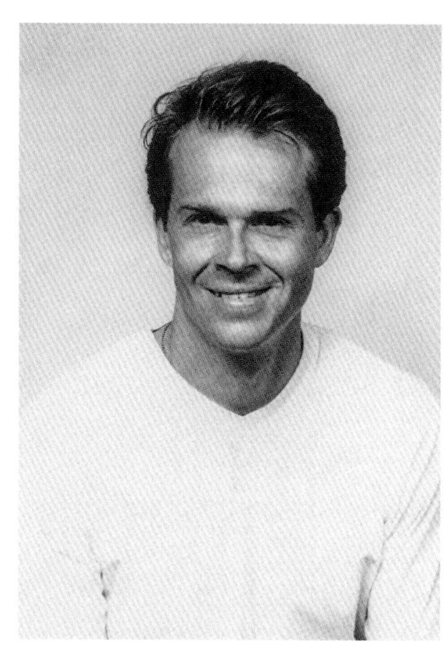

STEFAN EDBERG

Tennis player, 8 July 1998

Stefan Edberg came in with his daughter for her Swedish passport photograph. He didn't need one, but when I asked him if I could add him to our collection, he was more than happy to sit and have his picture taken (so it could be included in an archive like this book!).

KEINOSUKE ENOEDA

Karate master, 23 June 1983

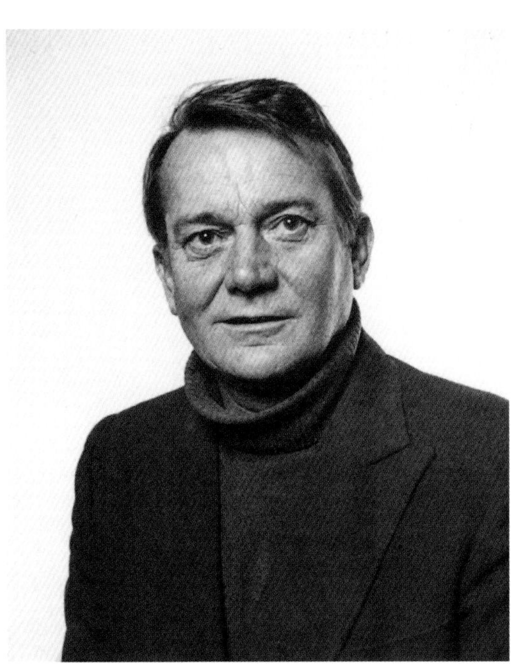

DENHOLM ELLIOTT
Actor, 29 November 1976

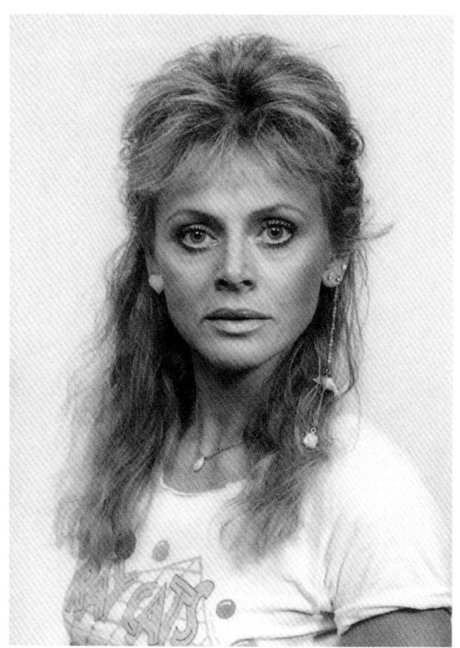

BRITT EKLAND

Actor, 25 August 1983

I was slightly terrified to take Britt Ekland's picture. She had been photographed by all the leading fashion and studio photographers, so I was worried she would be hard to please. How wrong I was – she was friendly, charming and happy with her photos. She is wearing a T-shirt for the band Stray Cats, which makes sense since at the time she was in a relationship with their drummer Slim Jim Phantom, whom I had also photographed a couple of years previously.

No. 75

CHRIS EUBANK

Pugilist, 30 May 1996

When the boxer Chris Eubank strutted into the studio in July 1992, he was the reigning World Boxing Organization super-middleweight champion and a well-known character in the media. Upon casting his eyes over our board of celebrities, he announced, 'I first came to this studio when I was nine years old, and I knew one day I would be added to your wall of fame.' Well, he was right, and when he returned a few years later, he spotted himself on the wall next to the popular dancer and television personality Lionel Blair (see p.36). Eubank remarked, 'That man is a "Bengal Lancer"' (Cockney rhyming slang for a dancer), and inquired with his trademark lisp, 'What has he done, on merit, to be next to me?' To placate him, Peter asked him where he would like to be placed. 'Between Terry-Thomas (see p.236) and Alastair Sim,' he demanded. Peter replied, 'Well, we can put you next to Terry-Thomas, but Alastair Sim never came up and he's dead!' So we duly rearranged the photos to place Eubank next to his hero. He shares with Terry a pronounced gap in the front teeth, and you can certainly see that he styled himself as an upper-class Englishman. He continued to drop in, often with his long-suffering trainer Ronnie Davies, who played along with his persona. Eubank would refer to him as 'Davies', as if talking to his manservant. He would come in with friends and colleagues to show them his picture and talk about the stars in our frames, always making sure to point to Terry-Thomas and proclaim 'He is the man!' Eubank once popped in just to have his photo taken with his Louis Vuitton bag, which had been autographed by Louis Theroux. A true eccentric.

No. 76

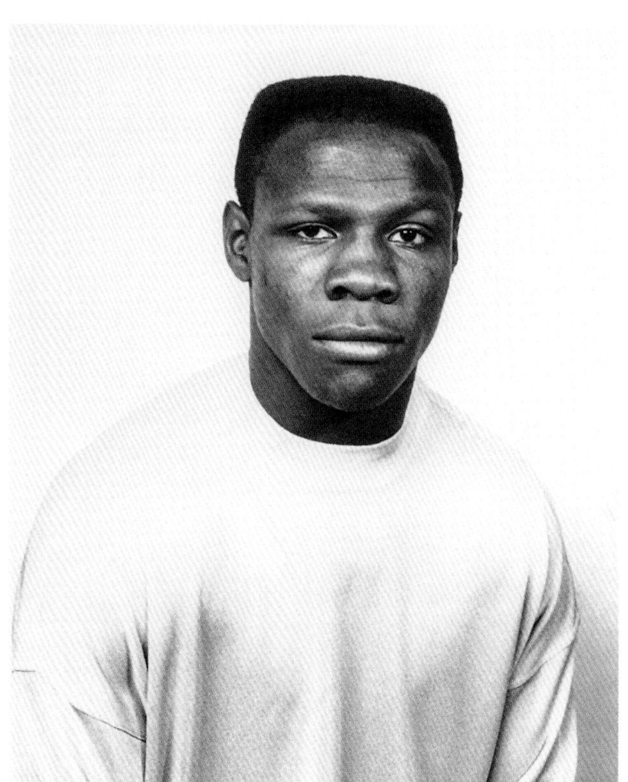

No. 77

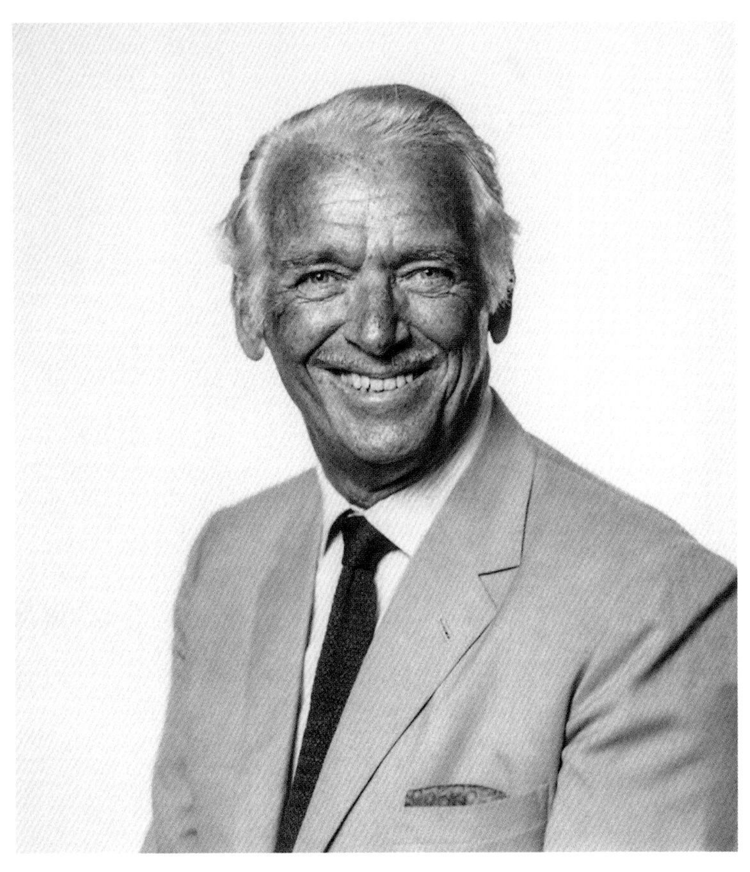

DOUGLAS FAIRBANKS JR
Actor, 12 June 1970

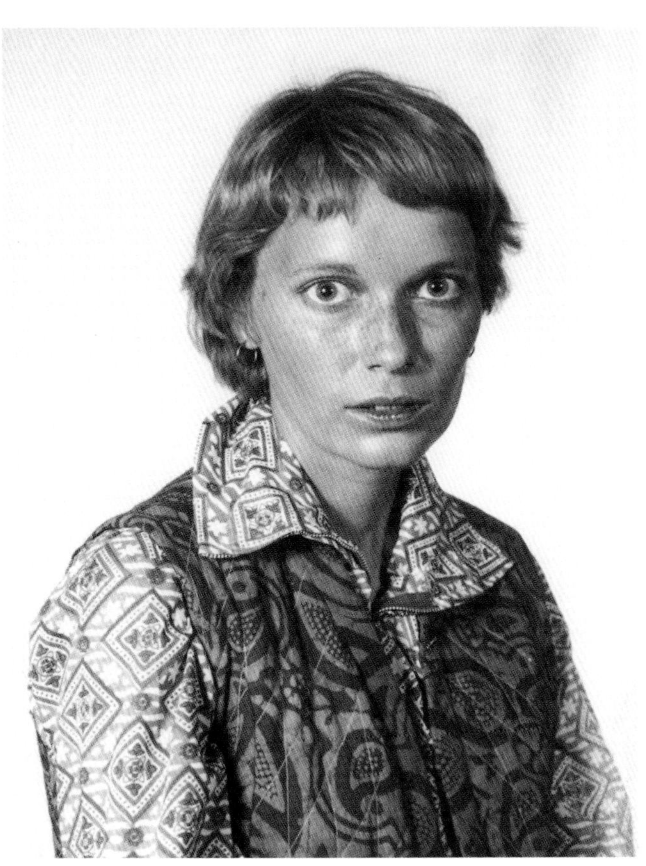

MIA FARROW
Actor, 30 June 1969

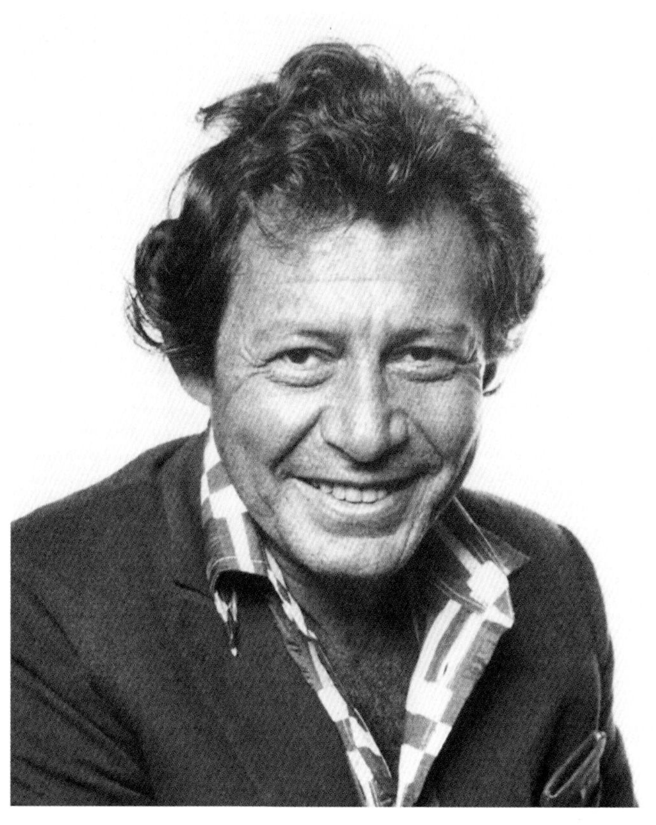

EDDIE FISHER
Actor/Singer, 20 July 1974

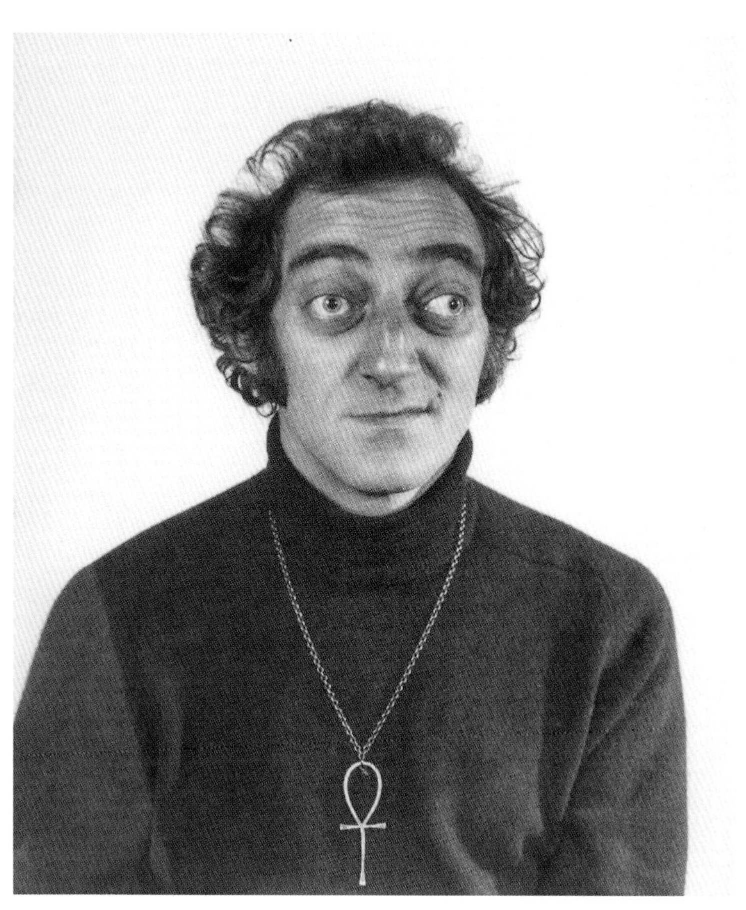

MARTY FELDMAN
Actor, 9 January 1969

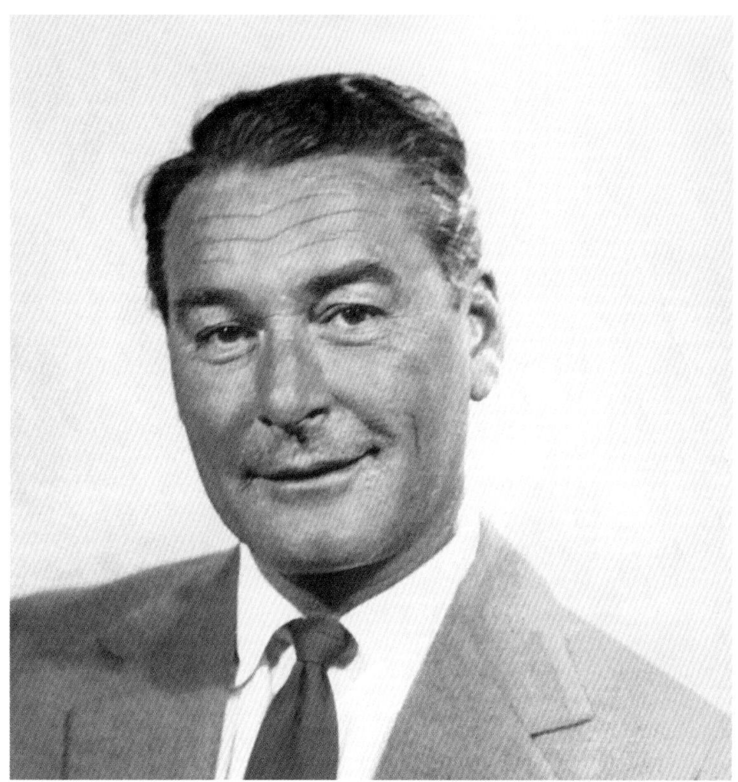

No. 82

ERROL FLYNN

Actor, Summer 1955

My father never forgot the first time Errol Flynn came into the studio, even writing down this account of it in 1980. The door opened with a kick and a tall, well-built man with dark glasses and a grey suit stood there, hands on hips, and boomed, 'Yep, it's me.' He had a good-natured smile, but a fairly aggressive stance. In the studio at the time there was an Irish girl who was unable to afford the seven shillings and six pence (37½ pence today) for her photos. When Mr Flynn overheard her plight, he said, 'Irish? I'll pay for them, a present from a fellow Irish.' He sat down for his photo and my father gave him a few directions, to which he grinningly replied, 'I'm the fucking actor, you're the photographer.' The conversation was lively, and he noticed everything, referring to people as 'sport', like Jay Gatsby. Of a British actress's wide-mouthed smiling portrait, for instance, he said, 'She didn't get that from sucking Coca-Cola bottles.' My father did not react to his vulgarity, and he became more serious. He even spoke of Polaroid cameras and instant films, asking my father if he had looked into this new technology. My father was one of the first people in London who had found a way to develop photos in ten minutes, and he offered a same-day service before anyone else. Curious, Mr Flynn came into the darkroom and was rapt as my father developed the photograph. He said photography was fascinating and would be especially useful in future technology. At this point, he very gently stroked the back of my dad's hand with a smooth, sensuous forefinger. My father acted as though he was completely unaware of the touch, but he was amazed by the action and not repelled, just registering how sensitive it was. The famous swashbuckler signed one of the photos and gave it to my father.

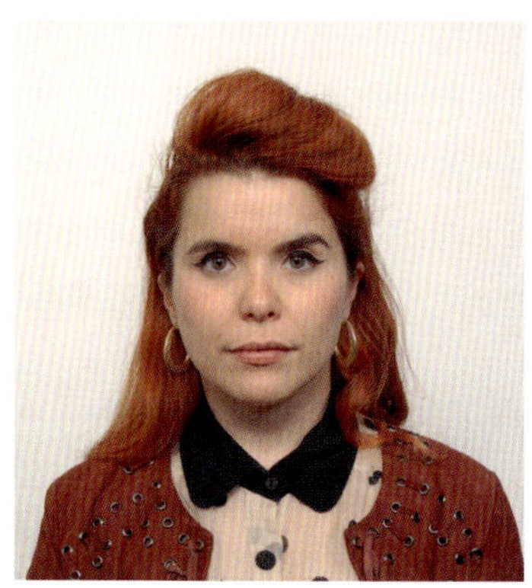

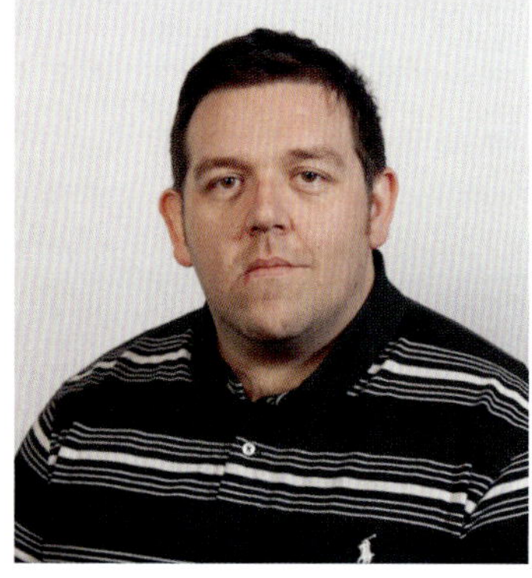

PALOMA FAITH

Musician, 20 July 2011

NICK FROST

Actor, 31 January 2011

Nick Frost could see I wasn't quite sure who he was, so he helpfully introduced himself, joking, 'I hope you think I'm famous enough to go in your frame of famous faces.' Well, mate, you've made it into the book as well!

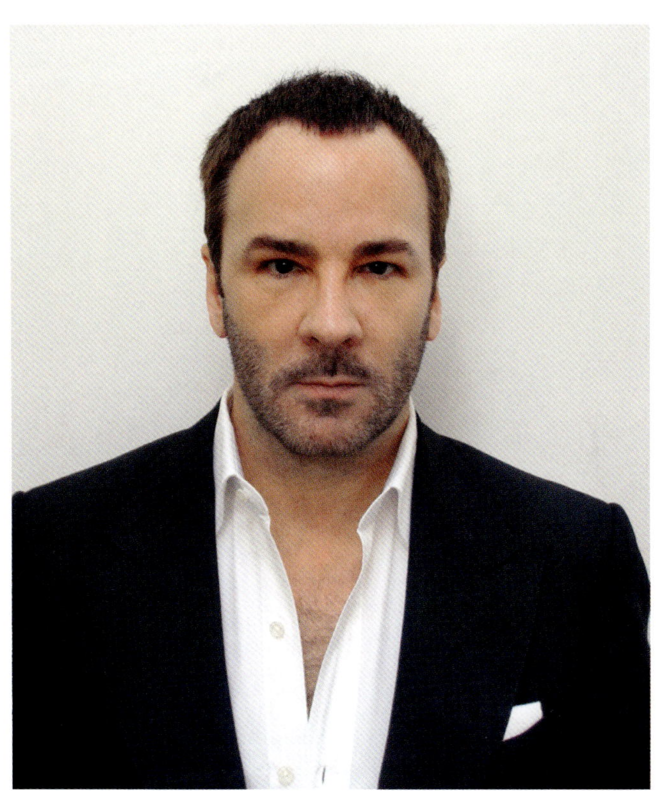

TOM FORD
Fashion designer, 18 November 2014

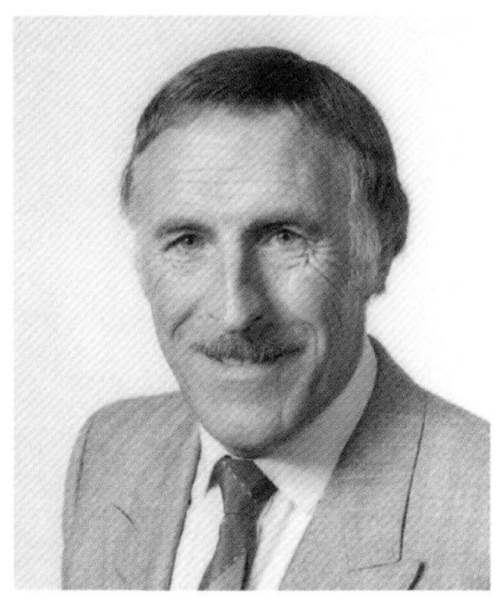

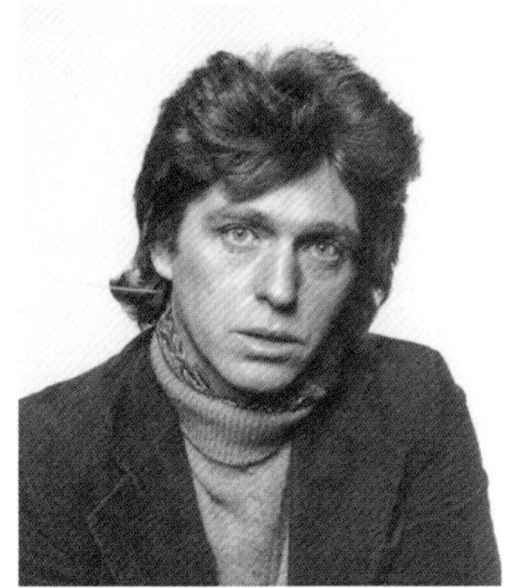

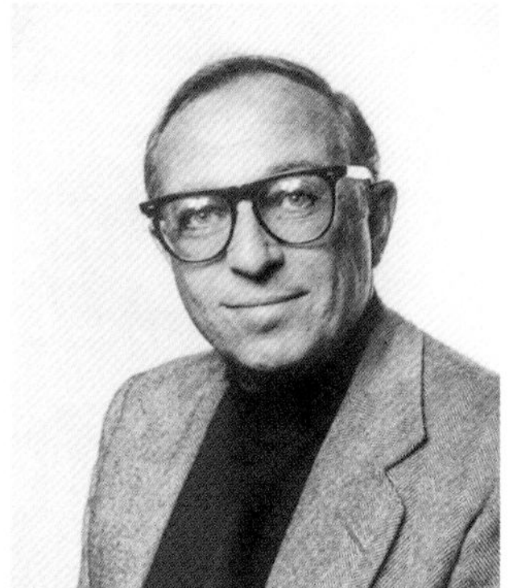

BRUCE FORSYTH
Entertainer, 19 September 1981

GEORGIE FAME
Musician, 1 March 1976

CARL FOREMAN
Screenwriter, 21 May 1975

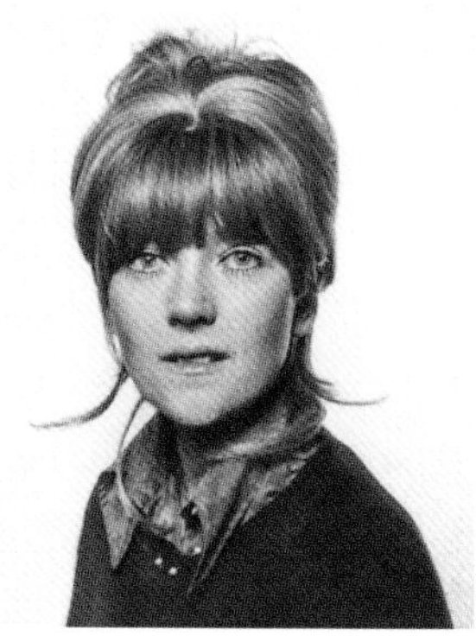

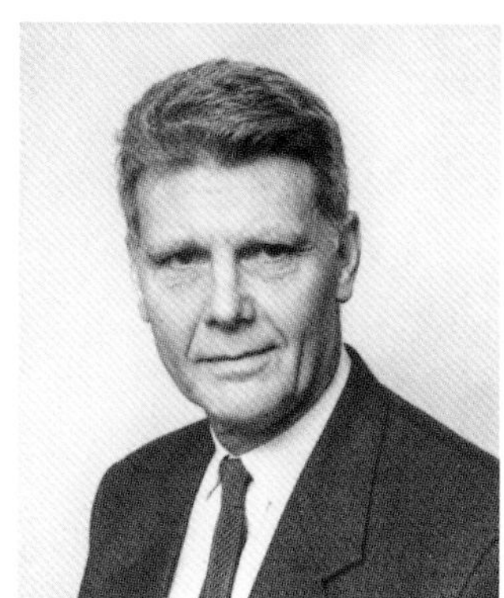

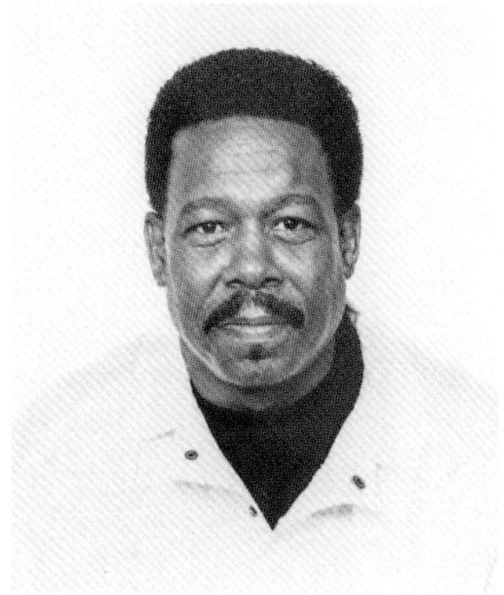

JULIA FOSTER
Actor, 14 May 1971

EDDIE FLOYD
Musician, 7 June 1991

JAMES FOX
Actor, 4 December 1996

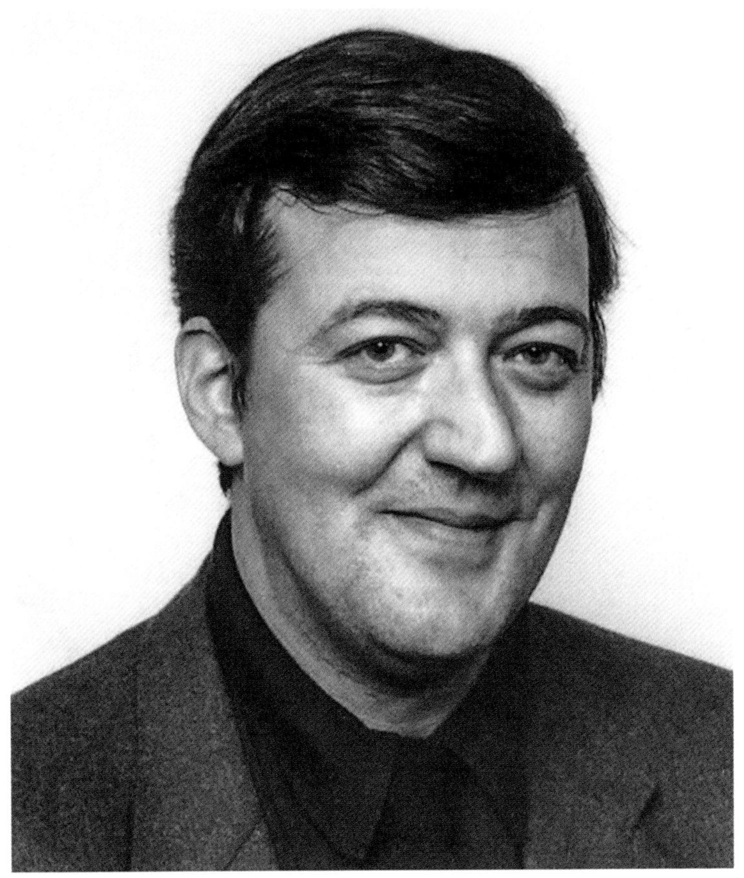

No. 88

STEPHEN FRY

Actor/Writer, 3 June 1986

Stephen Fry has been a regular in the studio since the late 1980s, as was his comedy partner Hugh Laurie (see p.145), although they have never come in together. Naturally, we have always placed their photos next to each other, leading to good-natured and often bawdy comments from both on seeing each other's images when visiting. Stephen has also accompanied his husband, Elliott Spencer, to the studio, and both used us for their passport and visa photographs. Always a delight to photograph and chat to, he is full of showbiz tales and stories about his travels.

No. 89

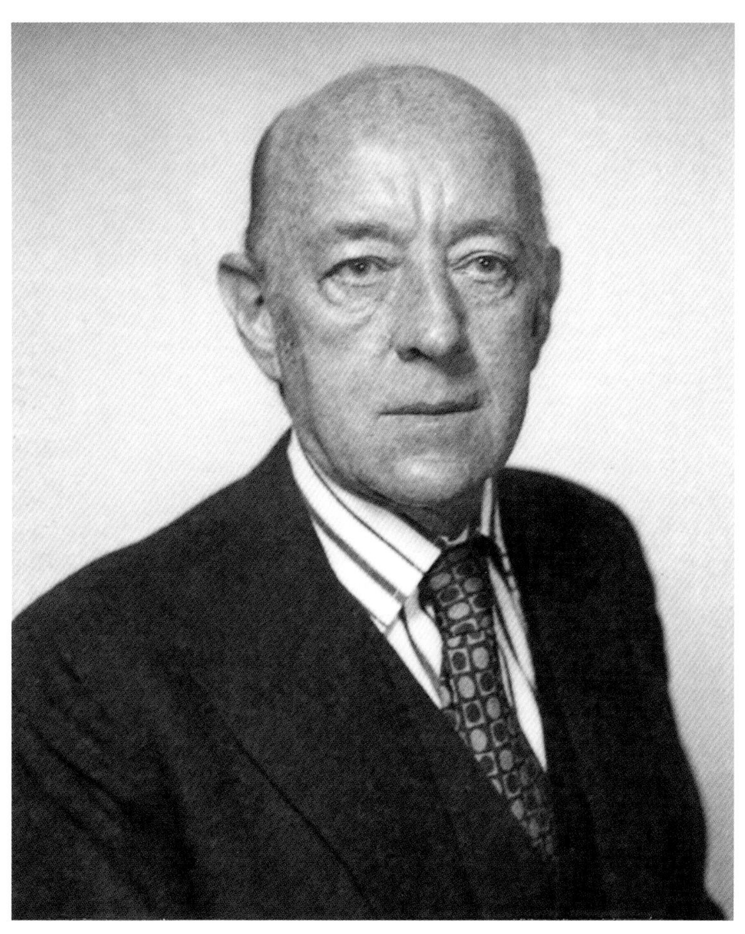

ALEC GUINNESS
Actor, 1975

No. 90

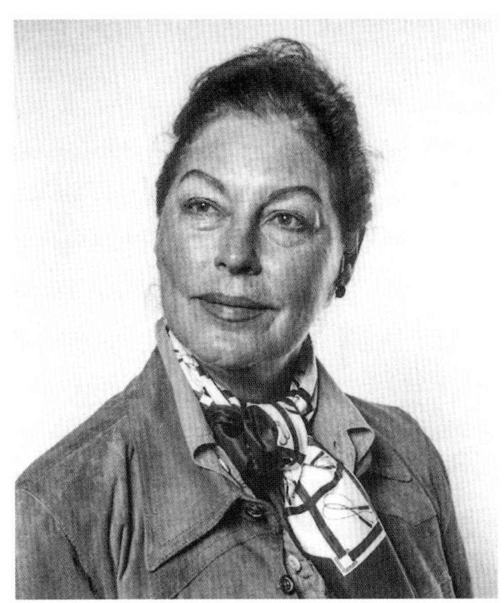

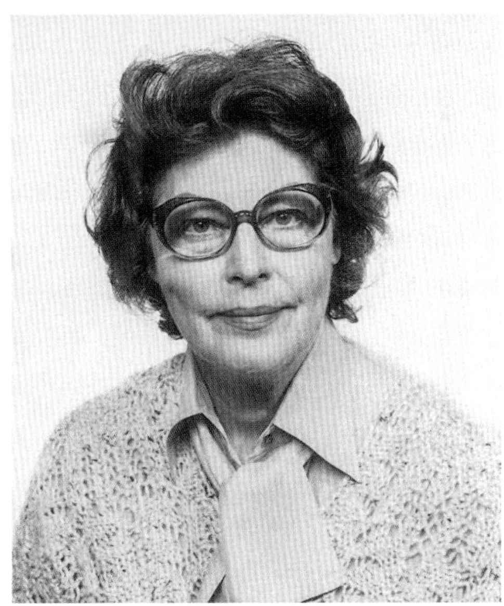

AVA GARDNER
Actor, 16 September 1976
and 2 April 1987

URI GELLER

Magician, 2002

As Uri Geller appeared, walking up the last few stairs into the studio, he looked around and took in the architecture, including the skylights of what had been the artist William Morris's workshop and, before us, the consulting room of a clairvoyant named Madame Sandra. 'I feel a very positive aura here,' he told me with a beatific expression. 'This space feels very special and gives off really positive vibrations.' The magician wanted to know when the studio started and all about the history of the building. I felt charmed and proud that he had picked up on how special our location was and understood how remarkable my father's journey from the East End to the West End had been. He was intrigued by everything, continuously talking as he came into the darkroom to watch me develop and print his photograph. Just before he left, he went into our little office, where we made our tea and coffee. On seeing a spoon, he picked it up and, standing directly in front of me, proceeded to rub it between his thumb and forefinger. Hey presto! It bent before my very eyes. He said it was a gift for my father and signed it to him. It was our only spoon. Some time later, Geller returned with his daughter for her passport photo. He was so pleased to see his picture on our 'wall of fame' that he produced a felt-tip pen from his pocket and signed the glass over his photo, being very careful not to obscure his face.

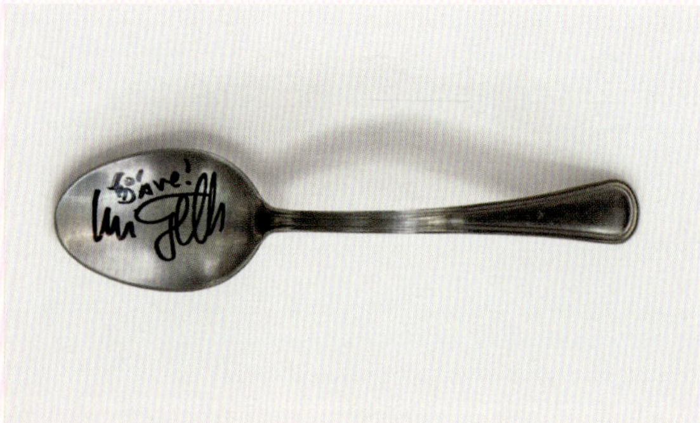

No. 92

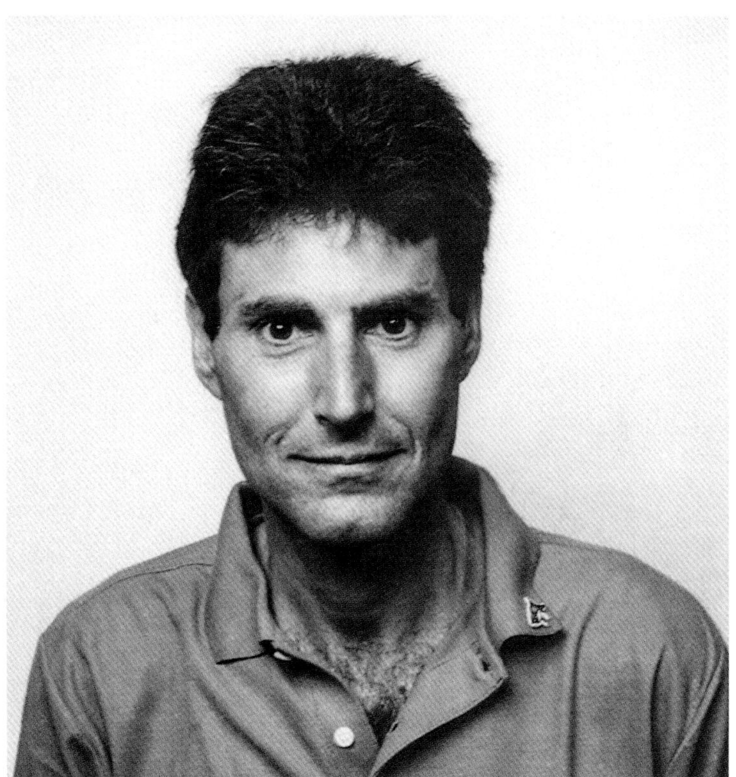

No. 93

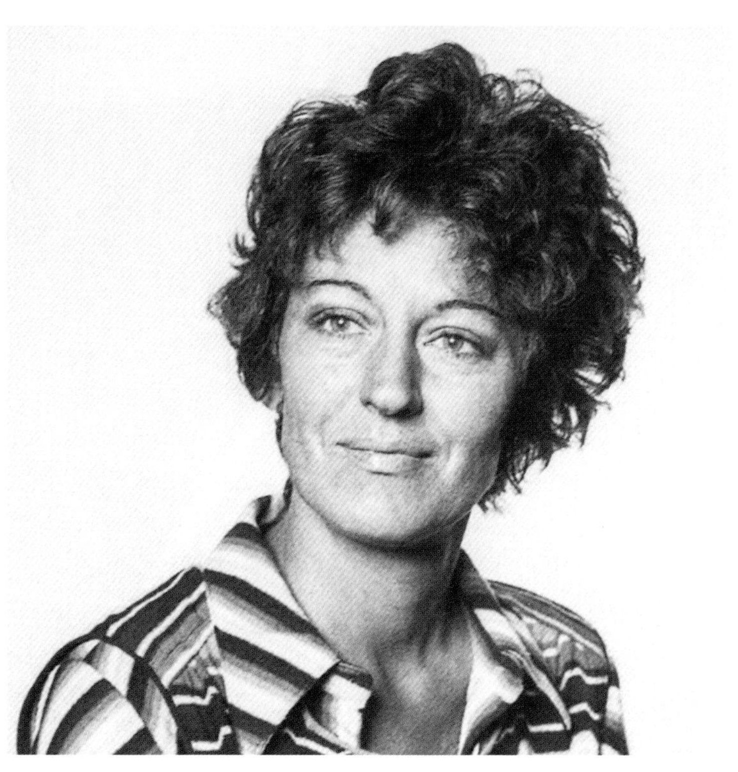

GERMAINE GREER
Writer, 3 October 1974

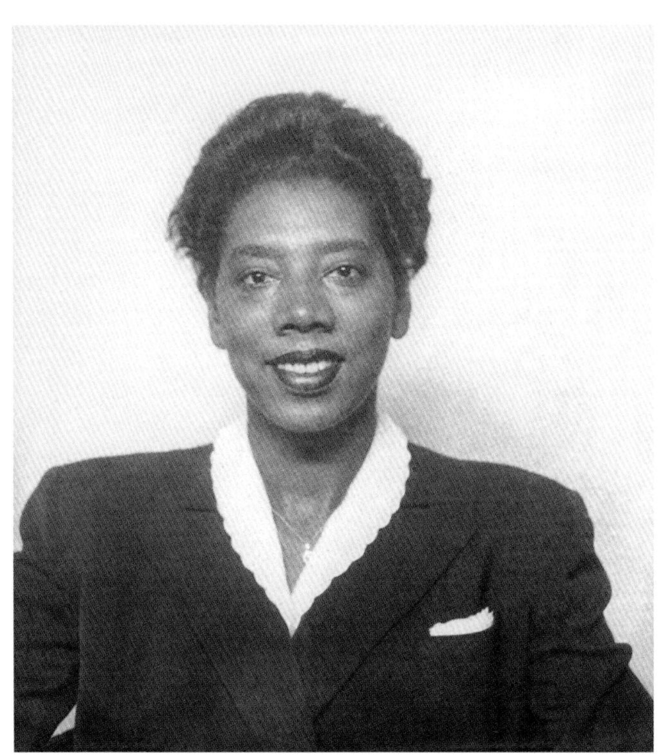

ALTHEA GIBSON
Tennis player, 8 July 1959

J. PAUL GETTY

Businessman, 1960s

When I was on my school holidays, I would usually be hauled up to the studio since both my parents were busy working there. One day, I remember a rather austere-looking man coming in. My father, who had just taken his photograph, told me, 'That's the richest man in the world.' Well, I was surprised because at that age I thought that if I were the richest man in the world, I would certainly be looking happier! J. Paul Getty ordered the minimum number of prints and, when his photos were ready, my father urged me to hand them to him in case he left a nice tip. ''Ere', I said as I thrust his photos at him. He handed me back the exact payment, a whopping seven shillings and six pence (37½ pence today). I suppose you don't become the richest man in the world by giving tips to nine-year-olds. Afterwards, Peter saw him heading the short distance down North Audley Street to the American embassy in his chauffeur-driven Cadillac.

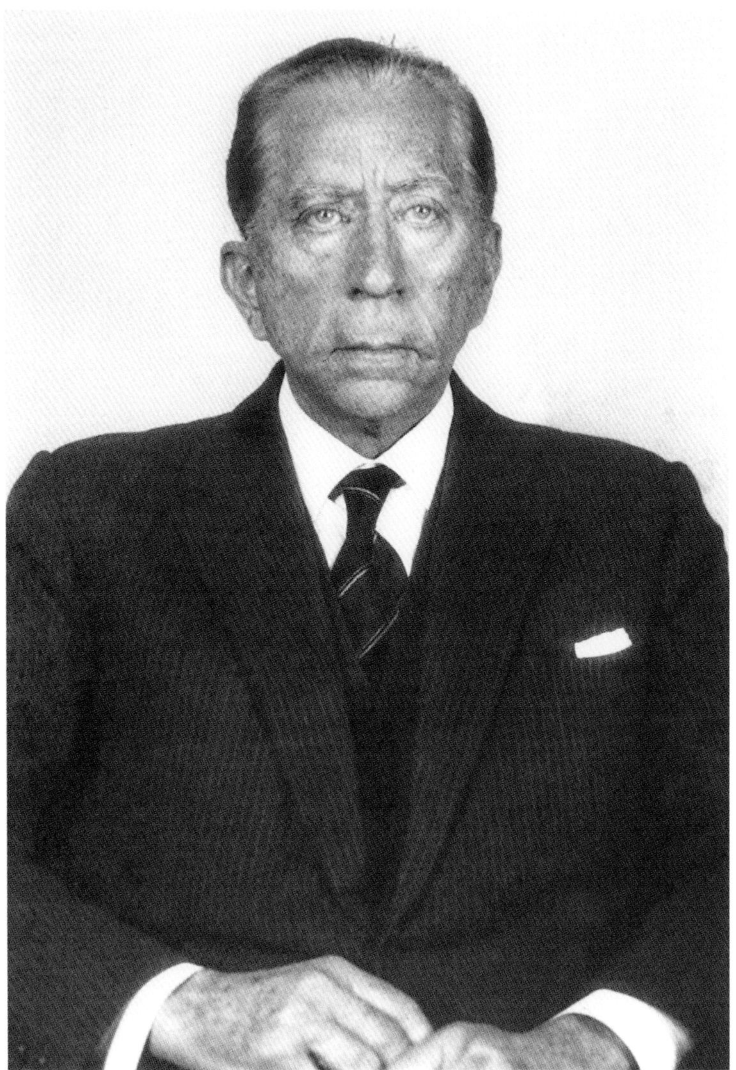

No. 97

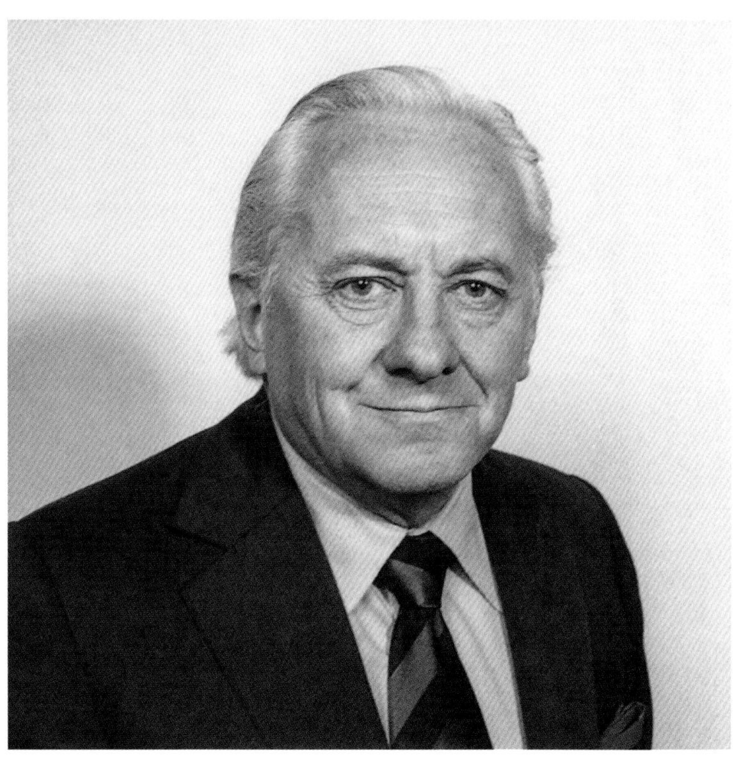

No. 98

HUGHIE GREEN

TV presenter, 8 May 1978

Hughie Green was possibly the person we photographed more than any other. As a Canadian, he needed to renew his passport every five years, and he lived very close to the studio, in Baker Street. Although he was a mainstream game-show host, it appears he was a bit of a Casanova in the 1970s, and it was quite a scandal when in the late 1990s he was revealed as the biological father of fellow TV presenter Paula Yates. His daughter Linda was also a regular at the studio, and whenever she came in, she would tell us that a few more people had come forward saying Green was their father. She said she welcomed them all and included them in her ever-growing family.

LEN GOODMAN

Ballroom dancer, 5 September 2012

An early-morning appointment for his visa at the US embassy hadn't started well for Len Goodman. He hadn't filled in his DS-160 form, and exclaimed wearily, 'I don't know why I'm still rushing about like this at my age. I should be putting my feet up. And don't talk to me about computers, I don't have a clue, you'll have to sort it out, son.' At the time, he was judging *Dancing with the Stars* in the United States, so he was across the pond often. By this point the studio offered a service to fill in the visa forms, much to Goodman's relief. 'Thanks, son,' he said as he left, sticking a £20 tip into my hand.

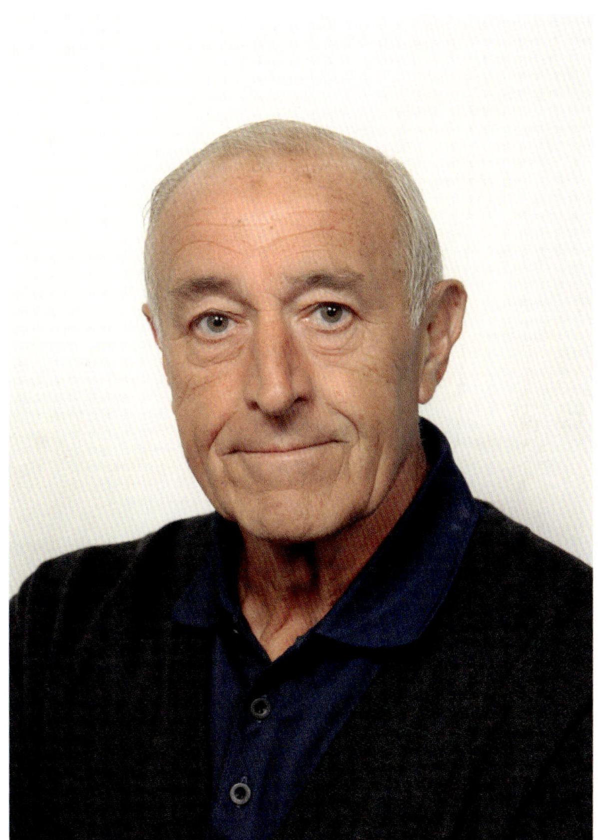

No. 101

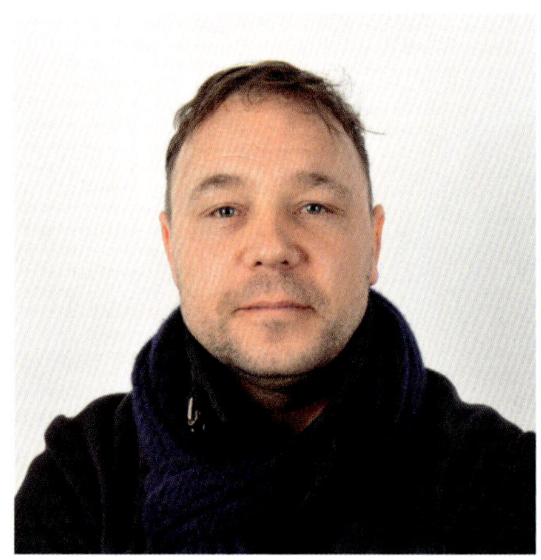

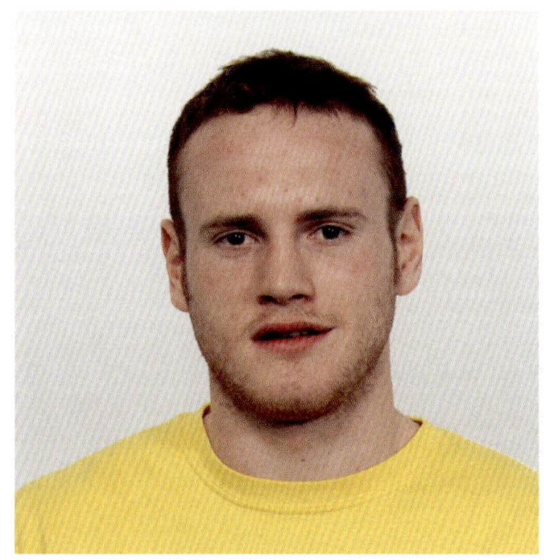

STEPHEN GRAHAM
Actor, 5 November 2015

GEORGE GROVES
Boxer, 28 April 2010

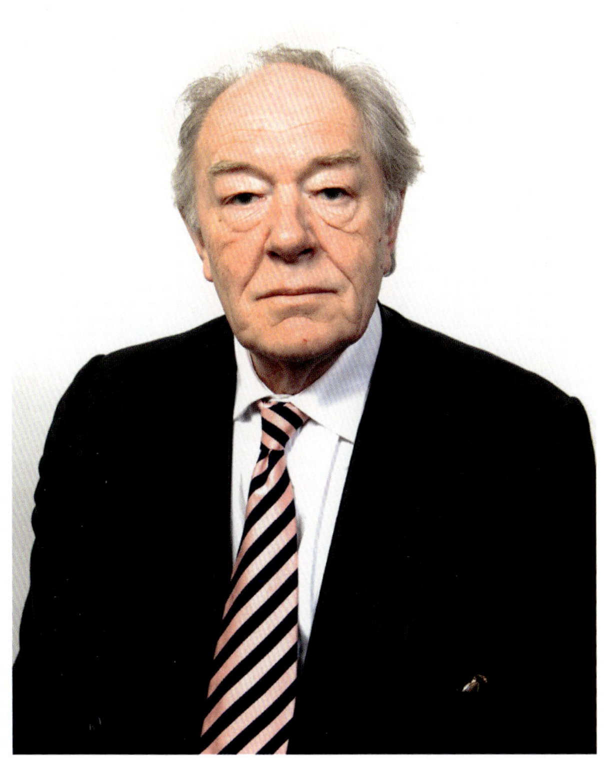

MICHAEL GAMBON
Actor, 9 March 2009

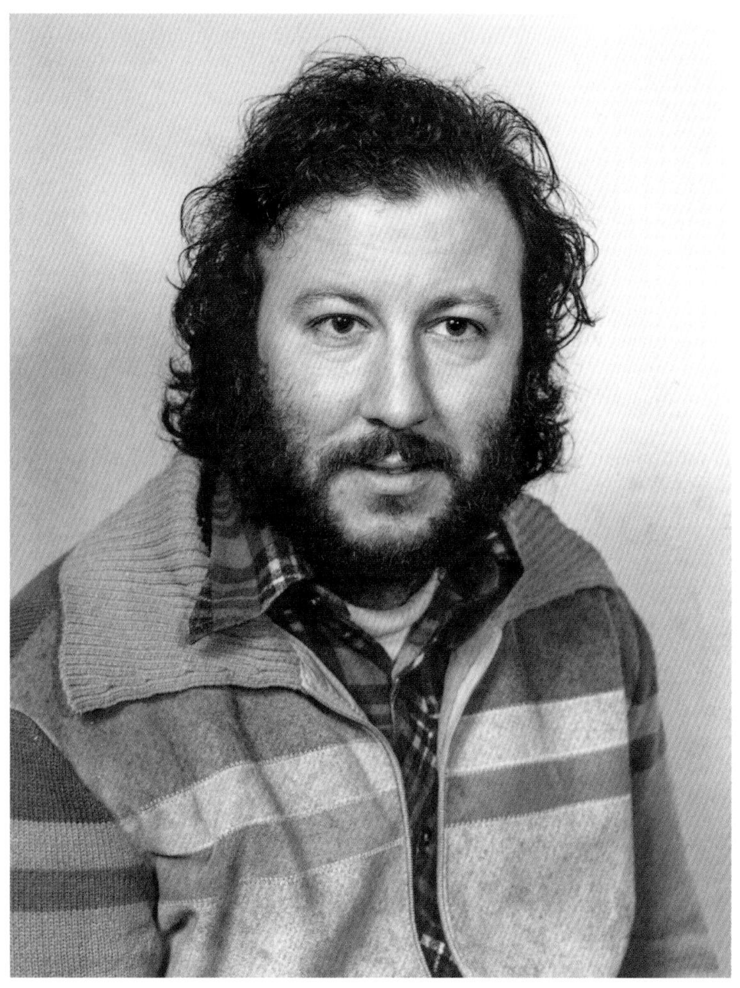

No. 104

PETER GREEN

Musician, 10 March 1978

The original Fleetwood Mac guitarist came in to have his photograph taken because he was going to relaunch his career and tour America, eight years after leaving the band. It was well known that he had suffered some seriously harmful side effects from taking large doses of LSD. Although he seemed pleased that I had recognized him and told him how much I loved his music, he really didn't seem ready to tour again, and he was nervous and quiet. I'm glad to say that he did recover well enough to return to playing live some time later.

No. 105

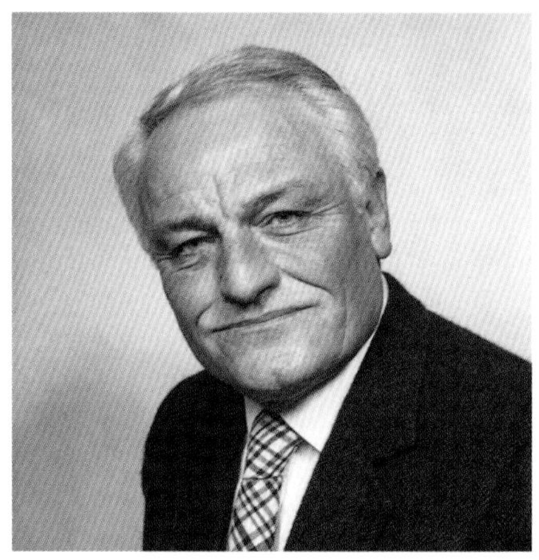

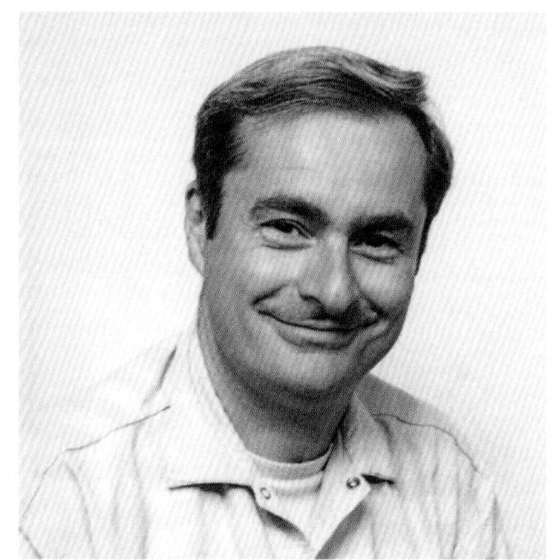

CHARLES GRAY
Actor, 3 February 1981

PAUL GAMBACCINI
Radio DJ, 20 June 1985

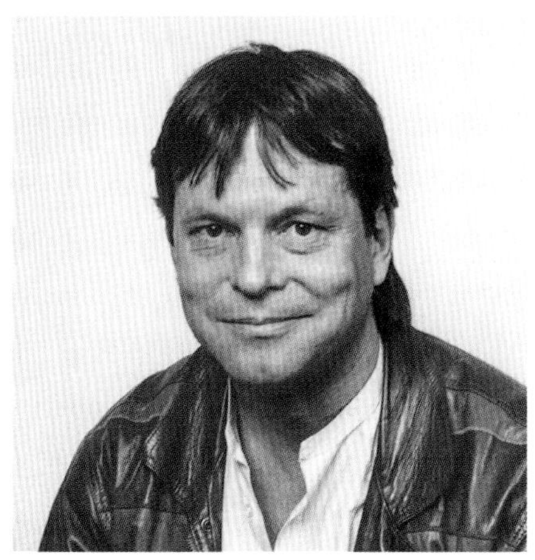

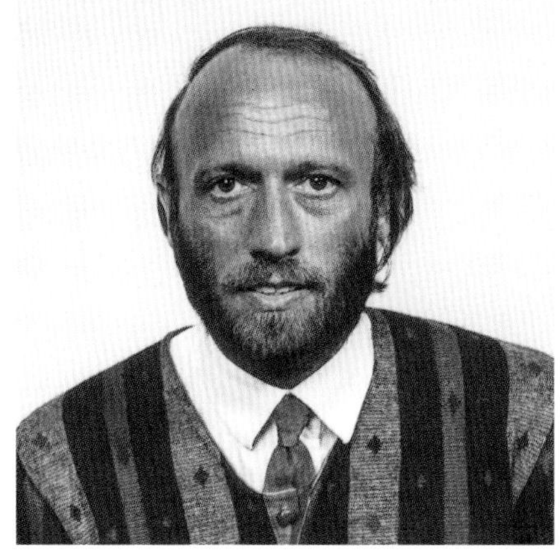

TERRY GILLIAM
Director, 9 May 1985

MAURICE GIBB
Musician, 11 January 1984

He rushed in, plonked himself on our stool and said, 'Quick, Concorde is waiting for me!'

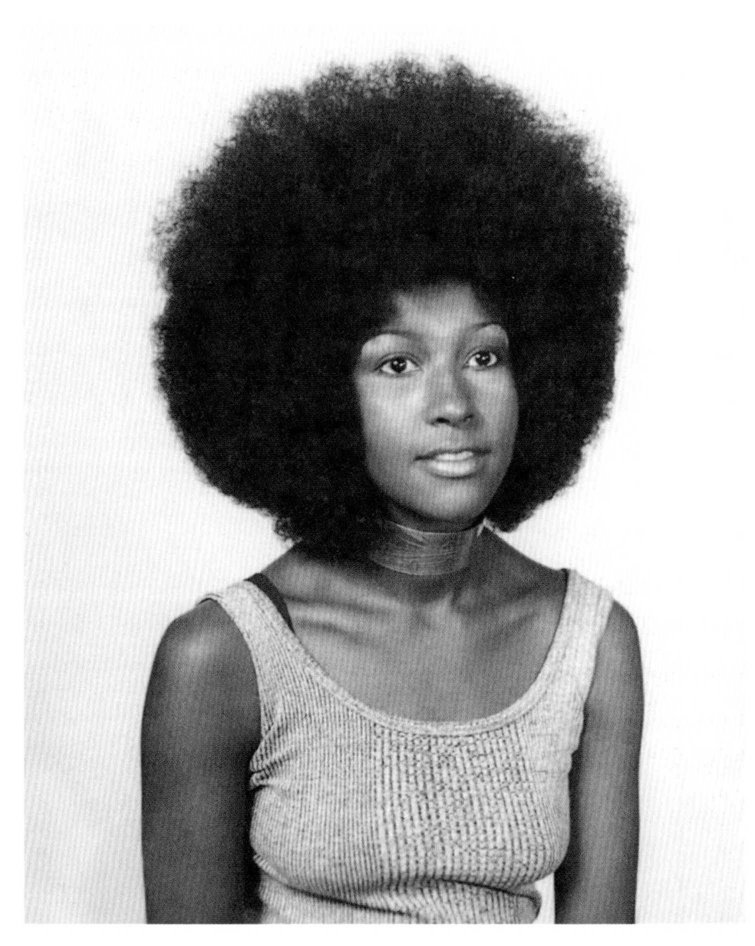

MARSHA HUNT
Actor, 14 July 1971

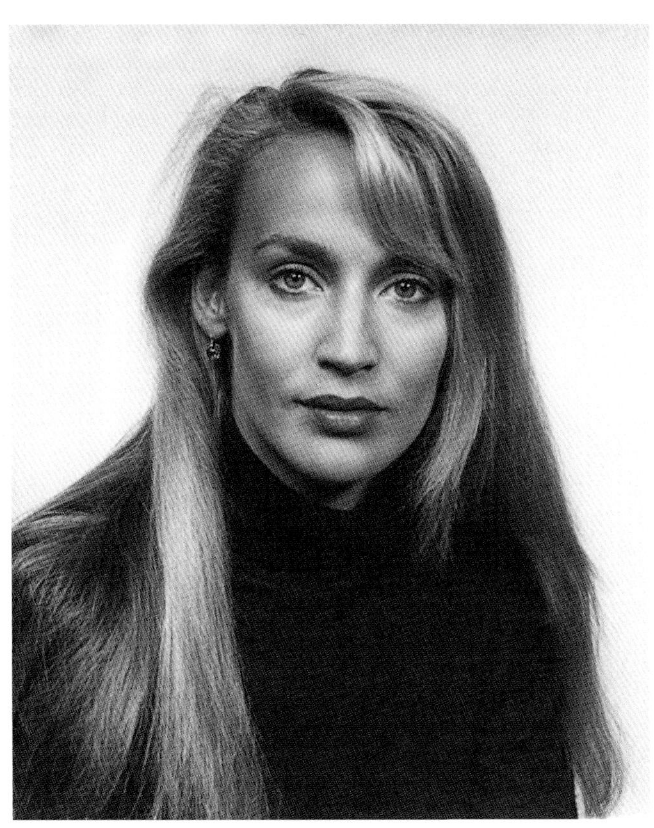

JERRY HALL
Model, 24 June 1983

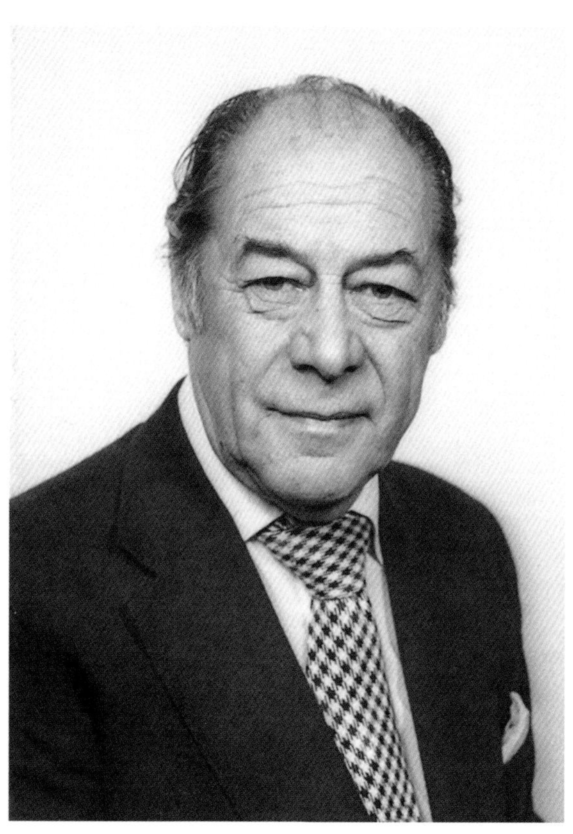

REX HARRISON
Actor, 21 March 1978

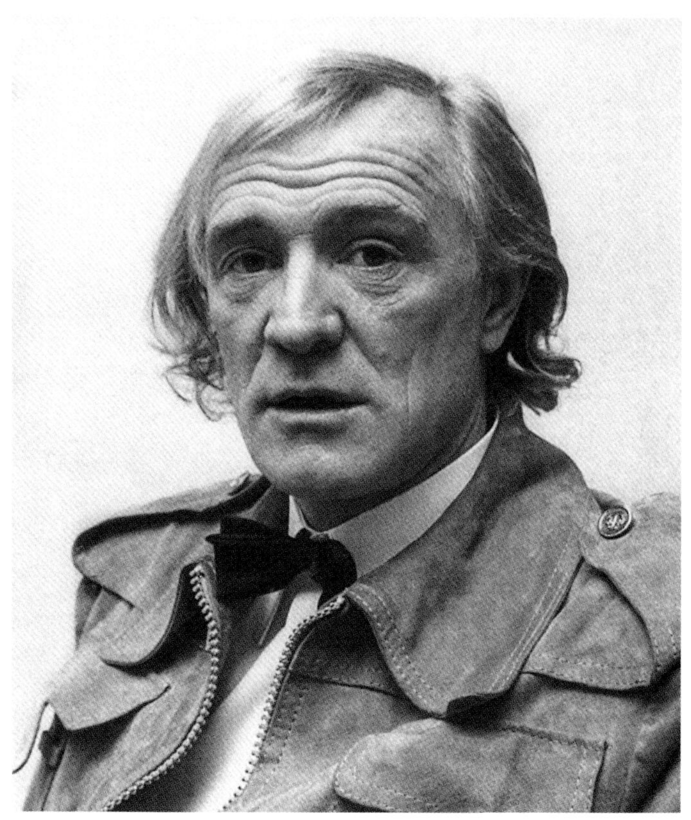

RICHARD HARRIS
Actor, 1976

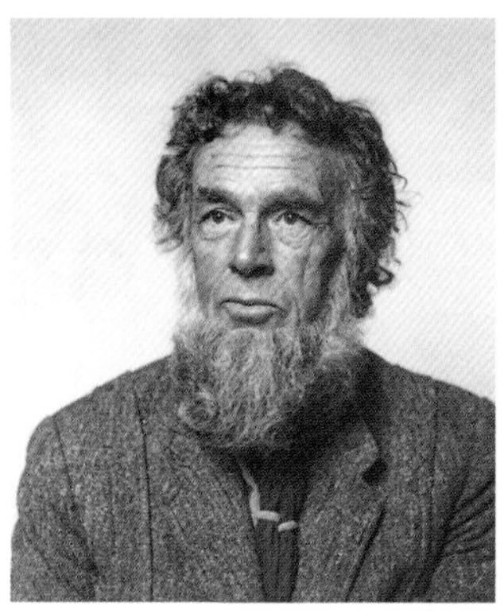

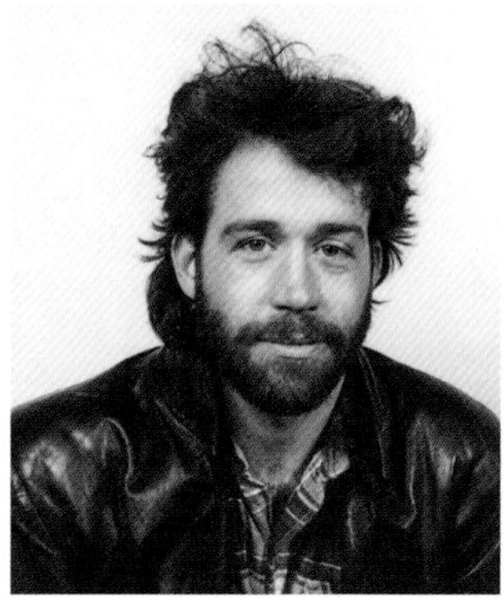

STERLING HAYDEN

Actor, 8 March 1973

TOM HULCE

Actor, 4 June 1986

Tom Hulce had gained worldwide recognition for playing Mozart in the film *Amadeus* two years earlier. He was in London for a more emotional role in 1986, appearing in *The Normal Heart*, the semi-autobiographical play by Larry Kramer about the HIV/AIDS epidemic in New York City.

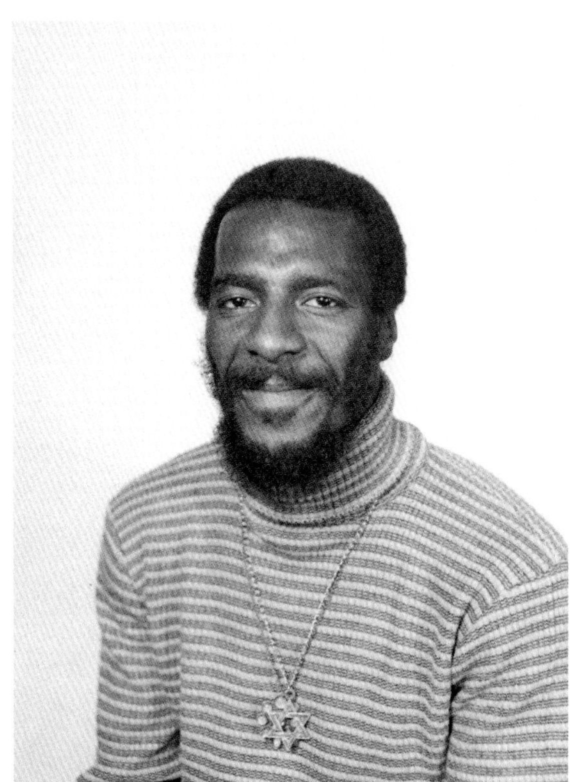

RICHIE HAVENS

Musician, 7 October 1971

Richie Havens was the opening act at Woodstock in the United States in 1969 and appeared two weeks later at the Isle of Wight festival in the UK. Taking the stage in front of more than 600,000 people on two different continents in only two weeks must be some kind of record.

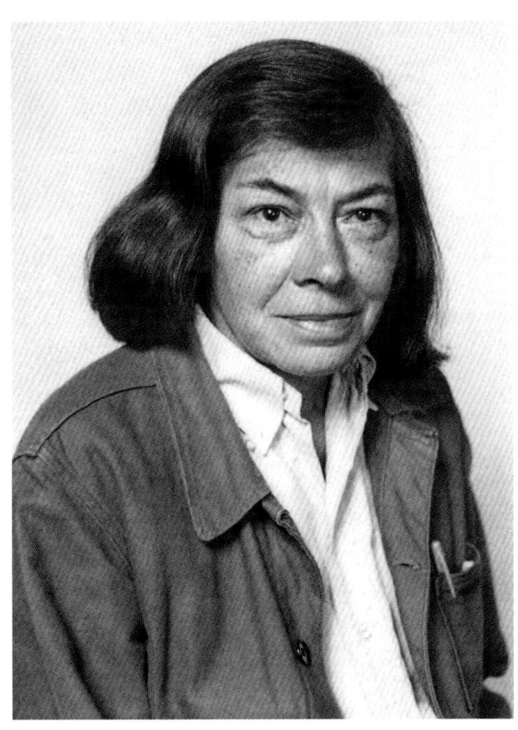

PATRICIA HIGHSMITH
Writer, 1970s

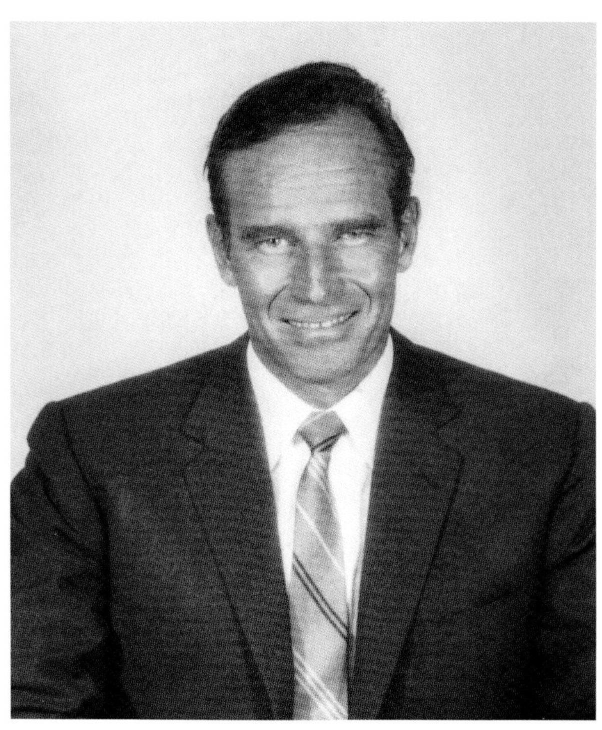

CHARLTON HESTON
Actor, 10 March 1965

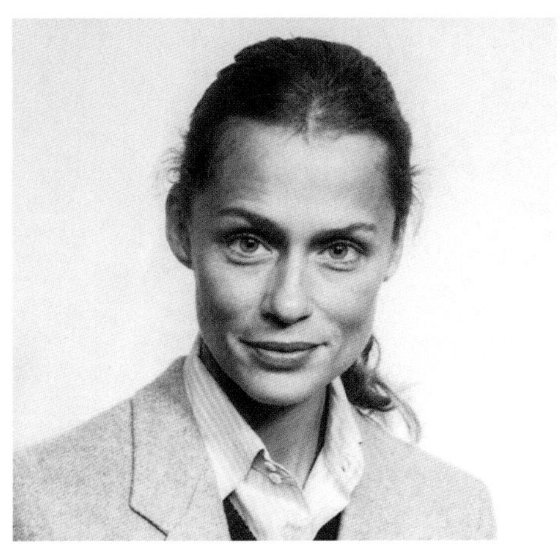

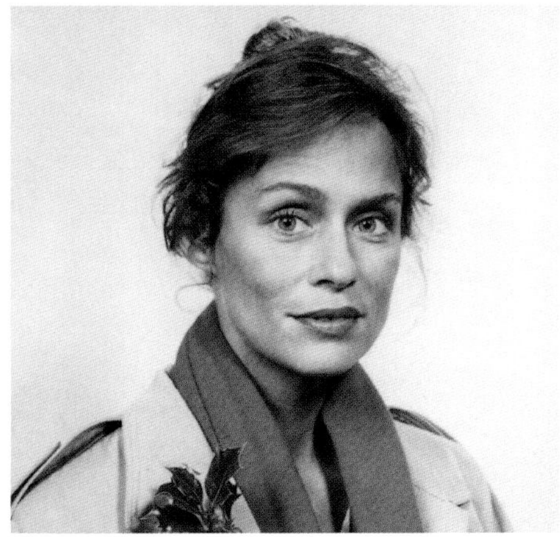

LAUREN HUTTON
Model/Actor, 7 December 1981

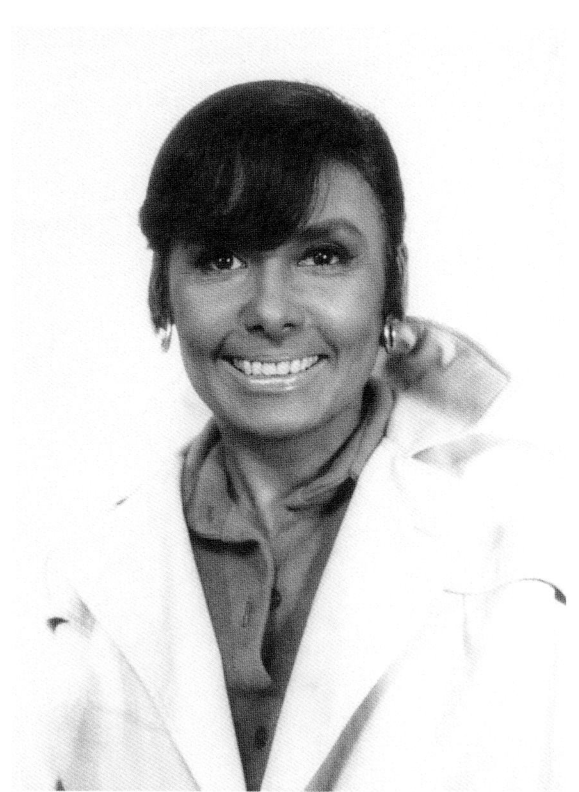

LENA HORNE
Singer, 11 May 1965

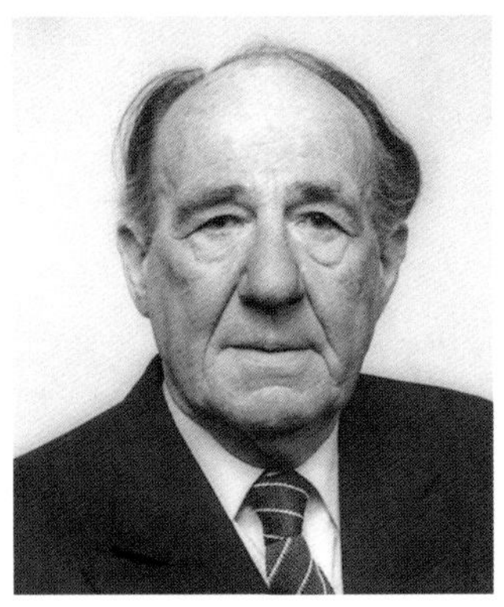

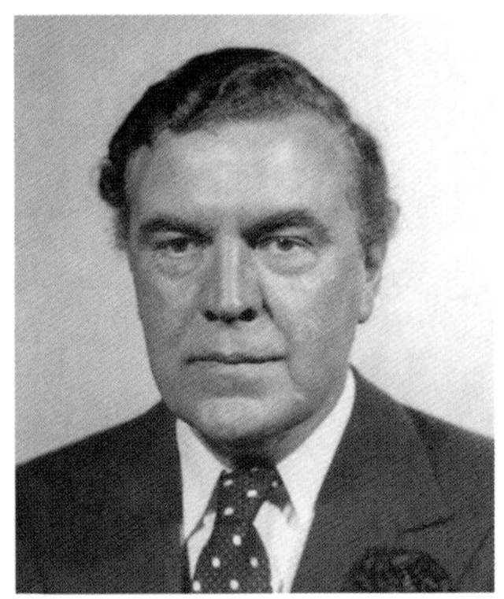

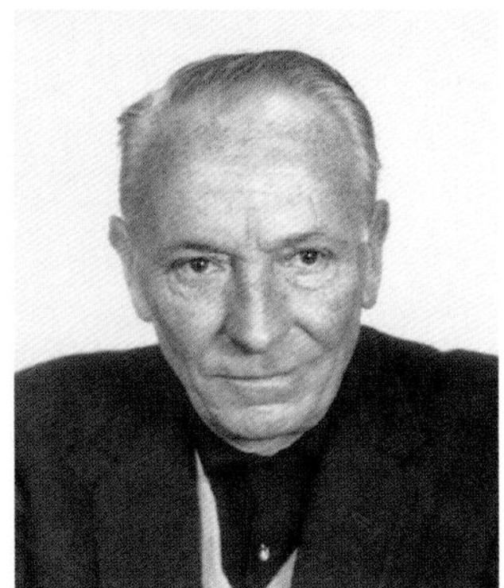

MICHAEL HORDERN
Actor, 1980s

NORMAN HARTNELL
Fashion designer, 1970s

WILLIAM HARTNELL
Actor, 6 May 1965

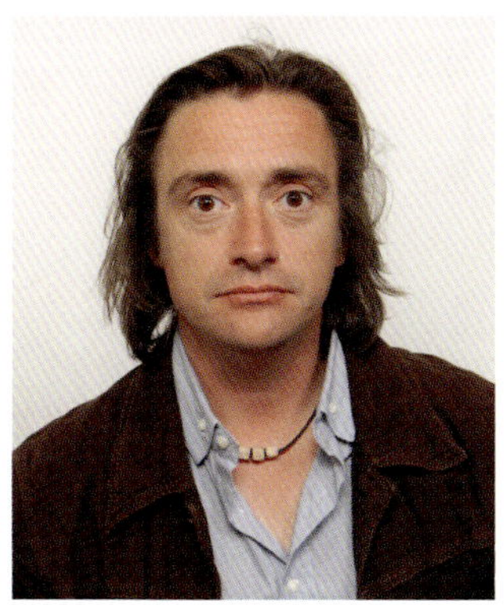

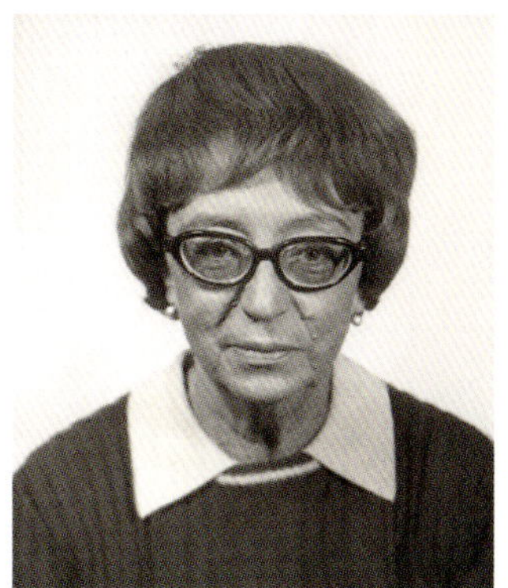

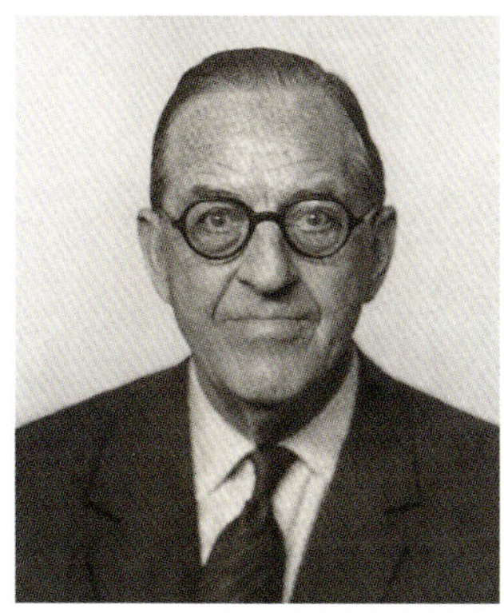

RICHARD HAMMOND
Journalist, 5 August 2010

STANLEY HOLLOWAY
Actor, 11 March 1963

THORA HIRD
Actor, 1970s

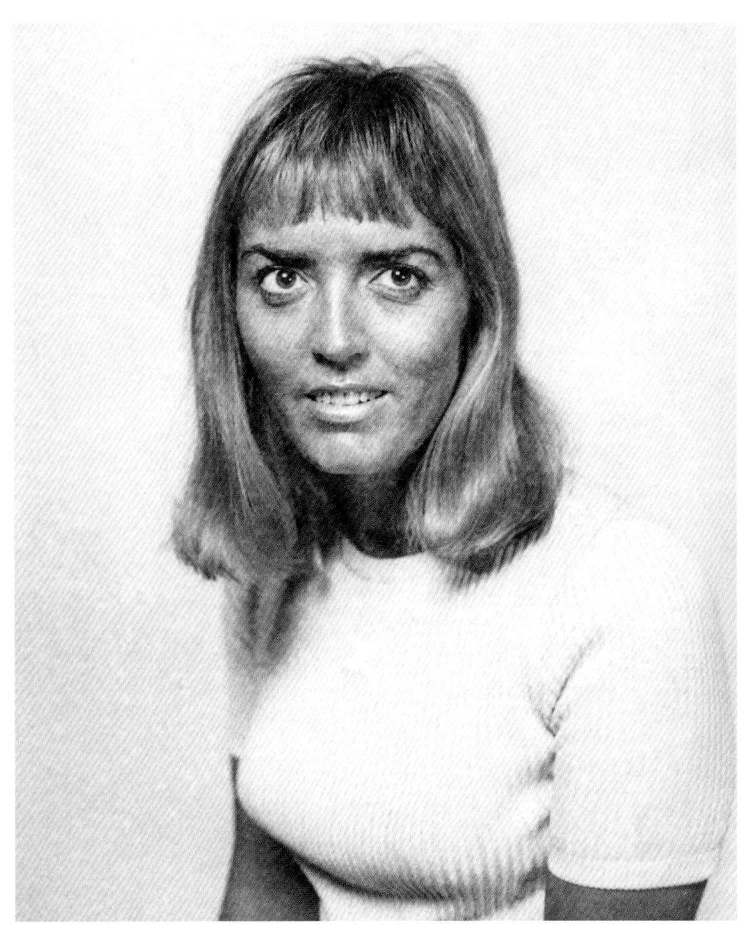

XAVIERA HOLLANDER
Writer, 3 September 1972

No. 120

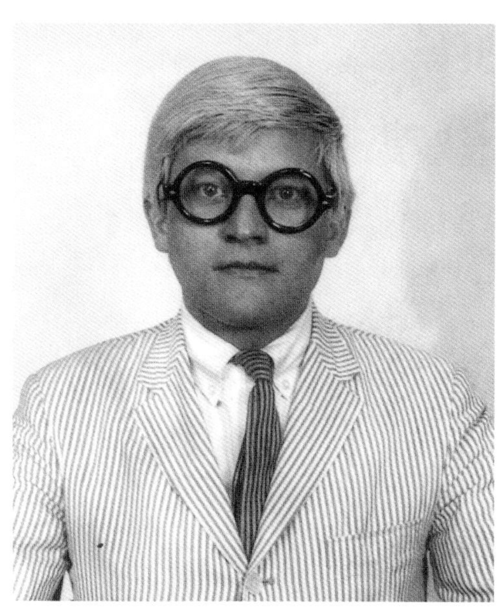

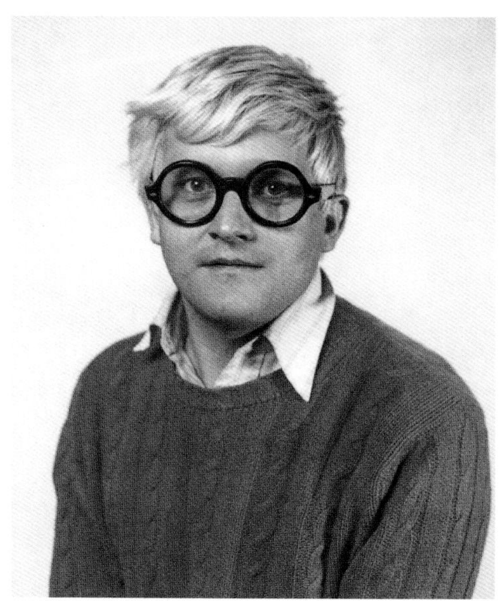

DAVID HOCKNEY
Artist, 22 June 1965
and 21 January 1970

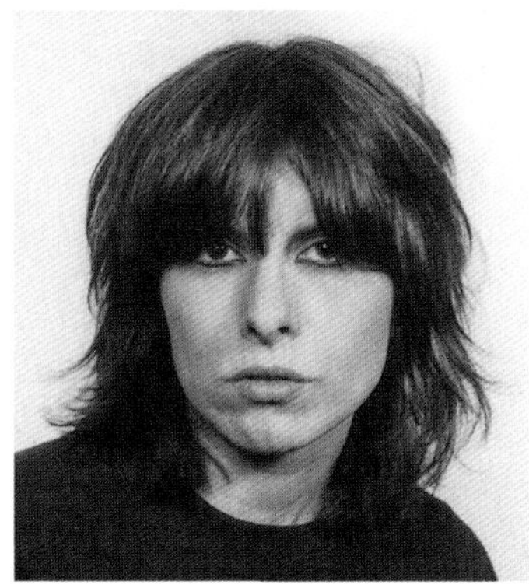
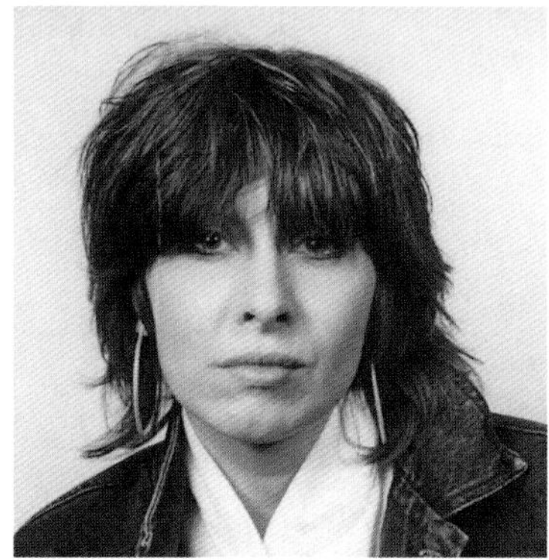
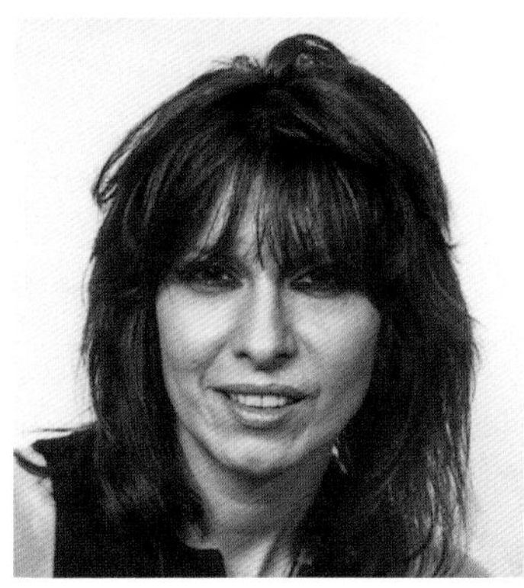
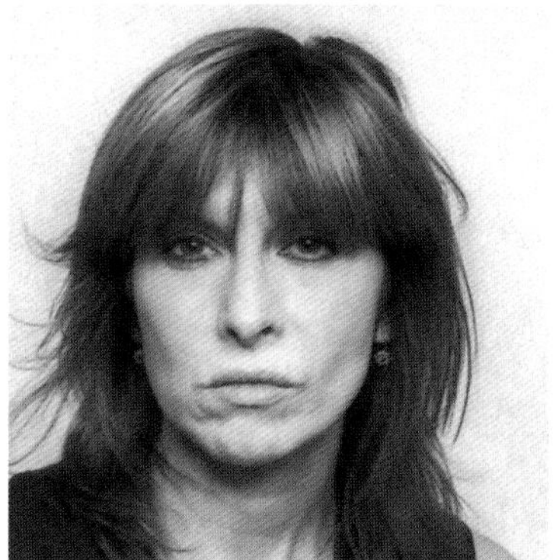

No. 122

CHRISSIE HYNDE

Musician, 23 June 1981, 13 June 1986, 13 July 1994 and 20 January 2004

I first went to Chrissie Hynde's Baker Street flat in 1978 to snap her, and have photographed her many times since. Once I went to her home in the elegant neighbourhood of Maida Vale and photographed her and her daughters. Her house had a sign outside that read, 'Don't bother me, I'm in vacation land.' She has even visited the studio for updates quite a few times. We spotted a photograph in the newspapers of her holding her passport aloft at Belfast airport, and there, stuck in it, was one of our photos of her.

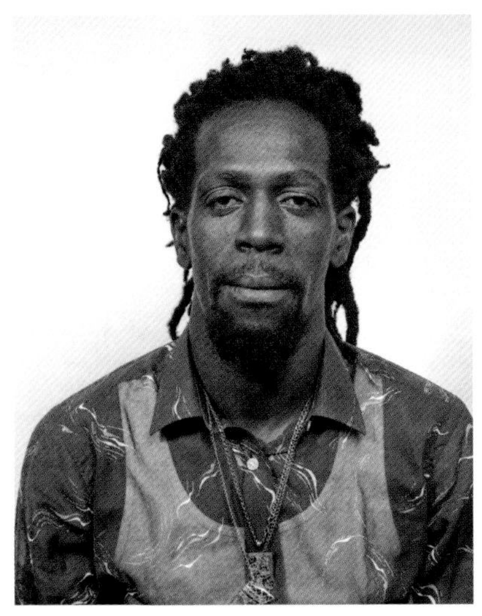

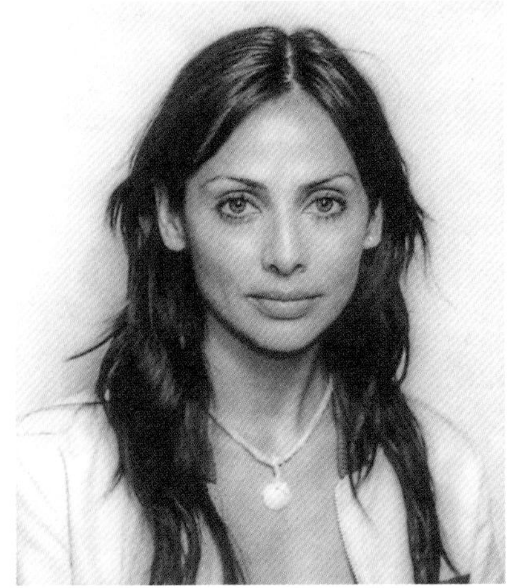

GREGORY ISAACS
Musician, 1979

NATALIE IMBRUGLIA
Musician, 25 July 2005

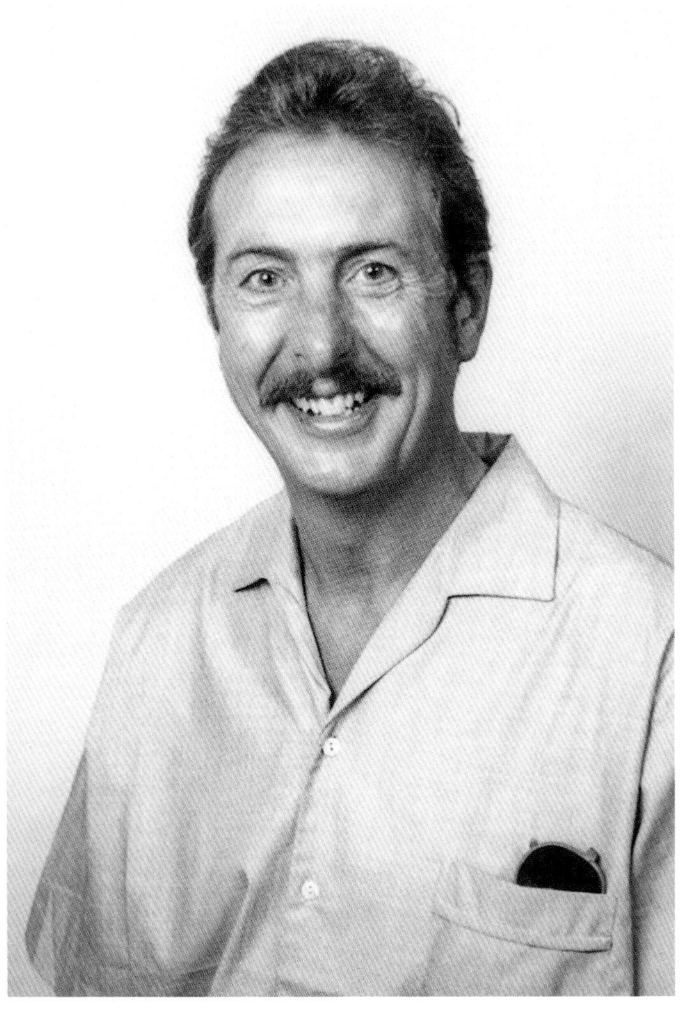

ERIC IDLE
Actor, 8 August 1988

BRIAN JOHNSON

Singer, 24 June 2003

You would never imagine that this casually dressed guy wearing a newsboy cap was a Rock & Roll Hall of Famer let alone the lead singer of AC/DC if you passed him in the street. When the chatty Geordie came in for his photo, he had just been to the Ferrari dealership in nearby Park Lane. He was still laughing as he told us how he had walked in and declared that he wanted to buy the Ferrari displayed in the window. 'Certainly,' replied the salesman, who at first thought he was joking. When Brian Johnson got out his black American Express card, the salesman's attitude changed immediately. He said he thought he could hop in and drive it away, but the smug salesman revealed that one in the same livery would be ready for him in nine months. Johnson was still laughing when he recounted that the salesman disclosed this only after he had charged that black card.

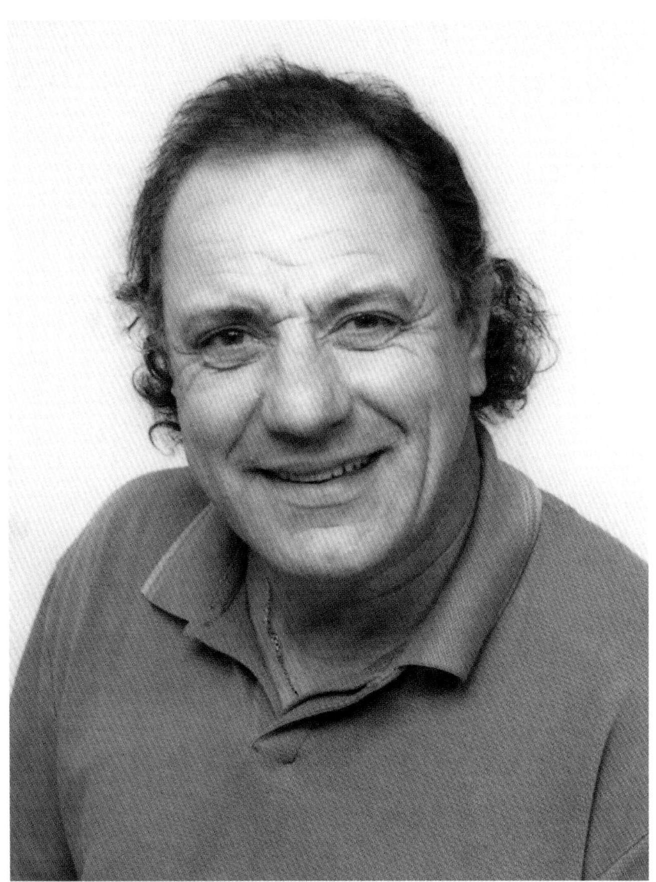

No. 127

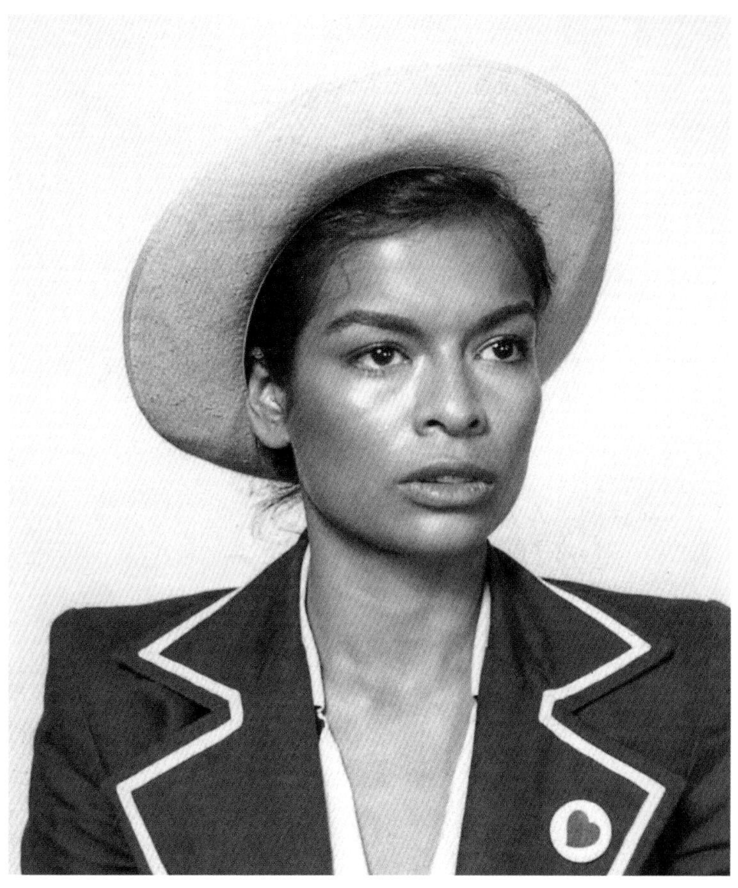

BIANCA JAGGER

Activist, 1 June 1976

'They won't accept a photo of you wearing your hat,' Peter tried to advise Bianca Jagger politely. 'They will for me,' she replied. Well, she didn't come to have her photograph retaken, so she must have been right about that.

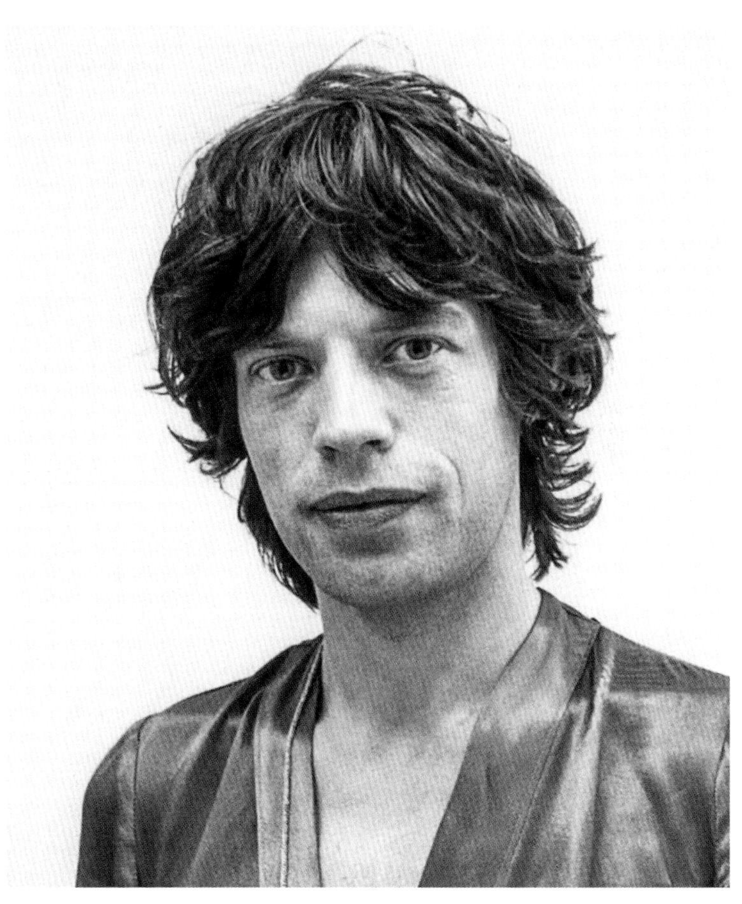

MICK JAGGER
Musician, 1 June 1976

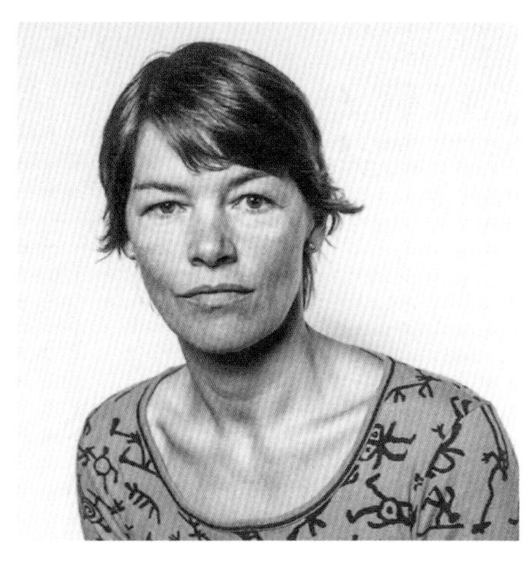

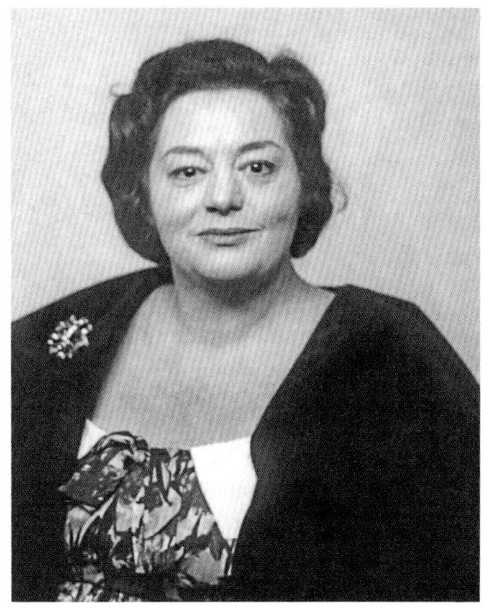

GLENDA JACKSON
Actor/Politician, 6 July 1977

HATTIE JACQUES
Actor, 3 February 1964

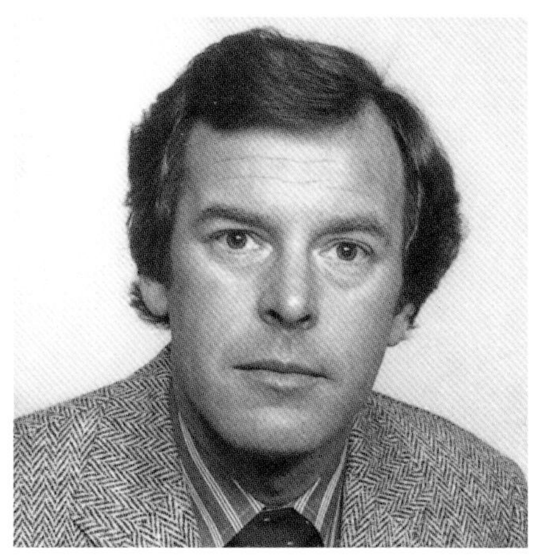

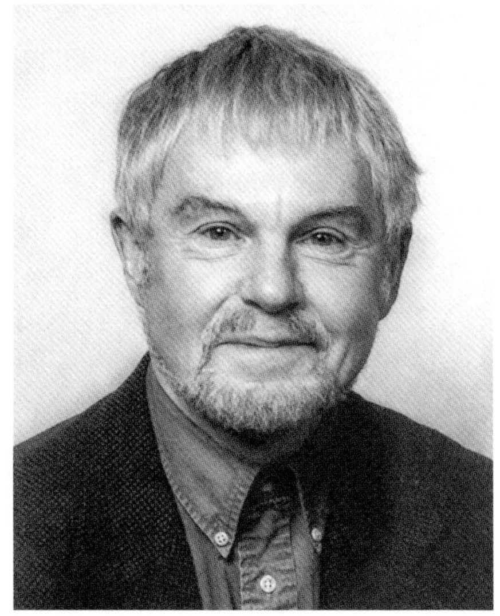

PETER JENNINGS
Journalist, 1977

DEREK JACOBI
Actor, 11 November 1998

WILKO JOHNSON

Musician, 10 April 2015

In our new premises at 39 North Row, where we had moved in 2014, I placed a mirror strategically at the entrance so that I could see when customers were walking down the stairs. Well, blow me down if one day I didn't see the guitarist Wilko Johnson coming in. He was in the legendary band Dr Feelgood, and later became well known outside the music scene as the mute executioner Ser Ilyn Payne on the TV series *Game of Thrones*. He was charming as I told him how the Feelgoods playing the Hope and Anchor in Islington was probably one of the best live shows I had ever seen. The well-built man who had come in with Johnson was looking at our board of celebrities and, on seeing the boxer John Conteh (see p.53), exclaimed, 'Oh look, there's Conteh! I used to spar with him.' Being a follower of the 'noble art' myself, I immediately started chatting to him, realizing that I had seen him fight a couple of times in London. Poor old Wilko then had to listen to all our boxing reminiscences.

No. 132

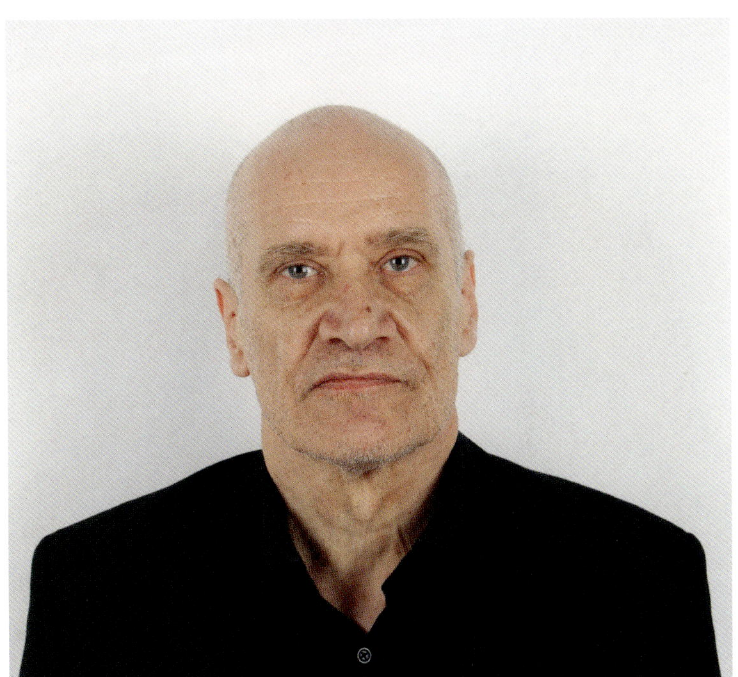

No. 133

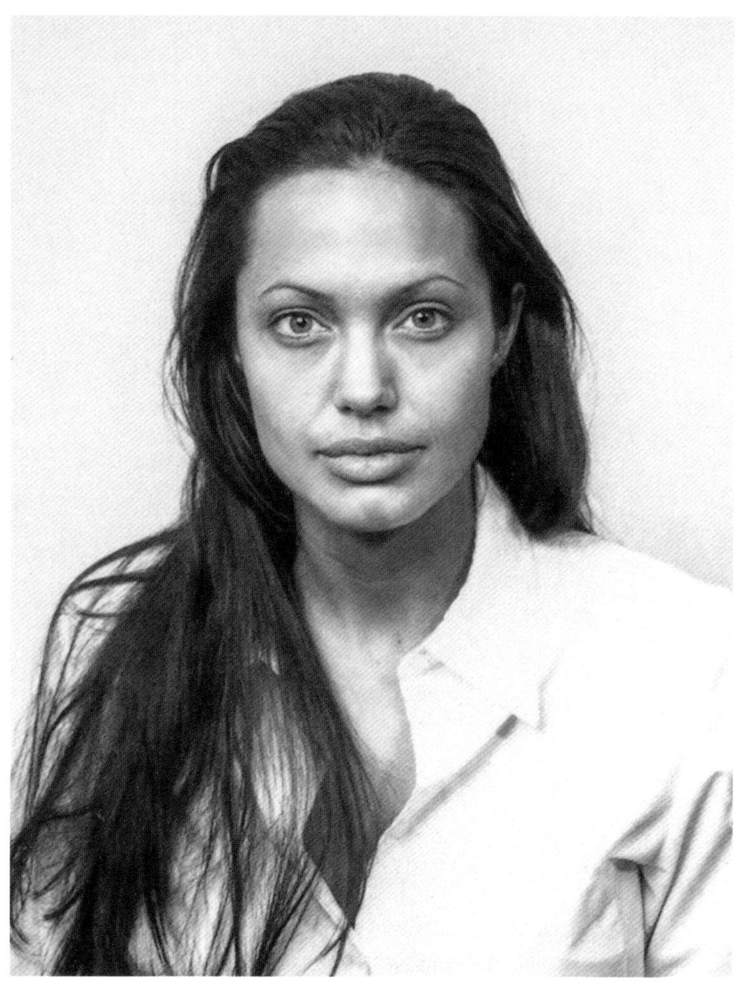

No. 134

ANGELINA JOLIE

Actor, 24 March 2003

'Blimey, she looks familiar,' I thought as Angelina Jolie walked in on her own one warm March afternoon. She was so petite and delicate that at first I didn't think it was the star of action movies such as *Lara Croft: Tomb Raider* (2001), but I could see her tattoos beneath her white shirt and, knowing she had many, that confirmed it for me. I must admit, I had not seen any of her films, so I didn't have very much to say to her. However, when she saw the other actors in our frames, she chatted about the ones she knew. Amazingly, no other customers came in while she was there, so had it not been for the passport photo it would almost have been as though I dreamed the whole visit.

No. 135

TOM JONES

Singer, 20 October 2009

We were often called to visit and photograph celebrities, royalty and business people who were too busy, too famous, too private or just couldn't be bothered to make it down to Oxford Street, so 'it's not unusual' to receive a call like the one we had in 2009 to photograph Sir Tom Jones at the Mandarin Oriental Hotel in Knightsbridge. He was appearing at the Brighton International Centre later that evening, so he was on a tight schedule and it was a sit down, face forward, snap snap encounter. However, Peter photographed his wife and childhood sweetheart, Linda (who had married him when she was sixteen and he was seventeen), at her flat in Park Street, Mayfair, in May 1997. In no rush that day, she invited Peter to stay for tea and biscuits after having her photographs taken.

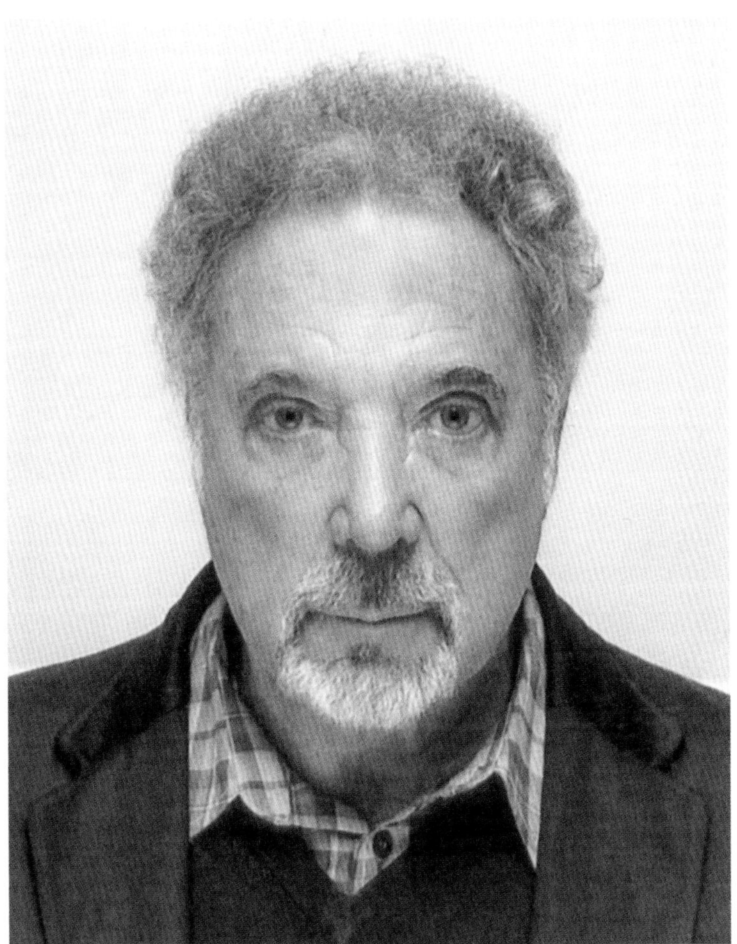

No. 137

CHAKA KHAN

Singer, 10 May 1990

When the great 'Queen of Funk' came in and introduced herself, I told her there was no need because I recognized her immediately. She was a delight to photograph. As you can see from her happy, natural smile, US passport regulations were not as strict then as they are now. Contrary to what the governments say, I believe you can still tell who someone is even if they are smiling, although I suppose international travel isn't as much fun as it used to be. A few weeks later she headlined the first Prince's Trust (now the King's Trust) Rock Gala to be held in Hyde Park.

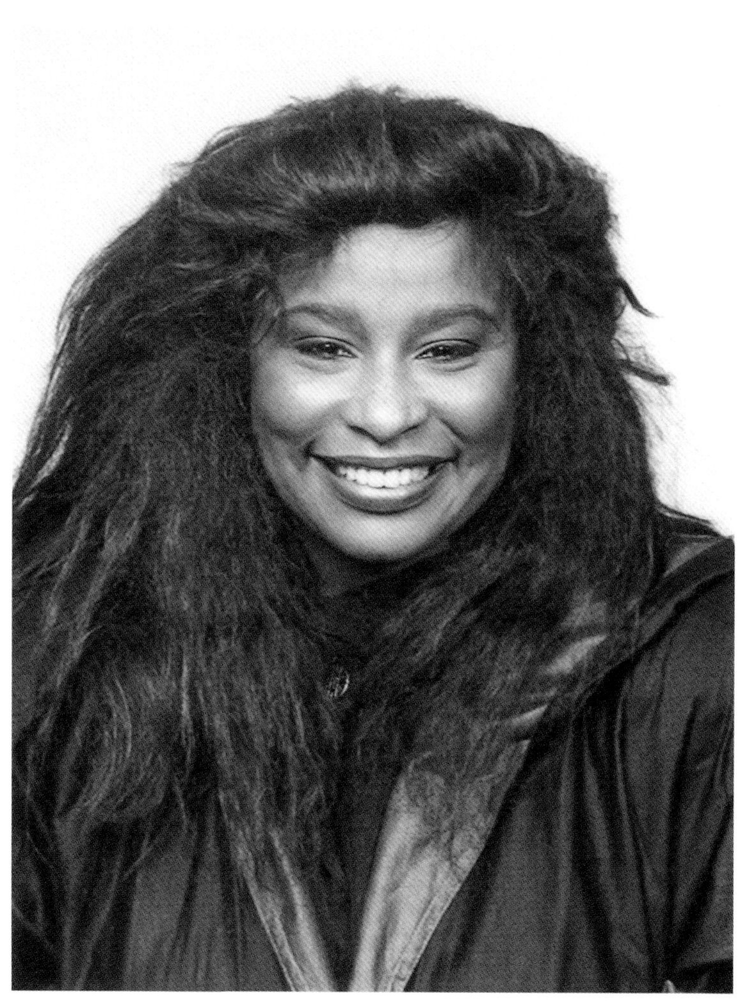

No. 139

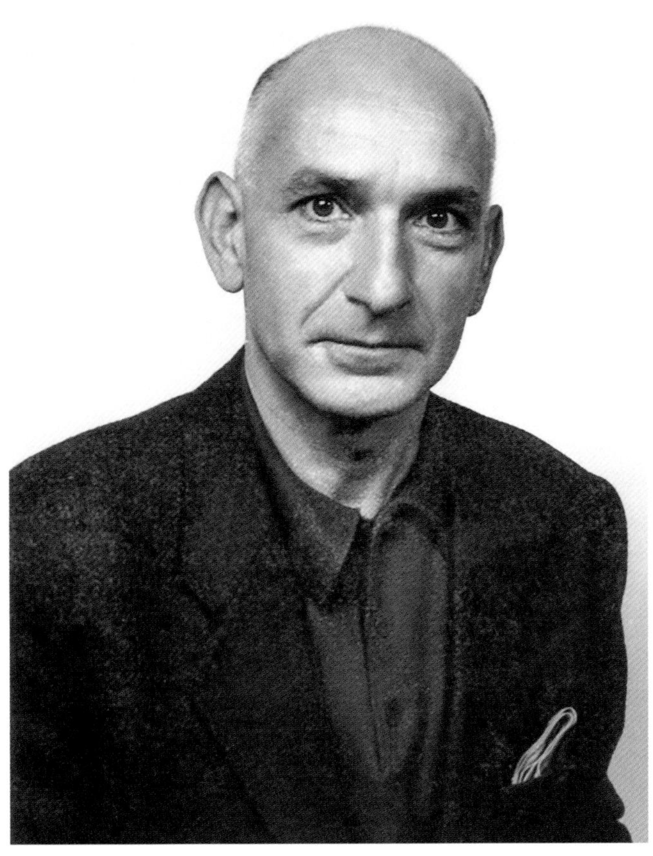

BEN KINGSLEY
Actor, 15 October 1992

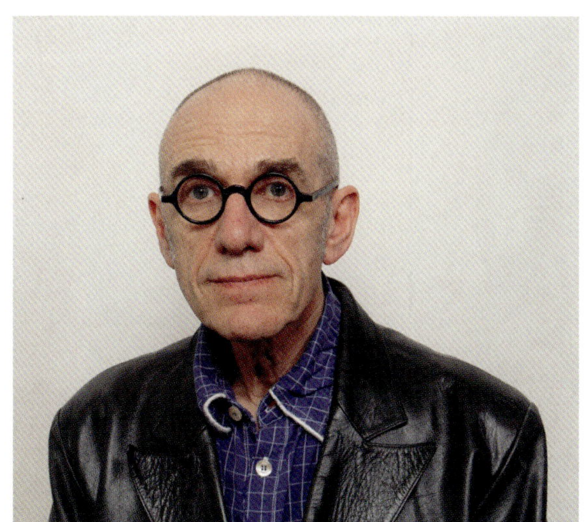

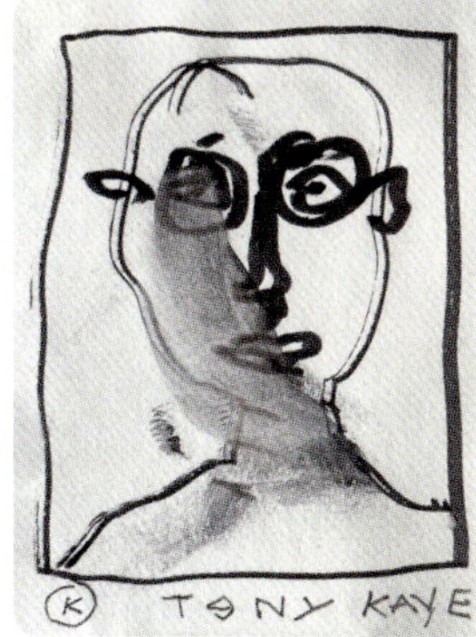

TONY KAYE

Director, 15 April 2013

I helped Tony Kaye with his US visa application. While filling it in, he had doodled a set of four passport-sized likenesses of himself, and he said he would prefer one of them to be added to the wall rather than the photo I had just taken. It's probably a better likeness!

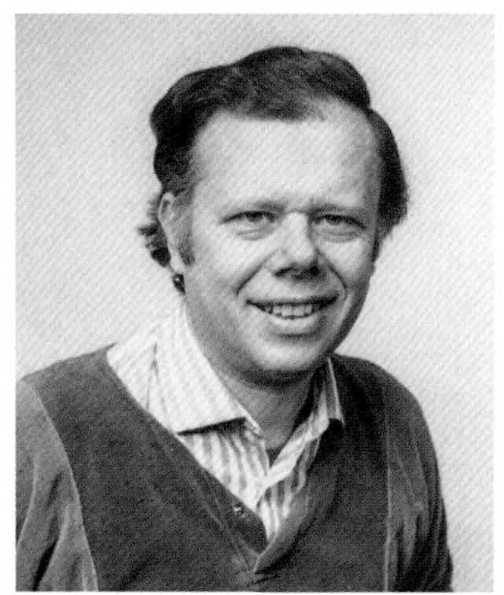

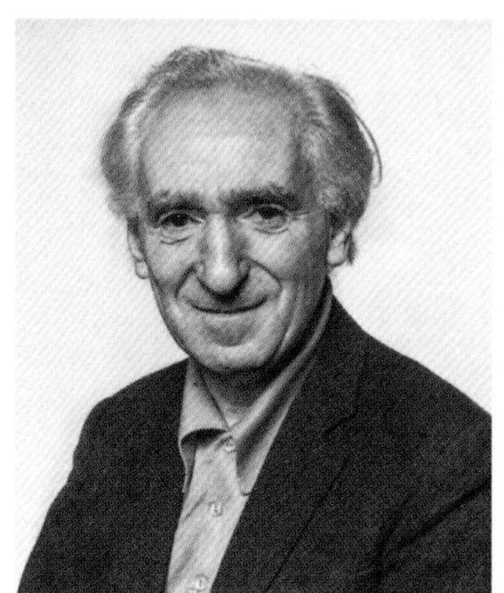

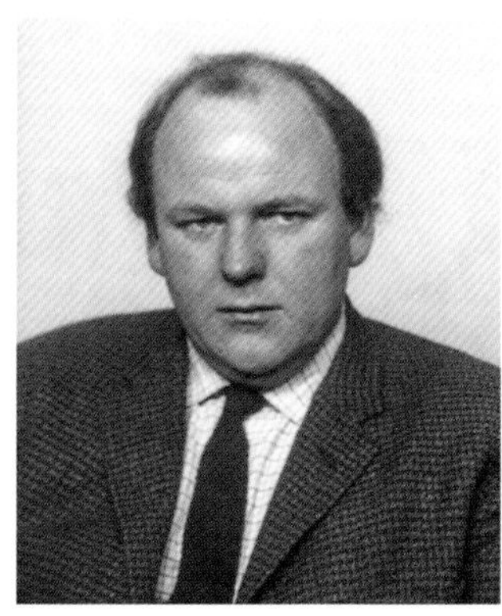

JOHN LAHR
Writer, 7 March 1996

ROY KINNEAR
Actor, 1970s

OSCAR LEWENSTEIN
Producer, 19 May 1976

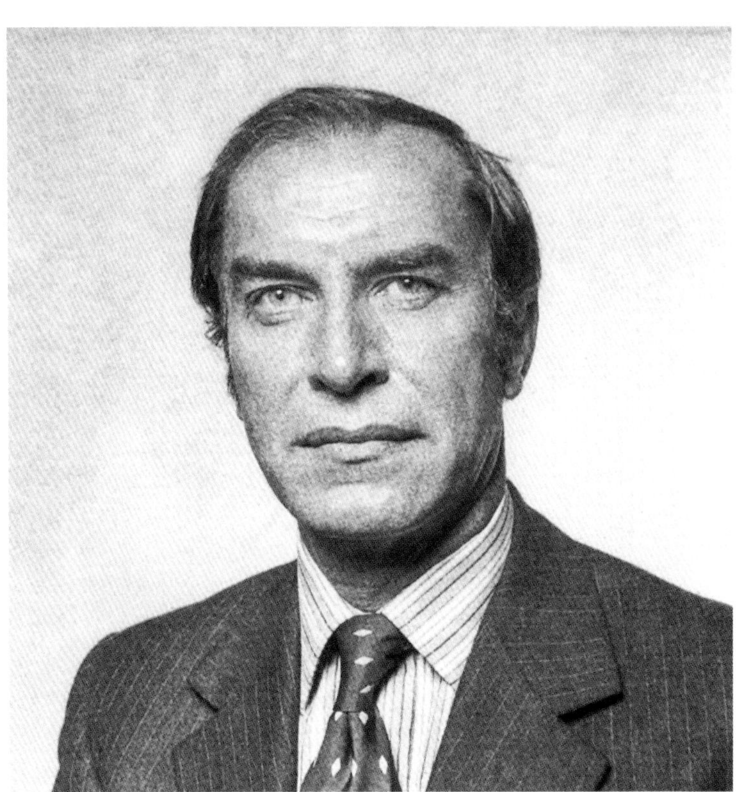

MARTIN LANDAU
Actor, 1970s

HUGH LAURIE

Actor, 2 August 1997

Hugh Laurie is another studio regular. This photo is from 1997, but when he entered the studio for the last time in 2011, all the waiting customers recognized him. To deflect their stares, he pointed to the framed 20 × 16 in (50.6 × 49.6 cm) prints hanging on our wall. One was of George Michael (see p.165) and the other of a boxer, former British bantamweight champion Martin Power. Everyone expected him to point out George Michael, but of course he cried instead, 'Oh look, there's Martin!' I was surprised that he knew Power, but he explained that they trained at the same St Pancras gym. Laurie was making a film with a friend of mine at the time, but our chat was cut short because everyone started getting their phones out to take his photograph, so he made his excuses and off he went back to the embassy.

No. 144

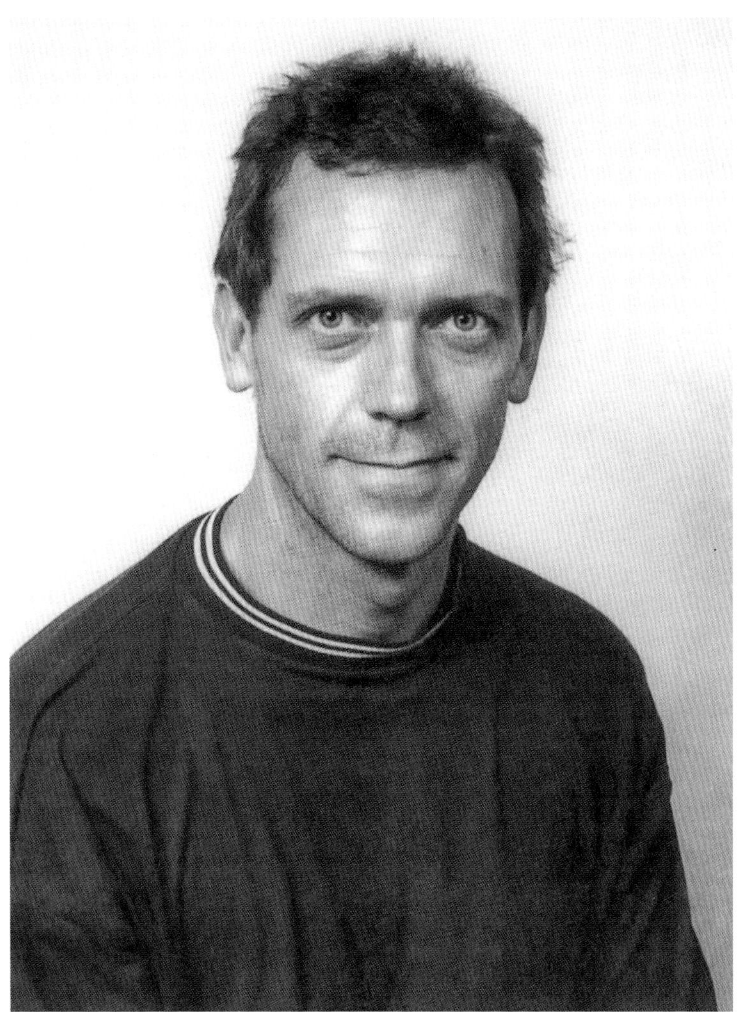

No. 145

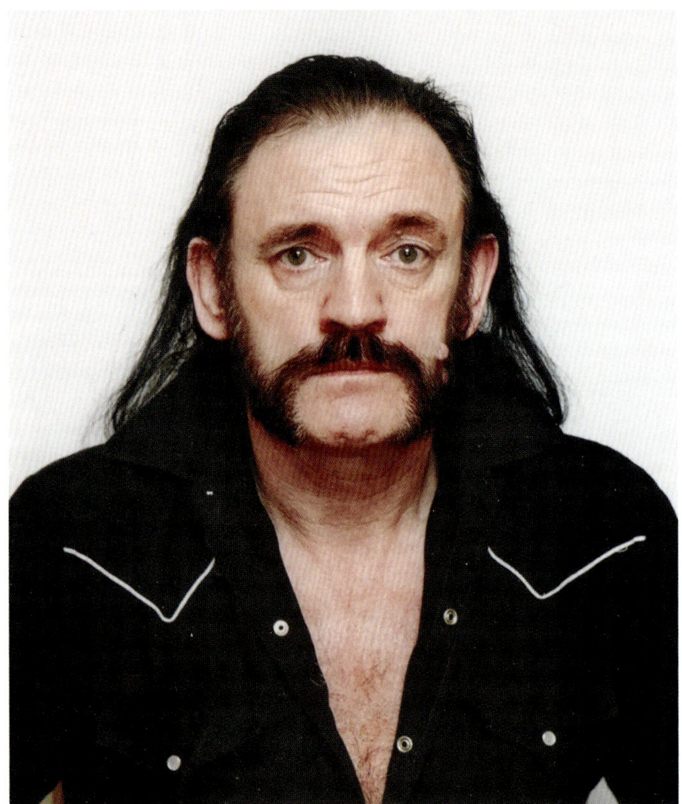

LEMMY

Musician, 27 June 2006

I photographed Lemmy at the Mandarin Oriental Hotel in Knightsbridge (as I did Sir Tom Jones; see p.137). I couldn't help noticing how clean and tidy his bedroom was, which was perhaps surprising for the mutton-chopped heavy-metal musician and singer of Motörhead. All his cowboy boots were in a neat row, and six bottles of Jack Daniels whisky were on the bedside table – all unopened and also in a perfectly straight line.

No. 146

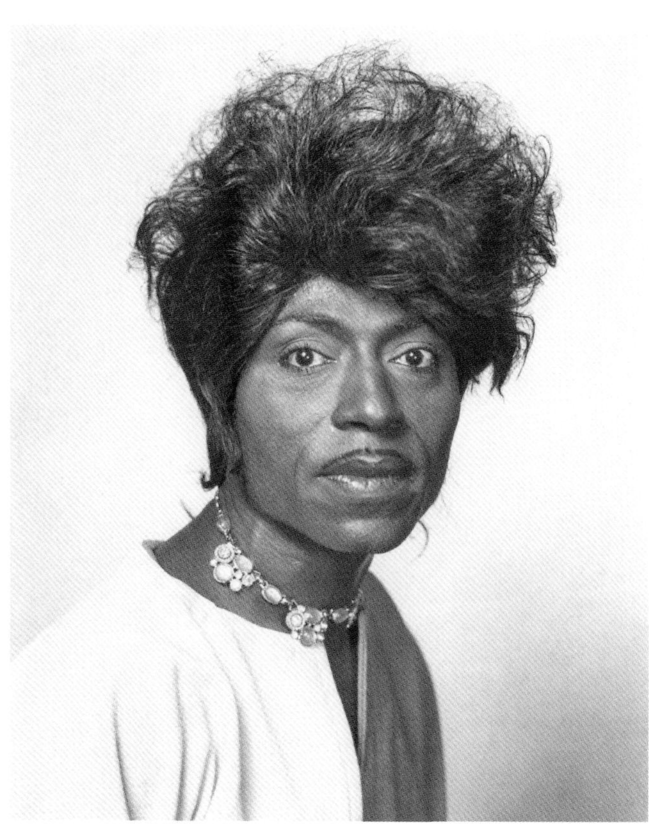

LITTLE RICHARD
Musician, 1970s

MATT LUCAS

Actor, 16 November 2015

Early one morning I had to put a 'Back in 2 minutes' sign on the studio door as I rushed around the corner on a quest to find Matt Lucas, after the person who was dealing with his visa had been delayed. We were eventually able to print both his pictures and his visa form, and I was pleased to meet him since we had an interesting family connection. Both his mother and his stepmother had cared for my father when he was ill, and they often met at the old persons' afternoons that were held near where he lived.

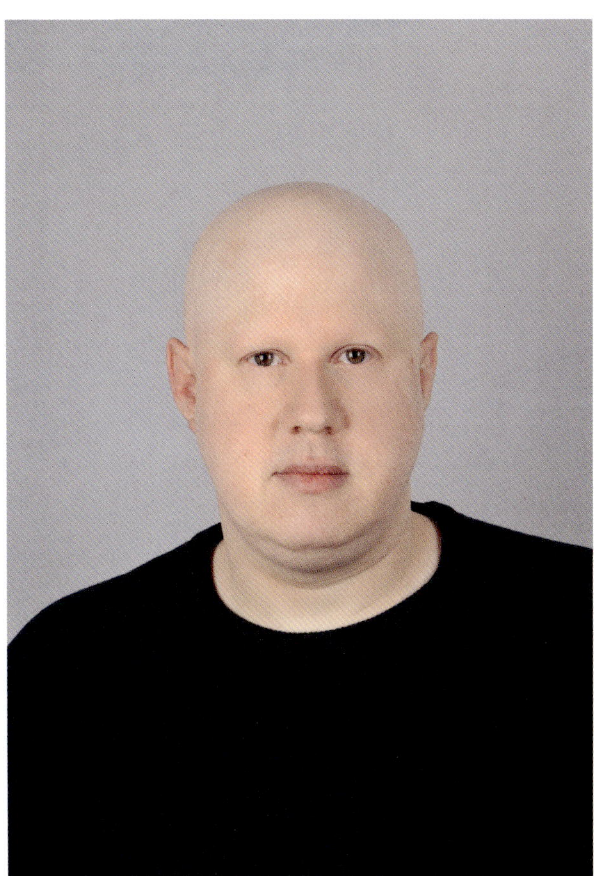

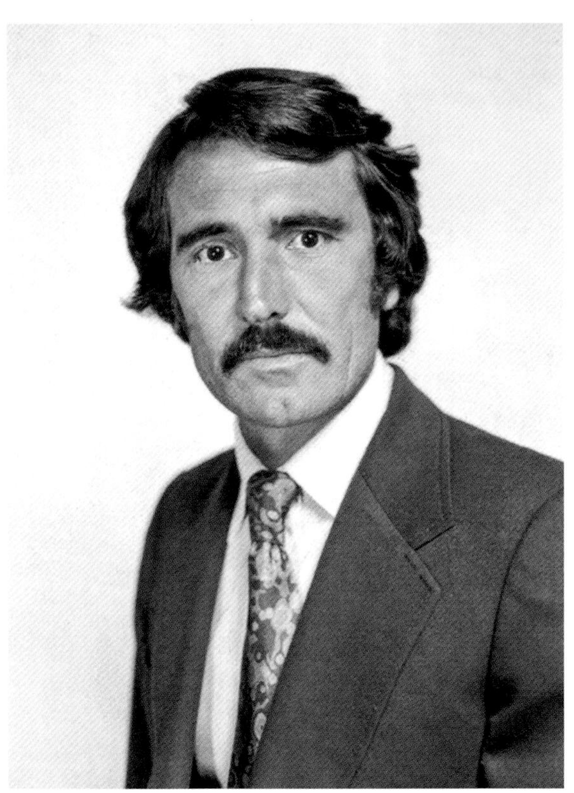

GEORGE LAZENBY
Actor, early 1970s

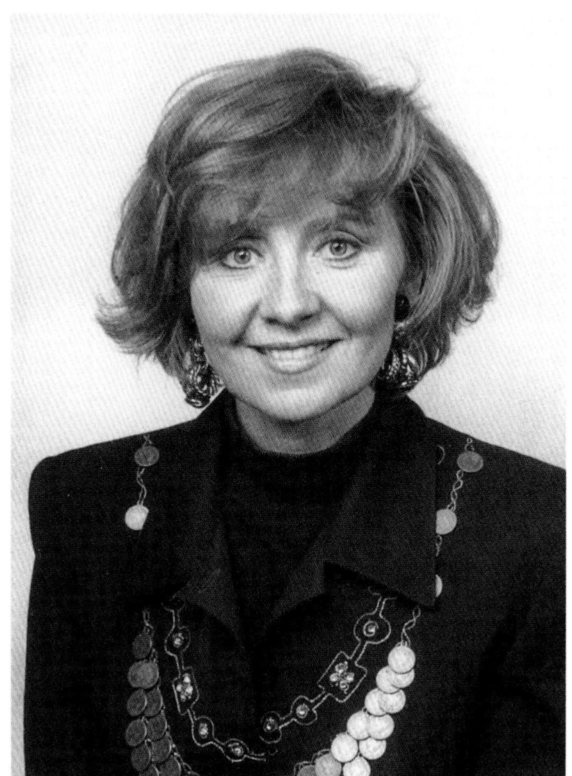

LULU

Singer, 24 April 1990

'Oh look, there's Maurice!' the singer Lulu remarked, pointing to the photo of Maurice Gibb (see p.107) on our wall of celebrities. Friendly and chatty, she confided – without a hint of animosity – 'He's my ex-husband, you know.'

No. 151

MADONNA

Musician, 26 November 2011

Peter went to Home House, the luxury private members' club in Marylebone, to photograph Madonna and her then husband, Guy Ritchie (see p.207), since their house around the corner in Great Cumberland Place was being renovated. They had just put their children to bed and sat themselves down unceremoniously on some flight cases for their portraits. I also photographed some of Madonna's children, who visited the studio with their nanny.

No. 152

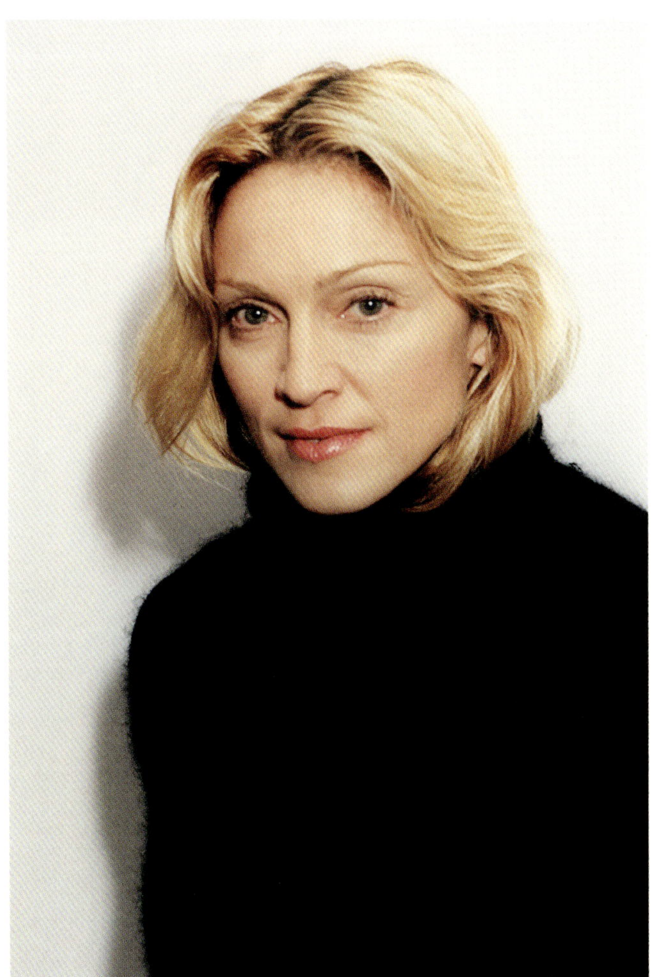

No. 153

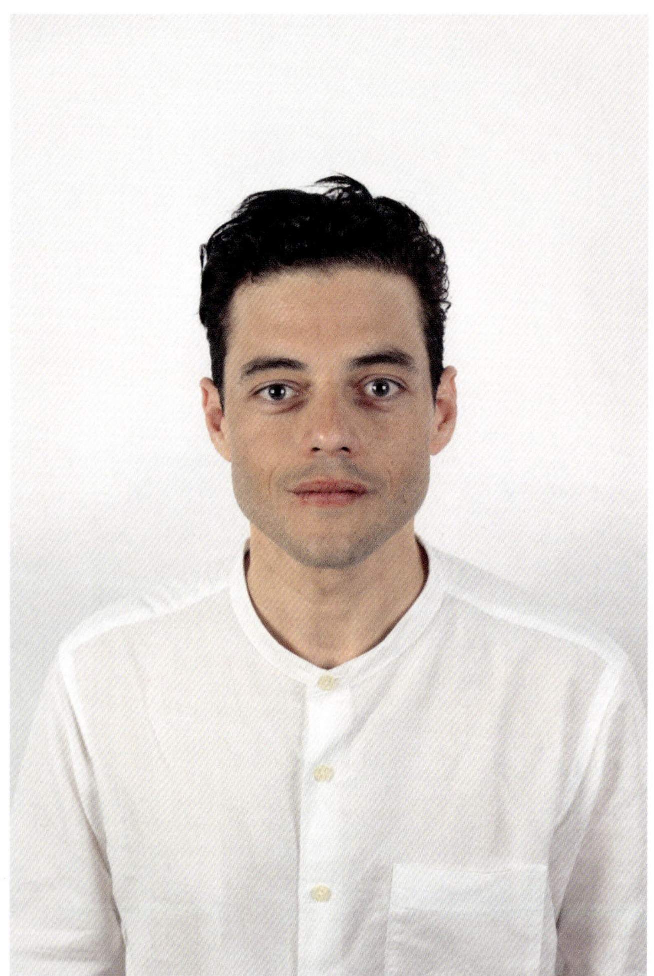

No. 154

RAMI MALEK

Actor, 6 July 2018

Ivo went to a rehearsal studio to photograph Queen in 2008, snapping their entire touring team, which included guitarist Brian May, vocalist Paul Rodgers and drummer Roger Taylor (see pp.157, 204 and 234), although Freddie Mercury had passed some years before. By coincidence, Ivo did ultimately get to photograph Freddie Mercury. Well, almost – it wasn't Freddie himself, but the actor who played him in the biopic *Bohemian Rhapsody* (2018). Although the film would not be released until October that year, Ivo recognized Rami Malek instantly. When he asked me where the nearest DX office was, I assumed he was just an American student, but when one of the waiting customers shook his hand and congratulated him on a previous role, I finally understood why Ivo was trying to catch my attention.

No. 155

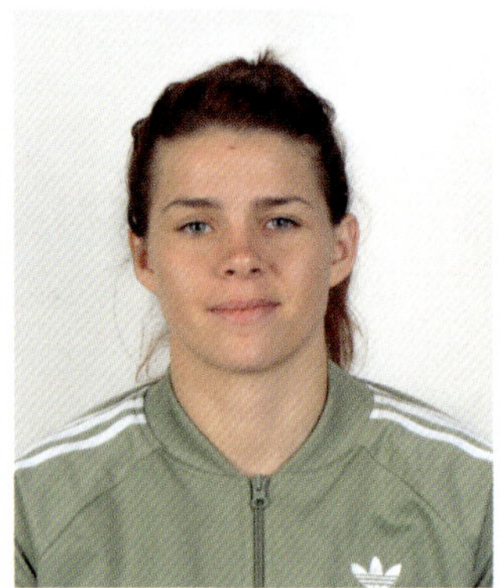

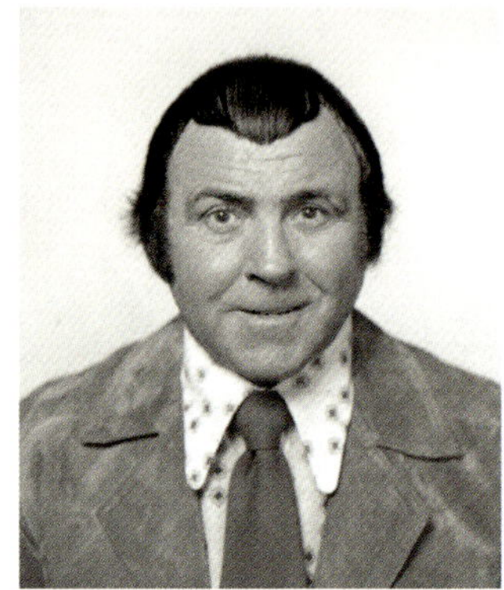

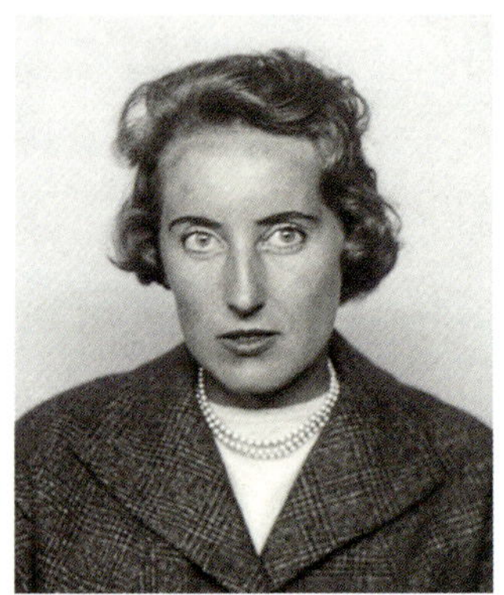

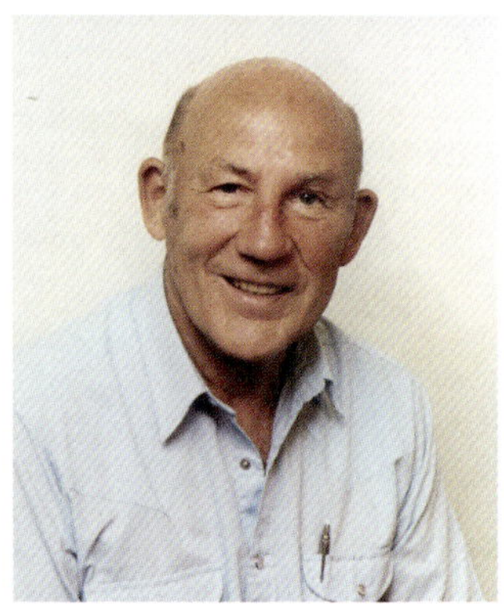

SAVANNAH MARSHALL
Boxer, 11 August 2017

ANGELA MORTIMER
Tennis player,
21 September 1960

MICK MCMANUS
Wrestler, 15 May 1973

STIRLING MOSS
Racing driver, 11 July 1994

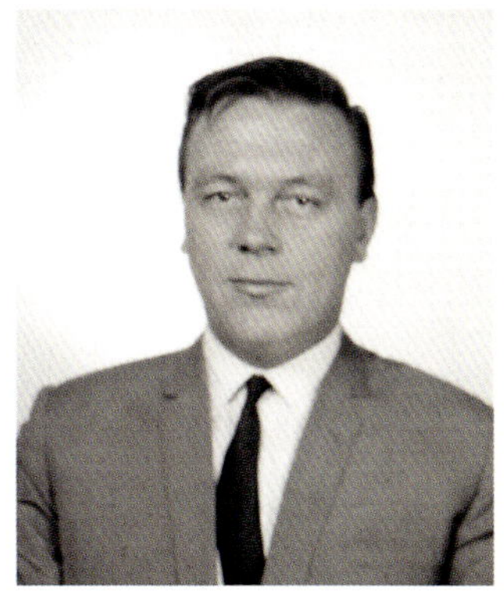

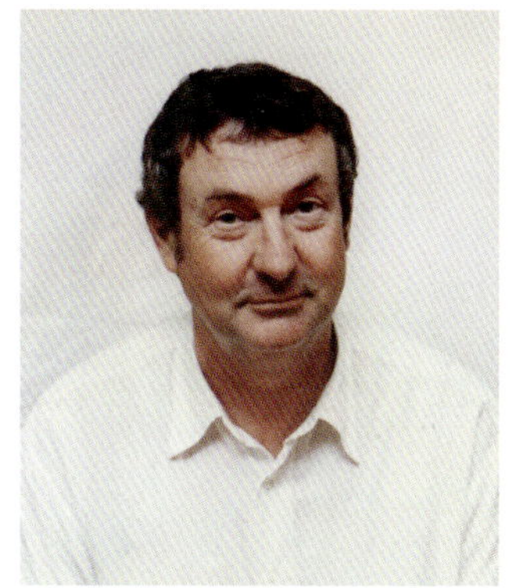

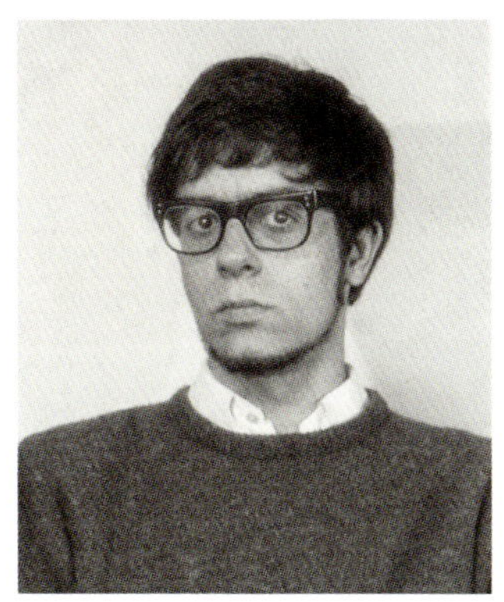

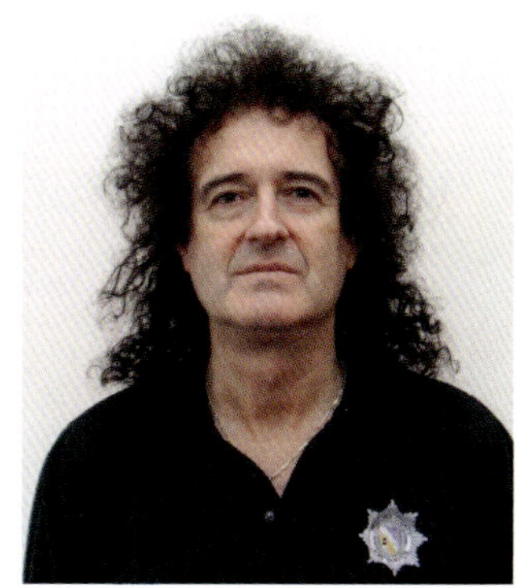

MATT MONRO
Singer, 24 September 1964

MANFRED MANN
Musician, 1960s

NICK MASON
Musician, 1 October 1997

BRIAN MAY
Musician, 1 September 2008

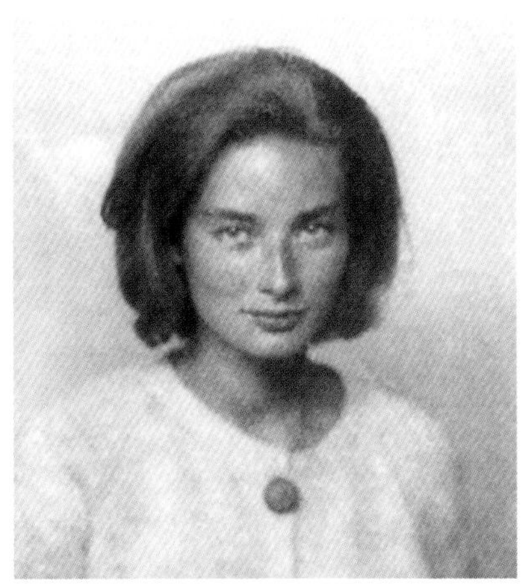

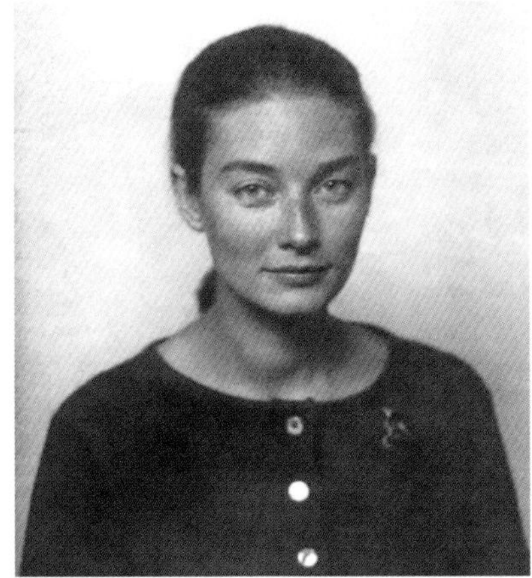

TANIA MALLET
Model/Actor, 5 July 1962
and 13 April 1964

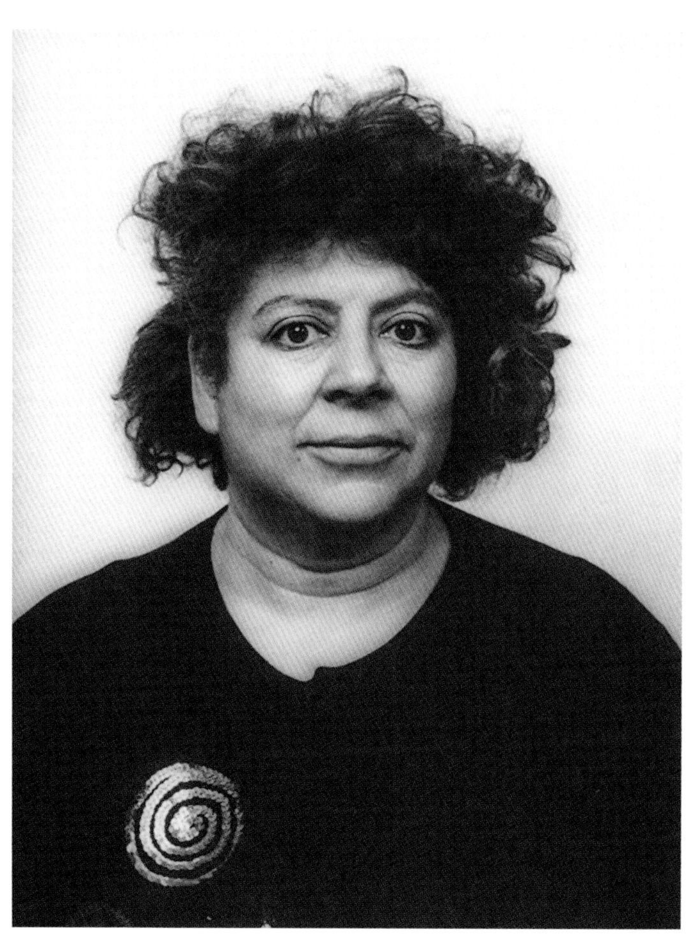

MIRIAM MARGOLYES
Actor, 9 December 1993

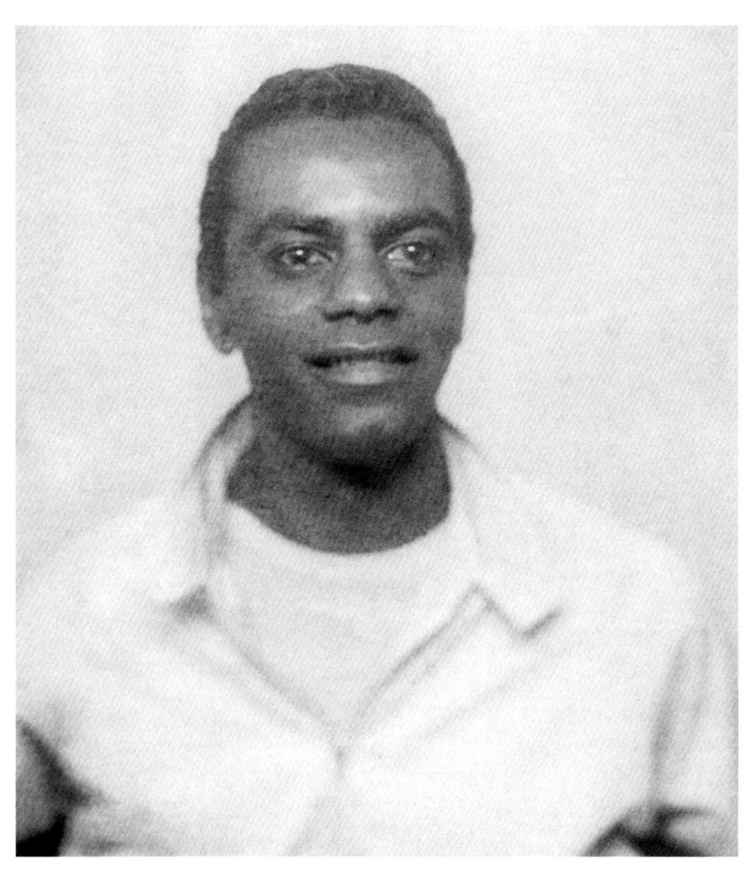

JOHNNY MATHIS
Singer, 10 December 1962

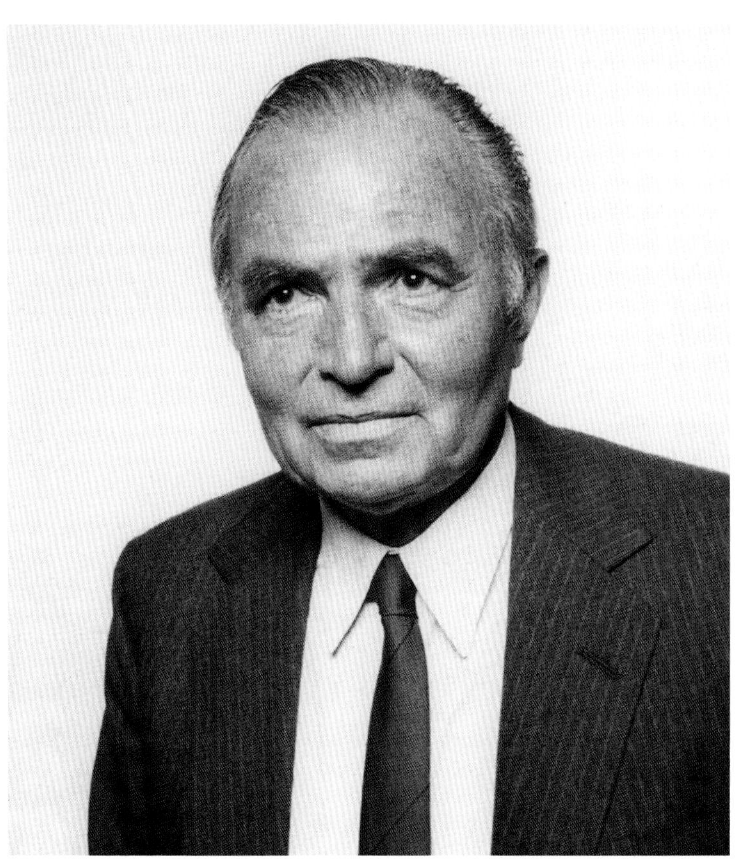

JAMES MASON
Actor, 7 August 1974

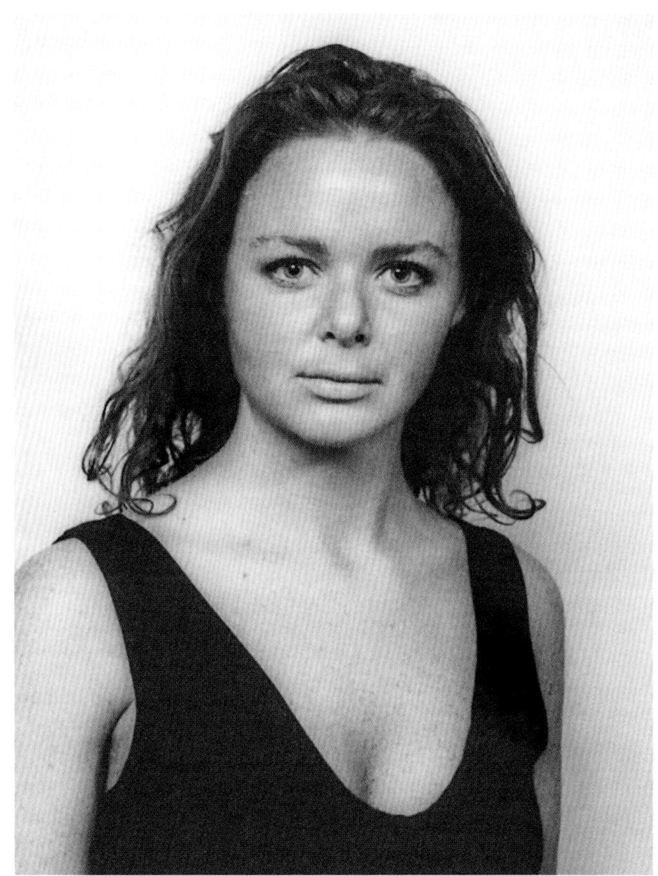

STELLA MCCARTNEY

Fashion designer, 22 July 2002

We have photographed all the McCartney offspring over the years, but alas never Paul or Linda. I guess that makes sense; Linda was a prolific photographer herself, so they probably didn't need to take the walk down Oxford Street to be mobbed by fans.

No. 162

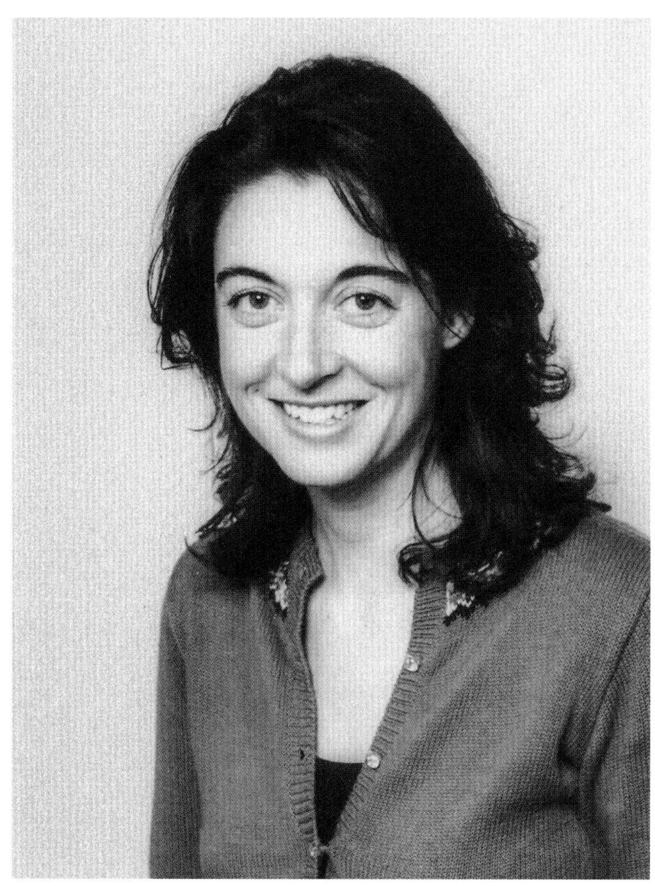

MARY MCCARTNEY
Photographer, 15 November 1989

GEORGE MICHAEL

Musician, 13 June 2006

I was pleased to get the call to photograph George Michael at a studio in Acton because we had grown up in the same village just outside London, although I never remember seeing him around since he was a couple of years younger than me. I didn't get very long to chat to him, but I had time to mention a few mutual friends that I was still in touch with, and we had a laugh about that. I next photographed him at his house in Highgate, where we had more time to reminisce, since he was on his own and in no hurry for me to leave. I was able to tell him how generous his father was. Their family house was at the end of a long, pretty steep road, and coming up to Christmas, all the kids who delivered newspapers would clamour for that round because Mr Panayiotou gave the biggest tip: £5 to the lucky kid who knocked on his door. George told me he also had a paper round in the village a few years later. In 2018, a couple of years after his passing, George's sister Melanie popped in for her photograph. She loved my newspaper-round story and was rightly proud of how generous her dad was.

No. 164

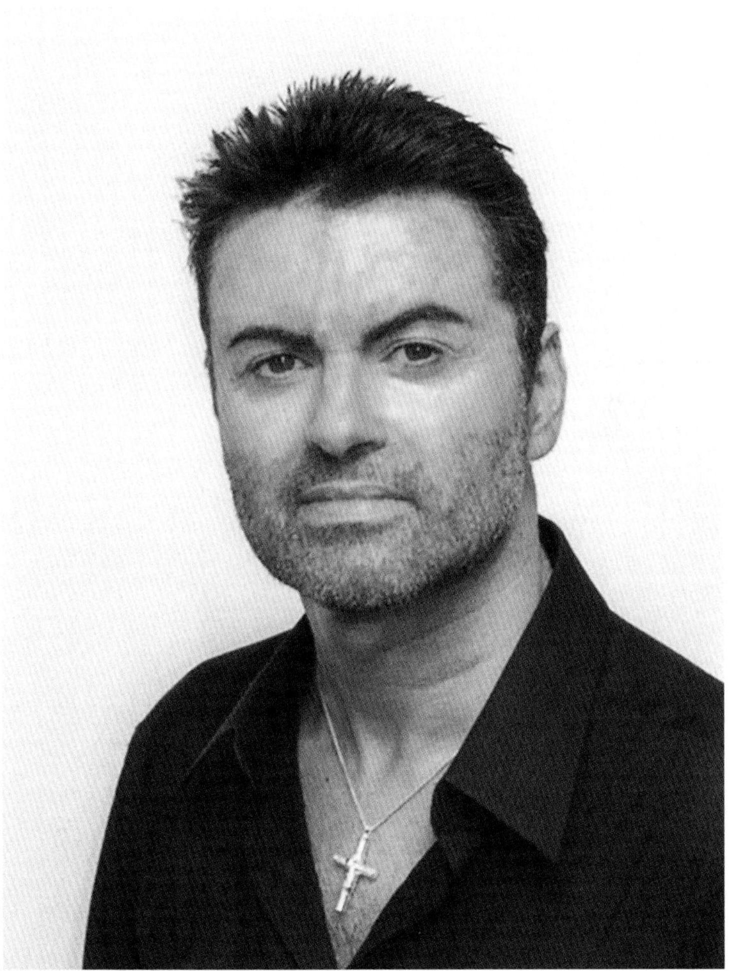

No. 165

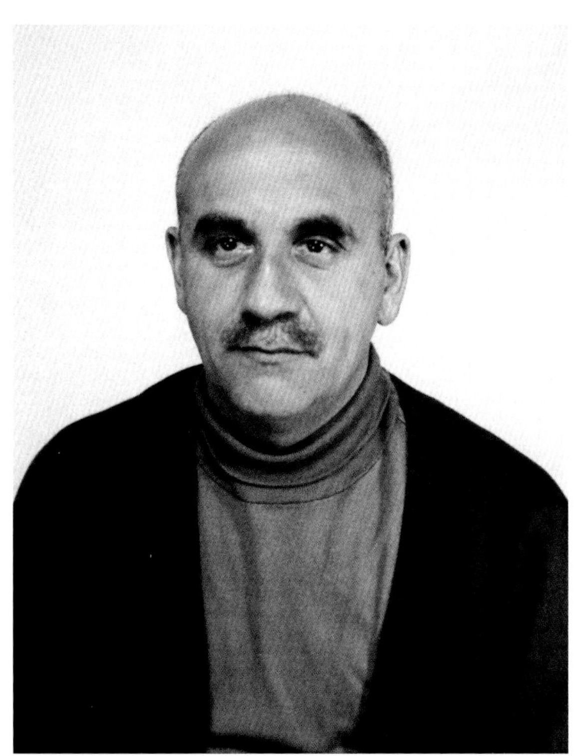

WARREN MITCHELL

Actor, 2 May 1968

Warren Mitchell played the bigoted Cockney Alf Garnett in *Till Death Us Do Part* (1965–75), a hugely popular and controversial TV sitcom and the inspiration for the American show *All in the Family* (1971–9). Another customer tried to make conversation by sharing her completed photos and asking his opinion. He just shrugged and replied, 'What do you expect for 10 bob, a Rembrandt?'

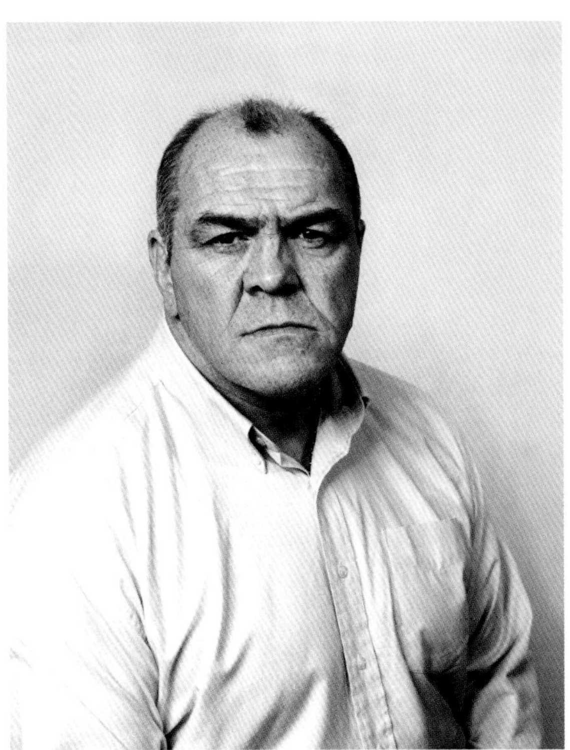

LENNY MCLEAN

Actor, 28 May 1997

When Lenny McLean, a nightclub bouncer-turned-tough-guy-actor, told Peter the headshots were for his acting work, Peter innocently asked which extras agency they were for, presuming he was a 'background artist'. 'They are for my agent ... I am an ACTOR!' he replied loudly as he smashed his huge fist into his palm. Well, who were we to argue with him about that? To prove his point, the next year he had his breakthrough role in Guy Ritchie's *Lock, Stock and Two Smoking Barrels*.

No. 167

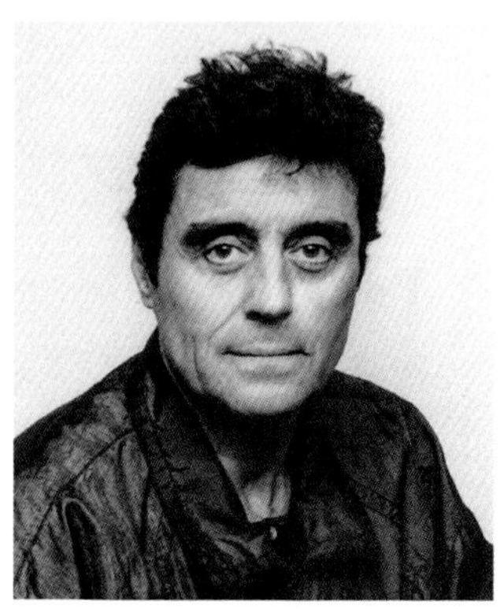

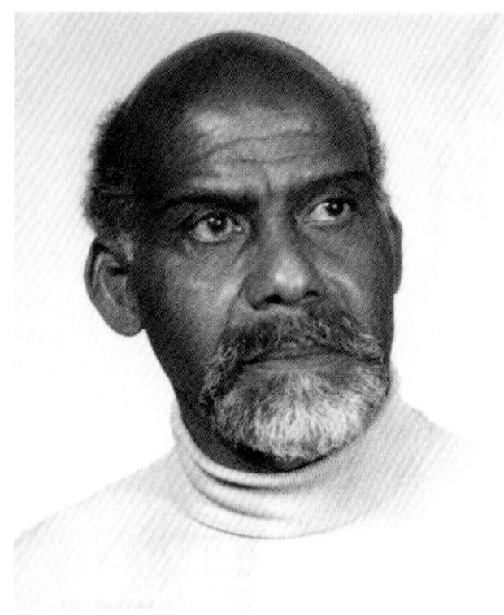

IAN MCSHANE

Actor, 3 October 1994

RONALD MOODY

Artist, 1970s

The Jamaican-born sculptor and artist became a great friend of my father's through their shared interest in the mystic philosopher George Gurdjieff. Ronald Moody's work was collected by Terry-Thomas (see p.236) and other celebrities, but only recently has he been more widely recognized. There was an exhibition of his work in 2024 at the Hepworth Gallery in Wakefield, and my father's photographs of Ronald were featured.

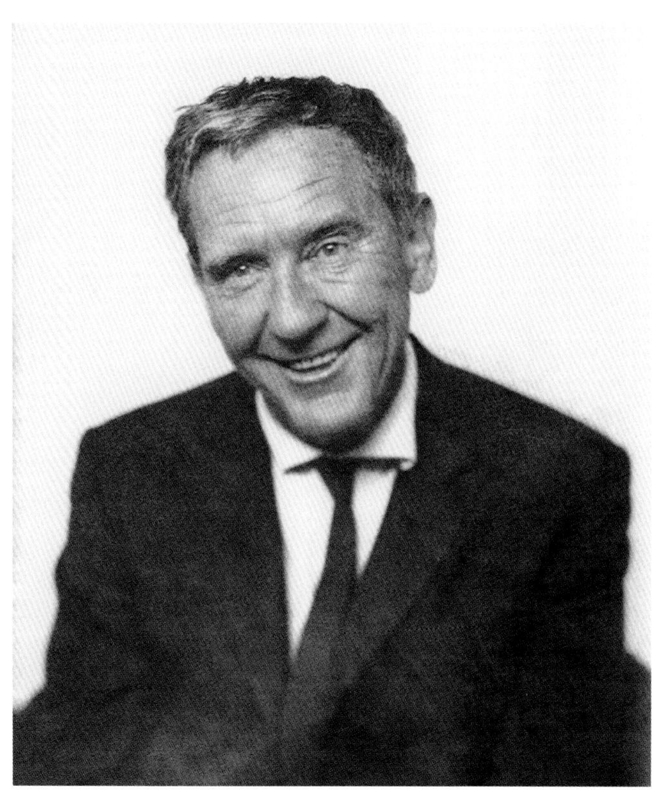

BURGESS MEREDITH
Actor, 6 May 1963

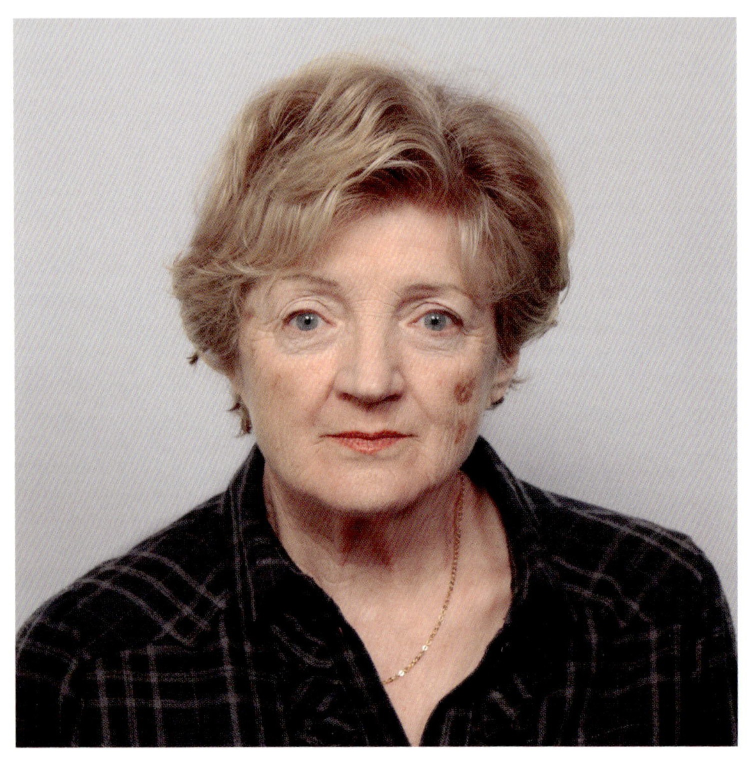

JULIA MCKENZIE
Actor/Singer, 5 September 2012

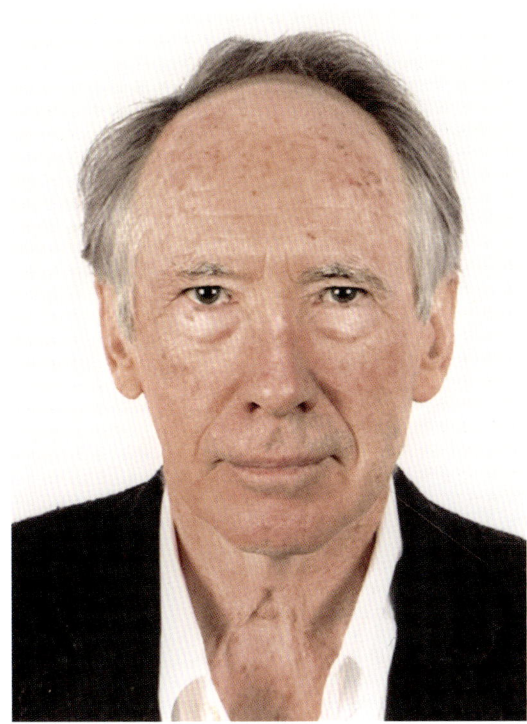

IAN MCEWAN

Writer, 20 January 2018

This writer, famous for such novels as *Amsterdam* (1998) and *Atonement* (2001), was almost the one who got away. I didn't realize who he was when we first took his picture. Thankfully, he ordered more photos of himself and his wife by post, so when I saw his name, I finally recognized him.

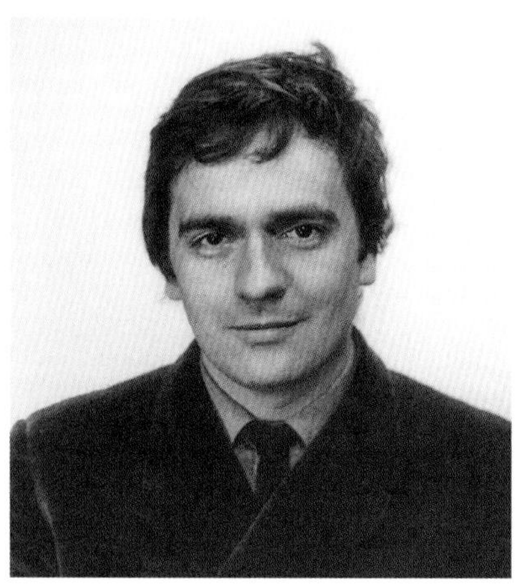

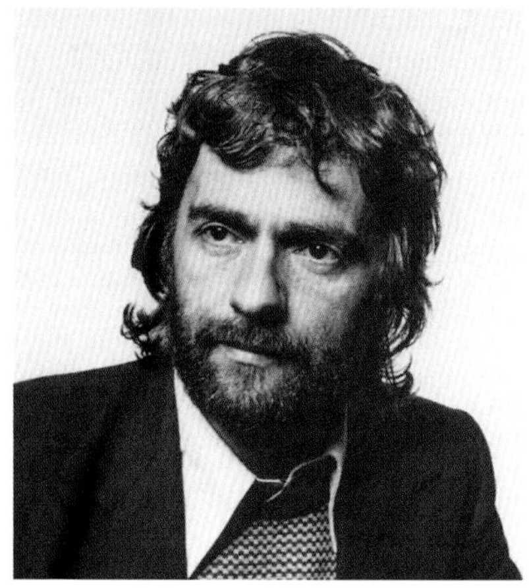

DUDLEY MOORE
Actor, 30 November 1967
and 28 January 1975

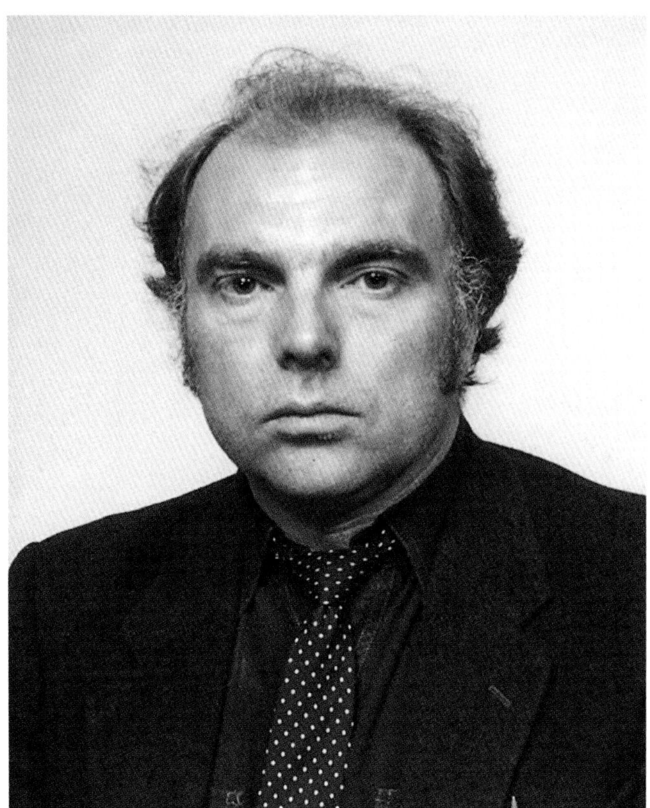

VAN MORRISON

Musician, 26 November 1988

Peter told Van Morrison that he had tickets to see him in a few weeks. 'Oh,' was all Van the Man said ... as he looked down and continued to stare at a piece of the carpet on the floor.

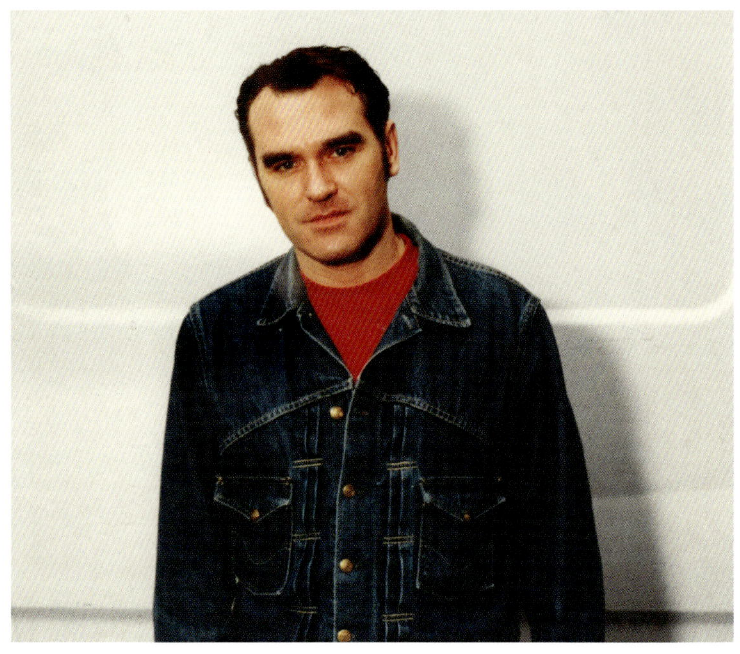

MORRISSEY

Musician, 1990s

Peter visited a rehearsal space in Holloway to take the portraits of singer Morrissey and his band. Every wall inside was black, so he had to snap them outside using the side of a white Transit van as the background. He was asked not to call the capricious singer 'Morrissey', but to address him only as 'Mr Morrissey'.

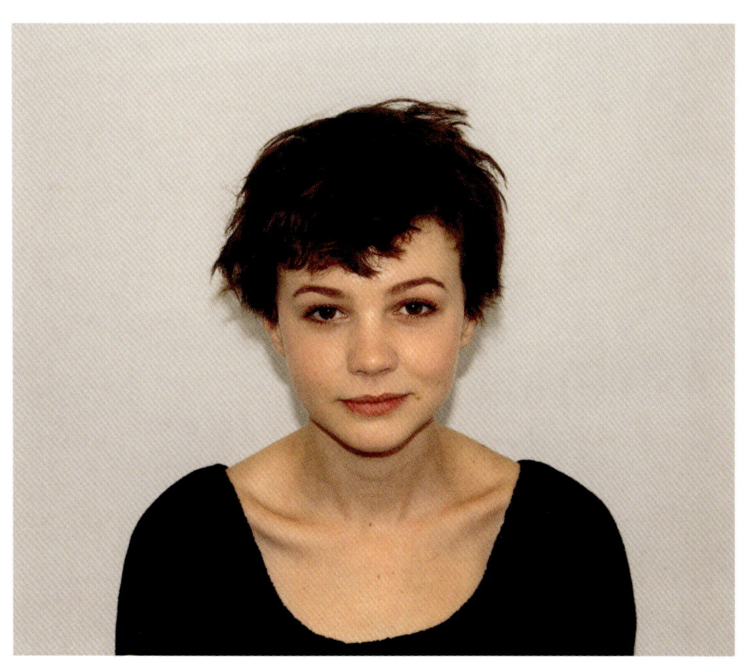

CAREY MULLIGAN
Actor, 27 August 2008

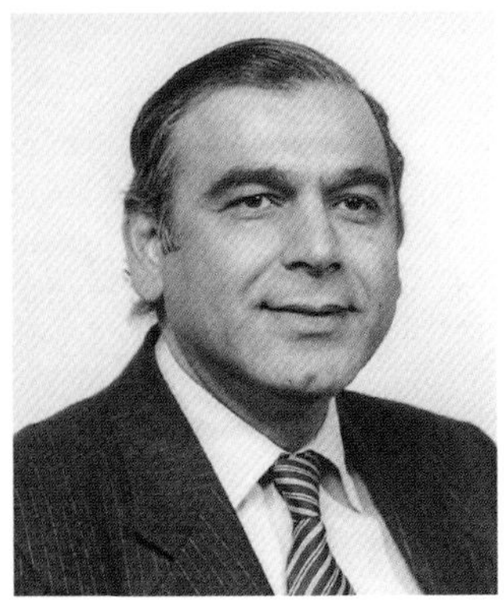

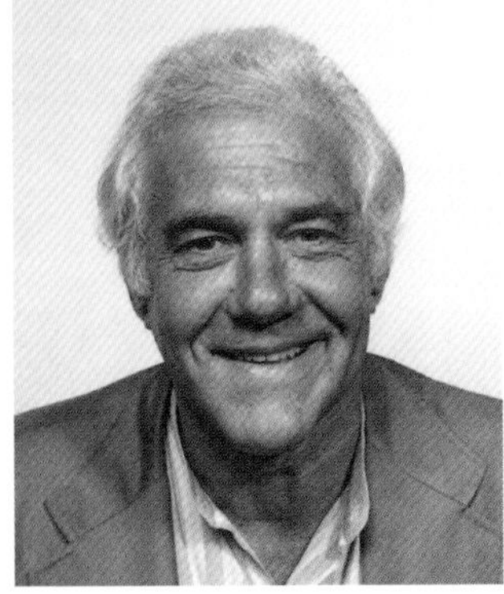

ISMAIL MERCHANT

Producer, 7 January 1986

MARVIN MITCHELSON

Lawyer, 26 July 1983

Dave only recognized this celebrity divorce lawyer – who came up with the idea of 'palimony' – when he walked into the studio because he had been interviewed on the news the night before, discussing his biggest cases. Mitchelson pointed out some of the famous clients he had represented on our wall, the fees of which seem to be reflected in the big smile in his passport photo.

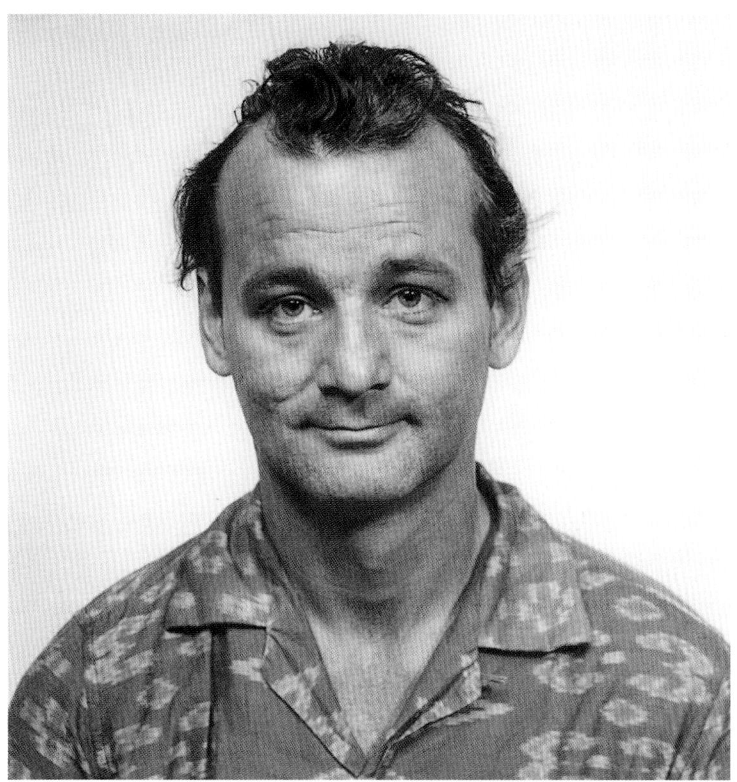

BILL MURRAY

Actor, 18 July 1983

While photographing this man, casually dressed in a Hawaiian shirt, I had the feeling I should recognize him, but I just couldn't place him. I remember he sat quietly reading a book while waiting for his photos. Two young American girls then came into the studio and, seeing him, screamed, 'It's Bill Murray!' Looking very uncomfortable, he raised his book to eye level to cover his face and continued reading.

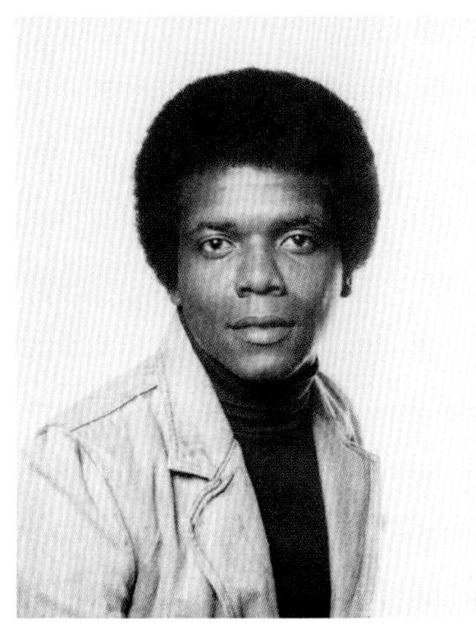

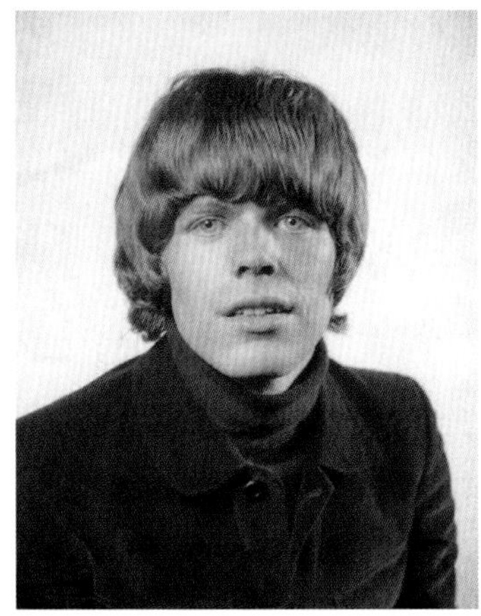

JOHNNY NASH
Singer, 22 September 1975

PETER NOONE
Singer, 5 May 1969

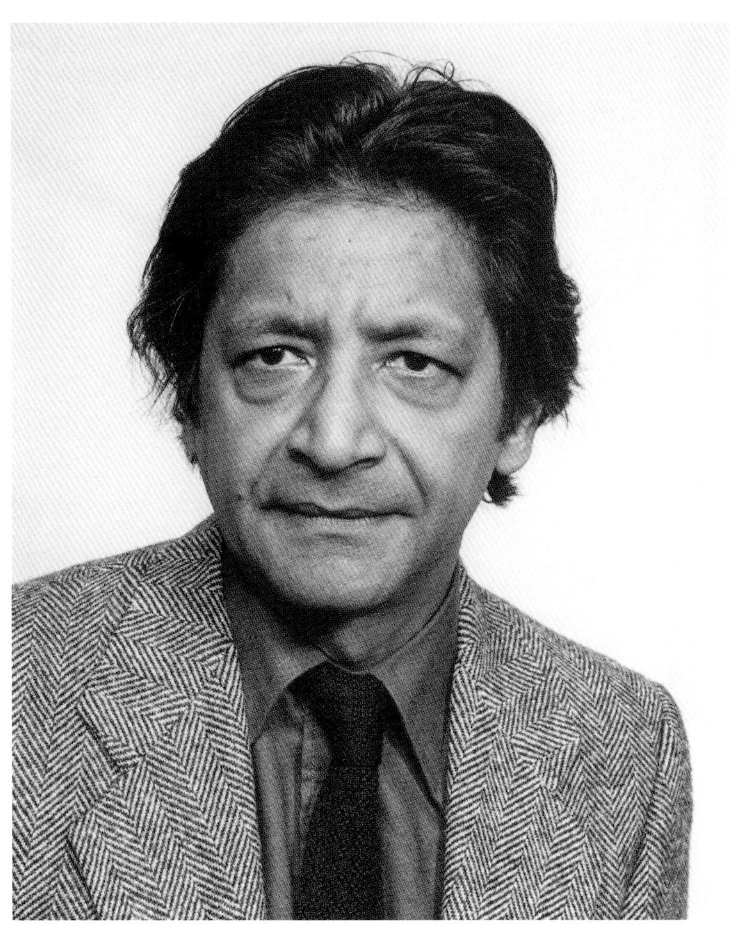

V. S. NAIPAUL
Writer, 29 October 1980

CHRISTINA ONASSIS

Businesswoman, 29 May 1987

One morning a couple of smartly dressed men in dark suits came to the studio and informed me that they had to do a security sweep of the building for a person who was coming in to be photographed that afternoon. When I asked who was arriving so that I could be sure to prepare properly, their tight-lipped reply revealed nothing. 'Fair enough,' I thought as they checked the windows and the small balcony, although it did cross my mind that they might have been casing the joint for other reasons. Anyway, at around two o'clock that afternoon, in walked the heiress Christina Onassis, her bodyguards standing discreetly by the door. The studio was busy with customers, one of whom had a young child whom Ms Onassis played with and read a little book to. Even with all the earlier hubbub, nobody in the studio knew who she was.

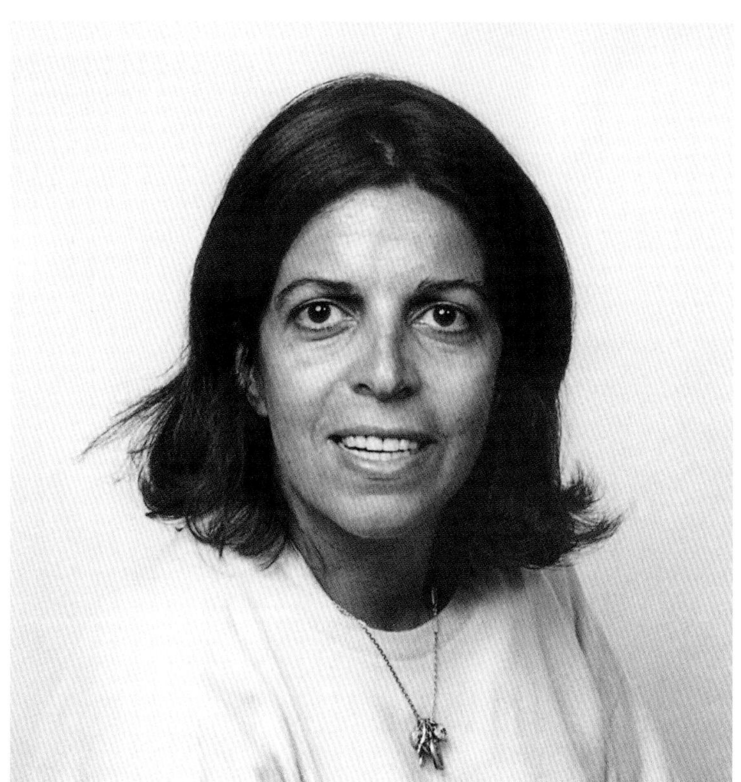

No. 181

ROY ORBISON

Musician, 26 August 1968

Peter photographed Roy Orbison in 1968, when he was touring the UK and living close by in Upper Brook Street. Sadly, his house in America burned down a few weeks later, destroying all his possessions, including photographs and memorabilia. Decades afterwards, in December 1998, I photographed a guy in his early twenties, who, just as he was leaving, spotted Orbison's picture. 'Wow, that's my dad,' he said. Sometimes I have a few jokers saying things like that, so I didn't believe him. But, strangely, I had just read a magazine article by Orbison's wife, who was a German au pair working in Leeds when they met in the 1960s. 'Is your mother German?' I asked. He was pretty amazed, and when he said yes, I knew he wasn't kidding. He told me he didn't have anything from his dad's early days because it was all lost in the fire, so I gave him an enlargement of his father's passport photo. He returned the next day with his brother Alexander, and they told me stories about growing up with their famous dad, and about another rock legend's daughter with whom Alexander shared his first kiss.

No. 182

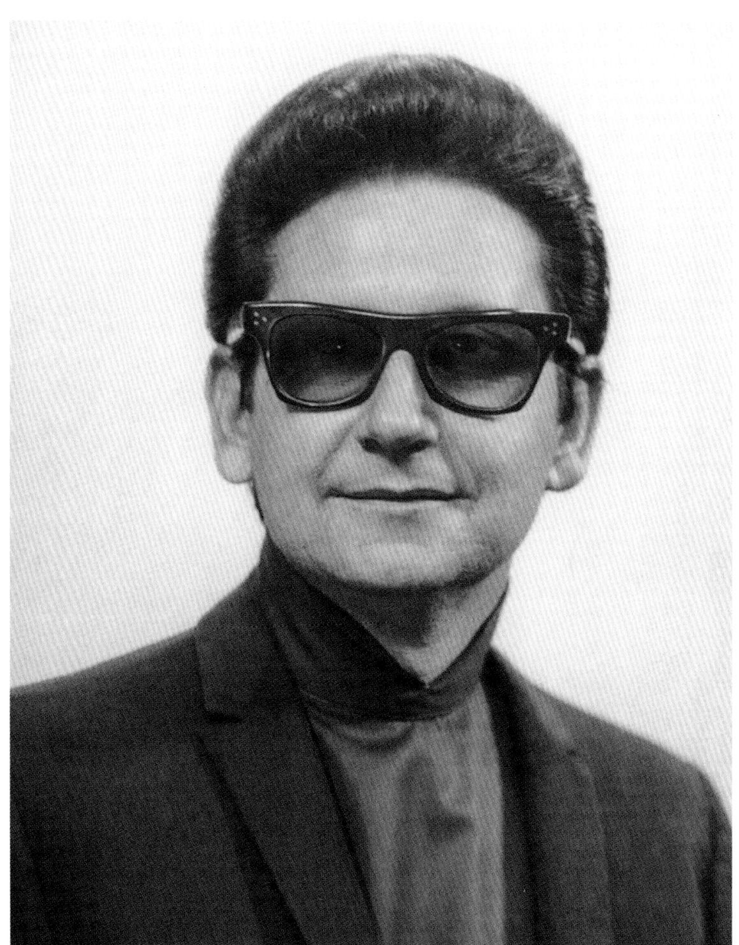

No. 183

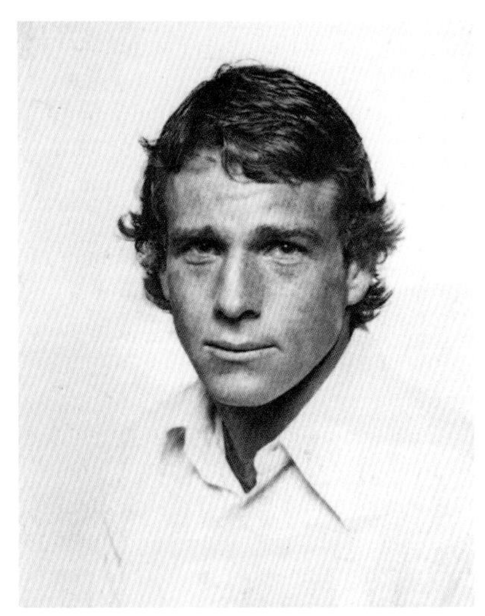

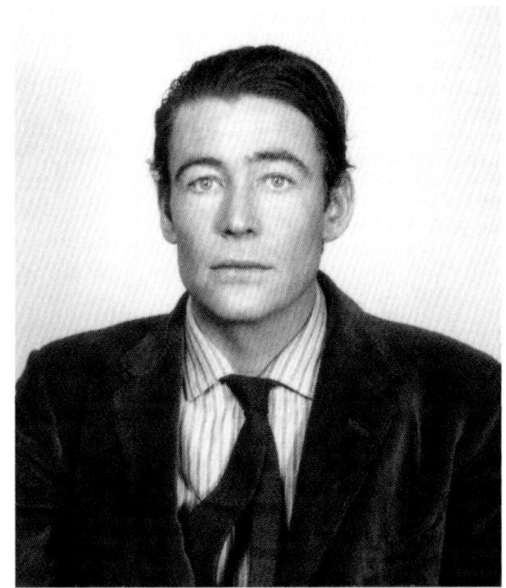

RYAN O'NEAL
Actor, 14 January 1975

PETER O'TOOLE
Actor, 1960s

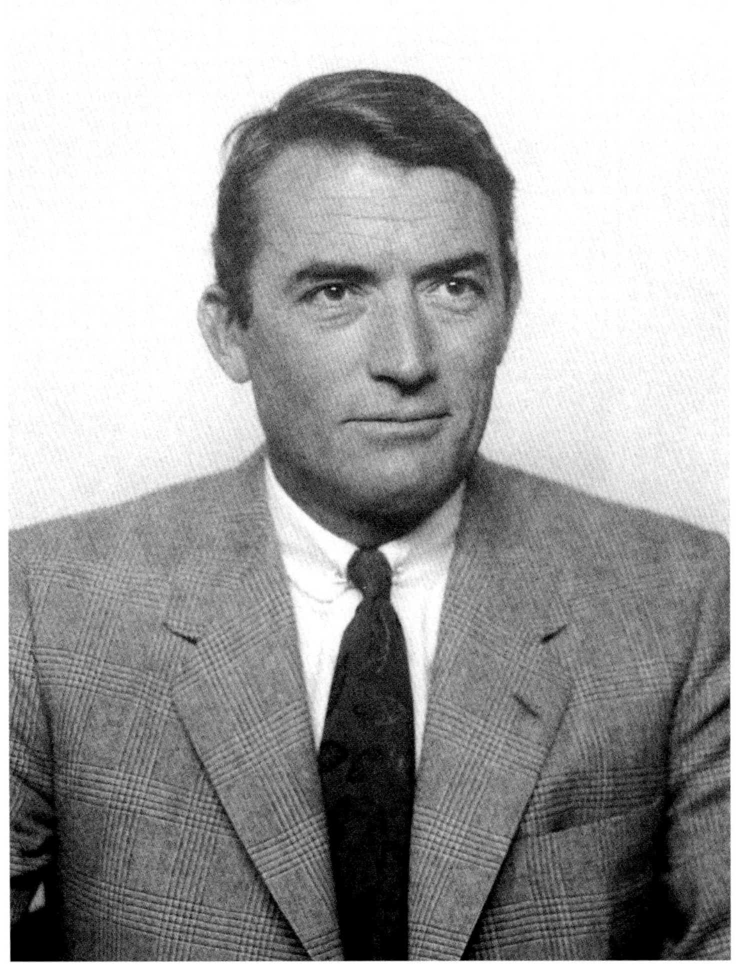

GREGORY PECK
Actor, 15 December 1959

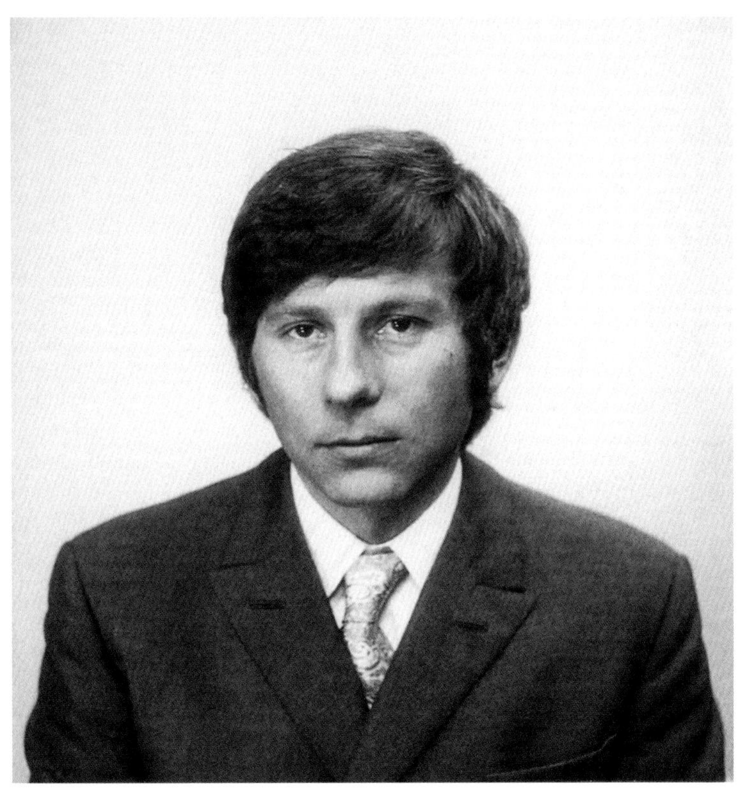

No. 186

ROMAN POLANSKI

Director, 23 January 1968

On a very busy morning at the studio, with many customers waiting the promised ten minutes for their finished photographs, we spotted Roman Polanski sitting patiently among them. Peter knew that Polanski was a photographer as well as a film director, so, since it was so hectic, he invited Polanski into the darkroom to develop and print his own photos, which the director was pleased to do. Polanski had married the actor Sharon Tate only three days earlier and was working on *Rosemary's Baby* (1968) at the time, so ultimately he didn't take us up on our jokey offer of a full-time job at the studio.

No. 187

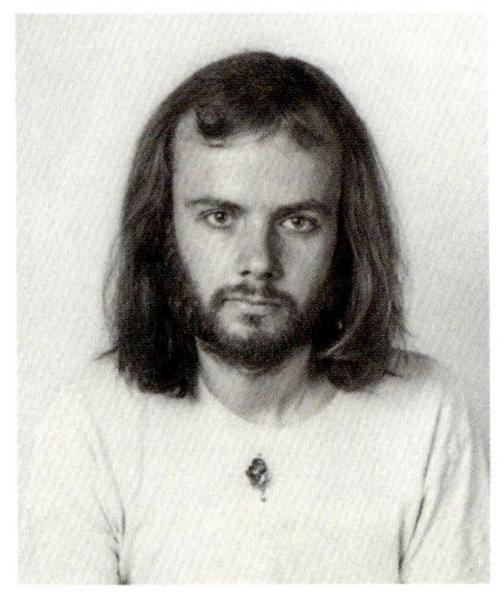

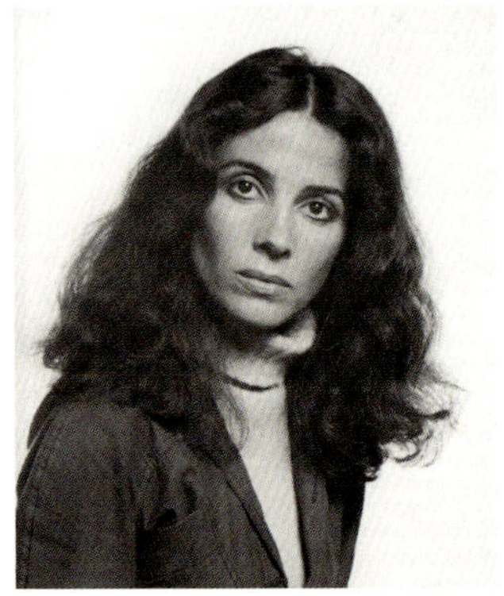

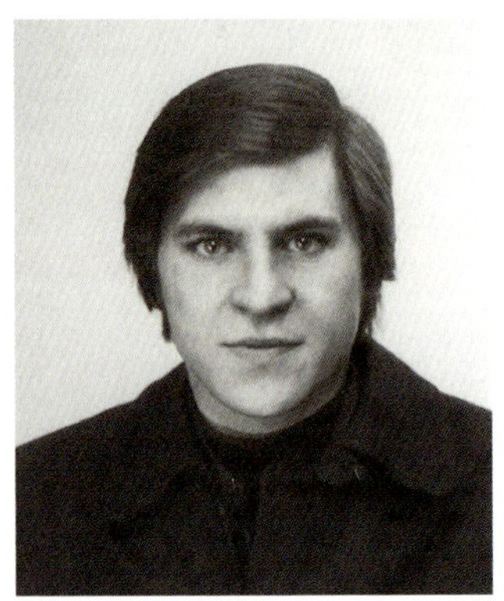

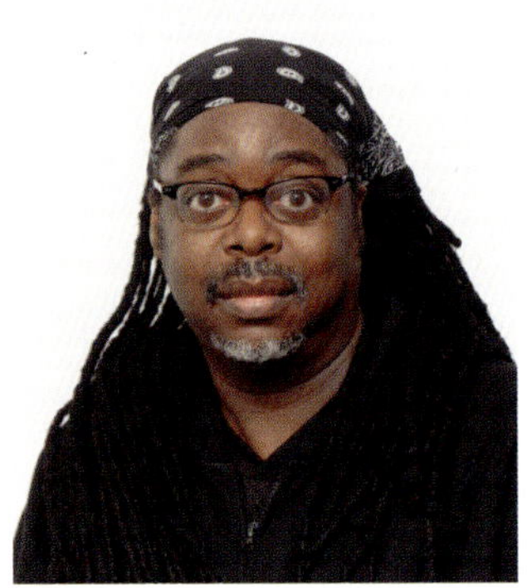

JOHN PEEL
Radio DJ, 8 August 1969

BARBARA PARKINS
Actor, 17 November 1975

ALAN PRICE
Musician, 26 January 1968

COURTNEY PINE
Musician, 16 April 2012

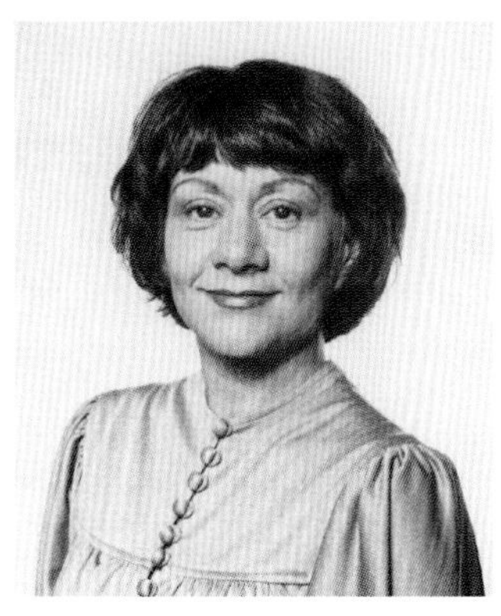

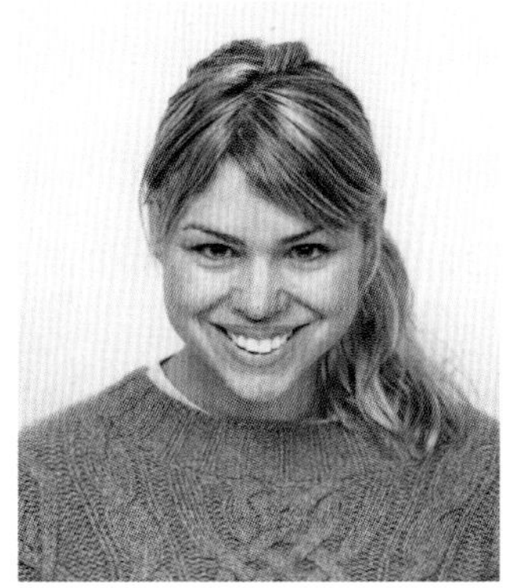

JOAN PLOWRIGHT
Actor, 16 July 1976

BILLIE PIPER
Actor, 19 December 2003

Billie Piper came in with her husband at the time, the radio DJ Chris Evans, for their US green card photos. I remembered that we had photographed Piper when she was at the Sylvia Young Theatre School, so I went through our files and pulled out the contact sheet of her and her classmates. Both roared with laughter at seeing her prancing about in a leotard, and they reminisced about the other pupils pictured.

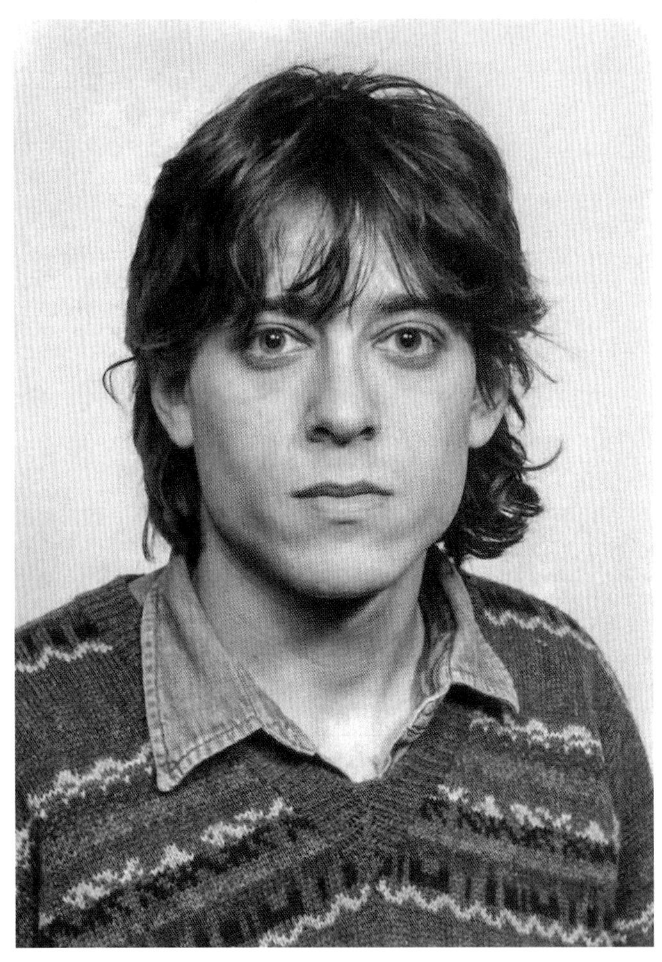

IGGY POP
Musician, 21 May 1981

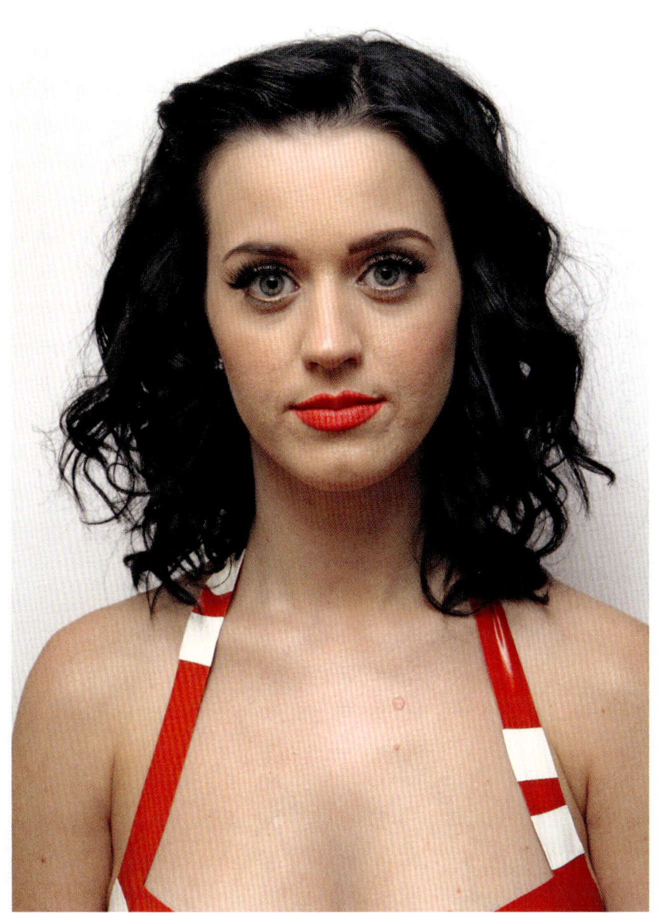

KATY PERRY
Musician, 25 June 2010

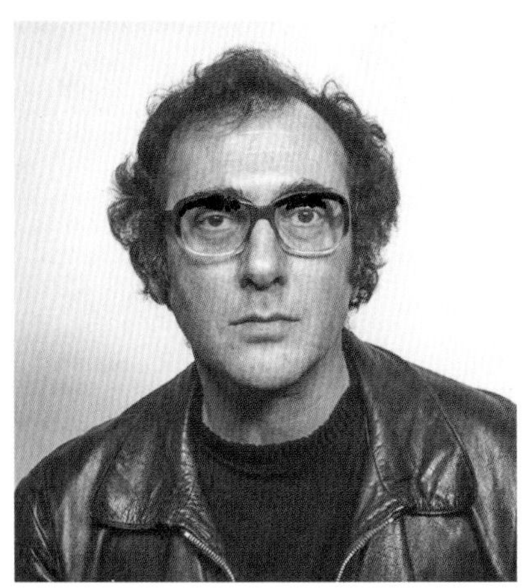

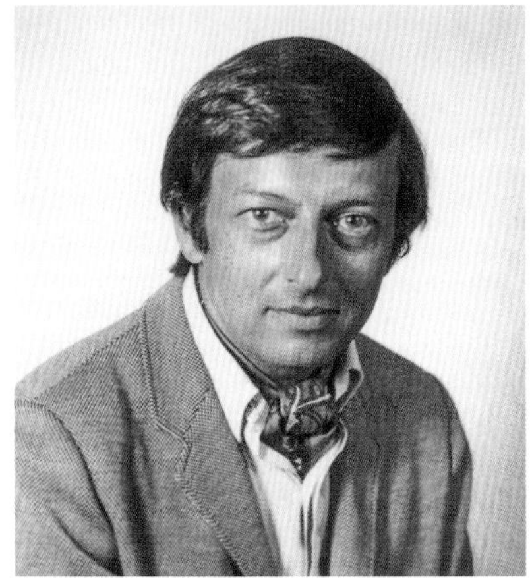

HAROLD PINTER
Playwright, 3 December 1979

ANDRÉ PREVIN
Conductor/Composer, 30 June 1969

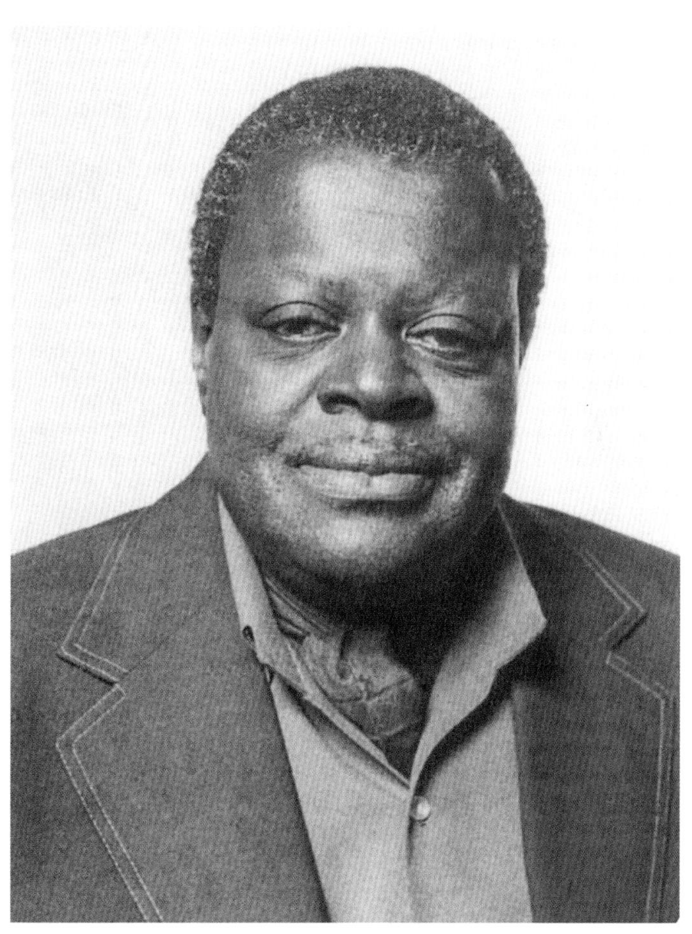

OSCAR PETERSON
Musician, 1970s

LUISE RAINER

Actor, 15 December 1959

Luise Rainer must be among our sitters who have visited the studio the most. Even when she was more than a hundred years old, she would dash up the forty-five steep stairs. Without needing to catch her breath, she would point at various celebrities and exclaim to all in her still strong German accent, 'Darlings, see these actors? They don't even come close to me, I won two Oscars in two consecutive years.' Of course, the customers waiting thought she was a slightly batty old lady, but indeed she was telling the truth. A bundle of pure energy, she lived to be 104.

No. 194

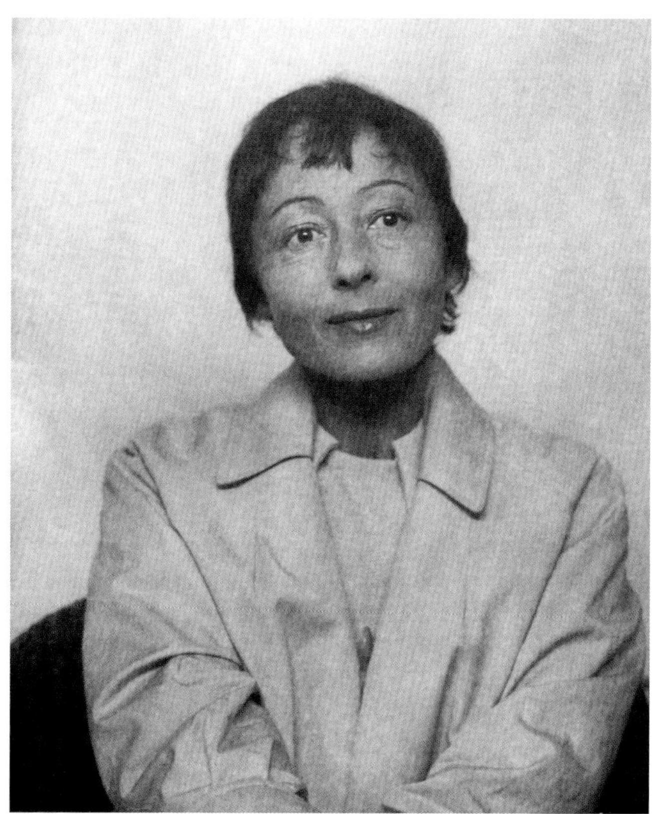

No. 195

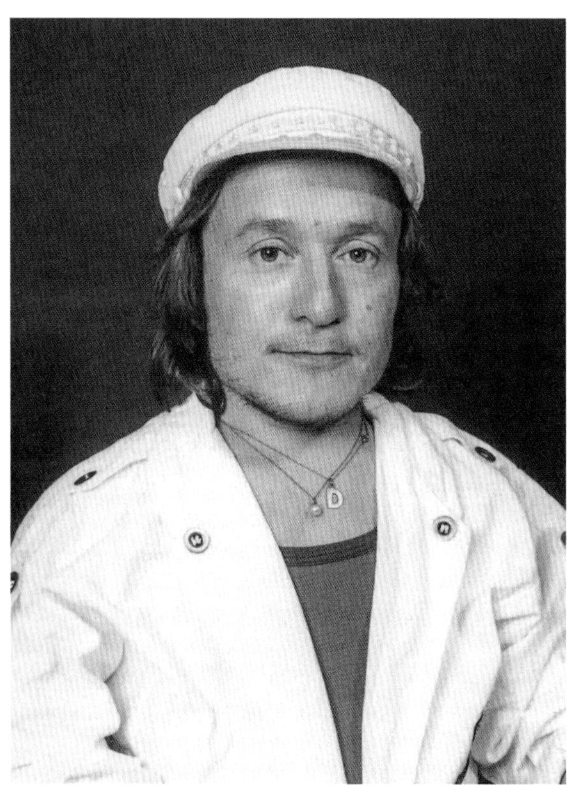

No. 196

DAVID RAPPAPORT

Actor, 9 July 1985

What a lovely, friendly man. We had a light-beam buzzer that would go off when customers entered, so that we would know if someone came in while we were working in the darkroom. David Rappaport was short enough not to set it off ... and he was wearing a hat! He found it funny that he had to knock on the darkroom door to get our attention. While Graeme was taking a portrait for his American visa, Rappaport quipped, 'I'm going to make it small in Hollywood.' He was looking at the framed celebrity photos, so we asked him if there was anywhere he would like to be placed. 'Well,' he laughed, 'I wouldn't mind being underneath Britt Ekland (see p.75),' so that is where we put him.

CHRISTOPHER REEVE

Actor, 25 June 1988

It was early one Saturday morning when Christopher Reeve and his two children came up the stairs. Reeve's impressive physique filled the doorway, and there was no hiding the fact that Superman had just walked in. After photographing his children, I asked him if he was ready for his picture. 'Oh no, I don't need mine taken,' he replied. I was crestfallen. How fantastic it would have been to add his picture to our wall. 'Look, Daddy, there's Arnold Schwarzenegger (see p.211) and Sean Connery (see pp.60–61) – you should be up there,' said one of his kids, coming to my rescue. 'Oh, all right then,' he replied, much to my relief. I think he could sense how disappointed I would have been if he hadn't sat for his snap.

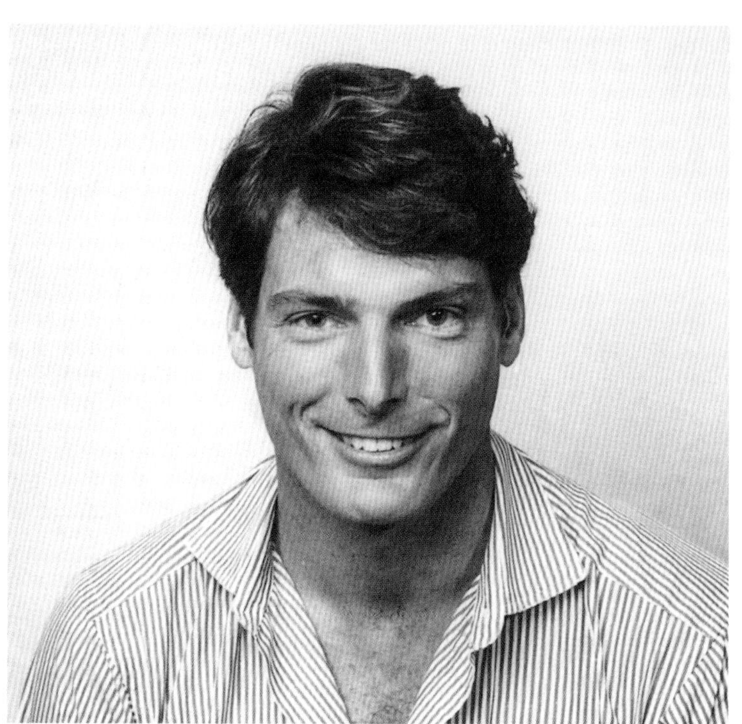

No. 199

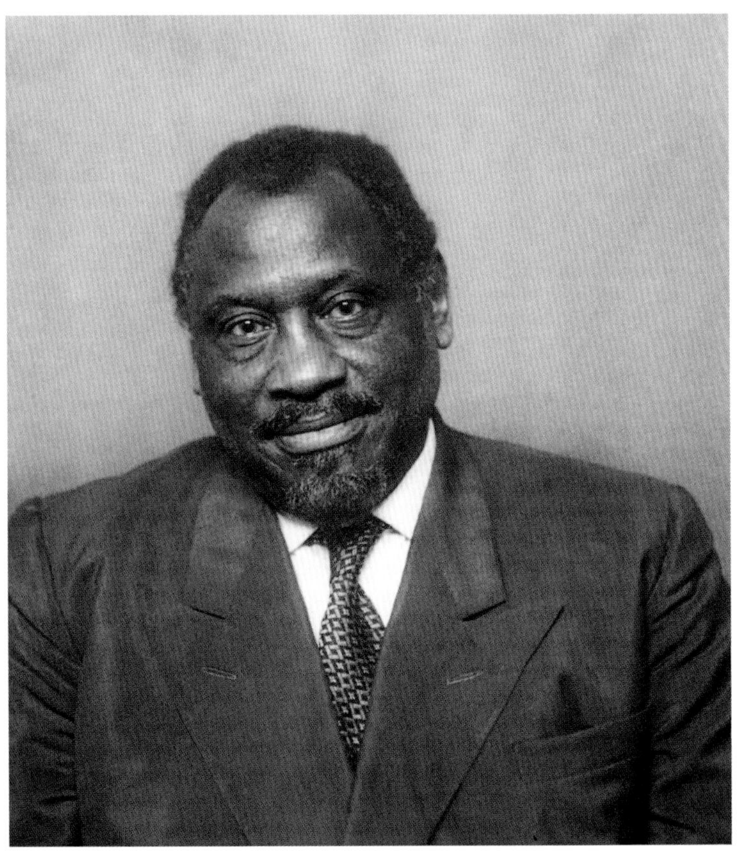

No. 200

PAUL ROBESON

Singer/Actor, 23 October 1959

My father wrote this account in 1980: he was a large man, and she was a small woman. He wore a battered brown hat and a loose, heavy overcoat. His face was sad, almost mournful, and he moved in a slow, ponderous fashion but was not clumsy. He seemed to be listening to every sound. He took one of the chairs, sat down and looked at the woman, who watched him all the time. She straightened his coat collar and spoke softly to him. I said 'Hello,' and when they both looked at me, I thought I recognized him. They both needed photos for their US passports, and they sat in the sparsely decorated waiting room after I had taken their portraits. I asked them how many prints they would like, and she replied, 'What is the charge?' I told them the prices, and the man said, 'Twelve, please.' As I walked into the darkroom, his wife thought I was out of earshot, so she said, 'You only need three, Pappy.' After a pause, he told her in his quiet, sad voice, 'The man's got to earn a living.' I came to give them their finished prints and, without looking up, the man began to sing. The woman (whom he called Essie) said, 'Pappy is going to sing for you.' He sang 'Sweet Chariot' in a deep baritone. I told them how pleased I was to meet them and how much I enjoyed him singing to me. We all shook hands as they left, and he signed one of the prints and gave it to me. It was a very moving moment, and it upset me greatly to hear of his subsequent health problems and his passing in 1976.

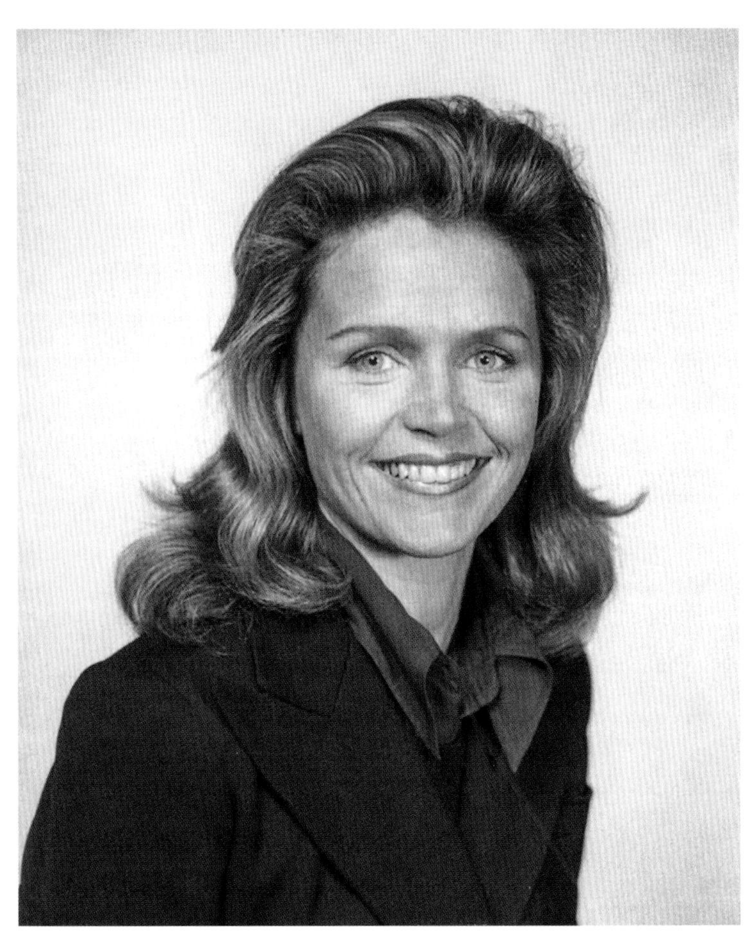

LEE REMICK
Actor, 8 March 1973

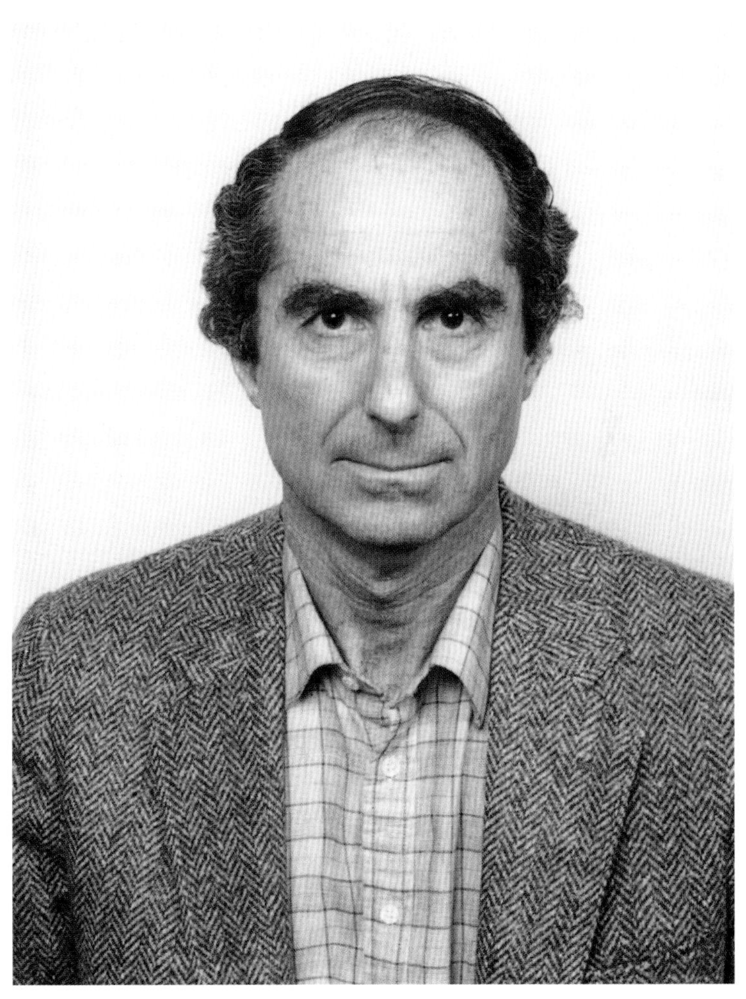

PHILIP ROTH
Writer, 5 February 1987

No. 203

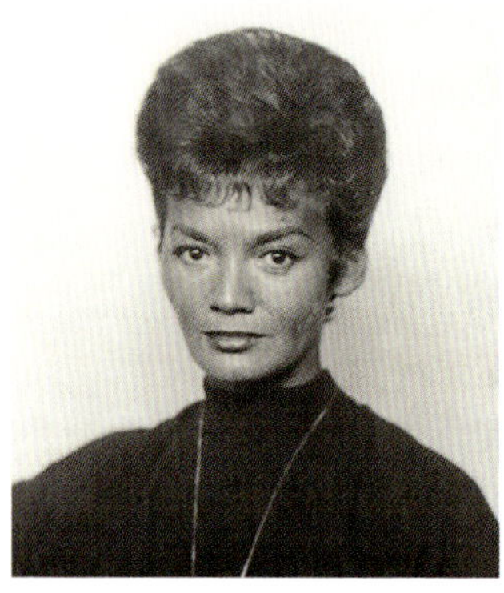

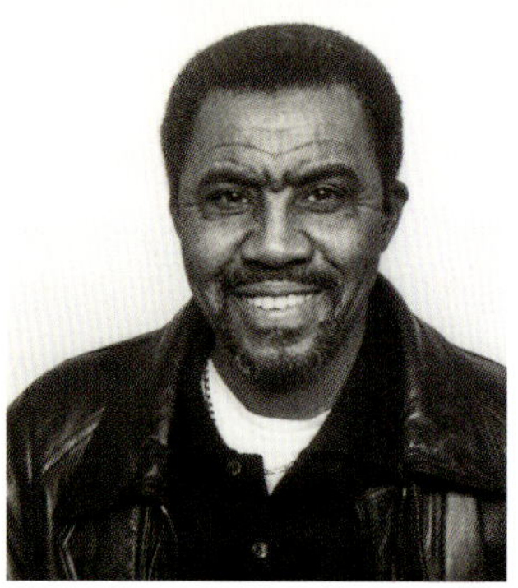

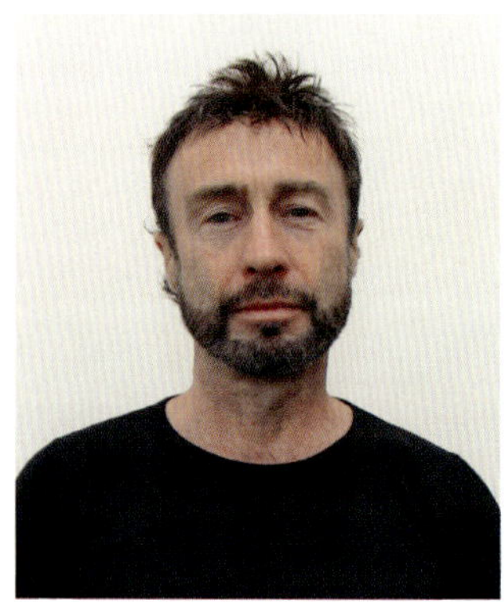

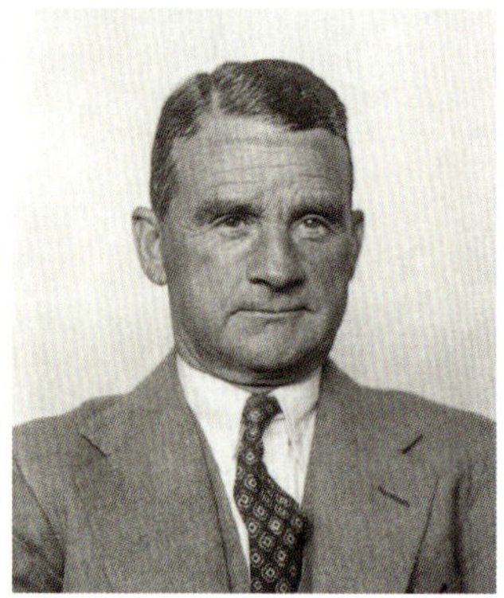

LITA ROZA
Singer, 11 October 1961

PAUL RODGERS
Musician, 27 August 2008

JIMMY RUFFIN
Singer, 1 April 1995

GORDON RICHARDS
Jockey, 15 December 1960

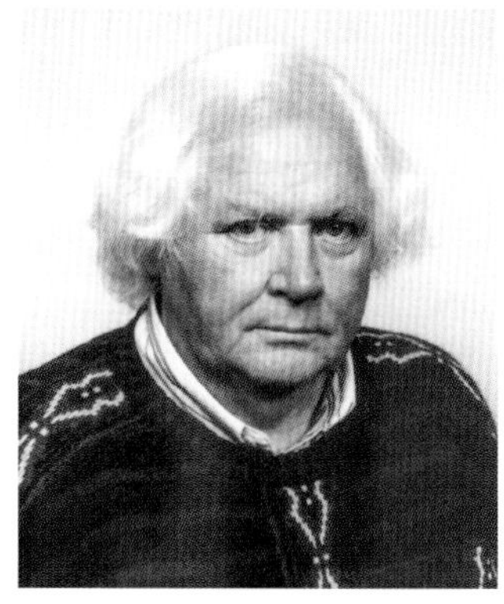

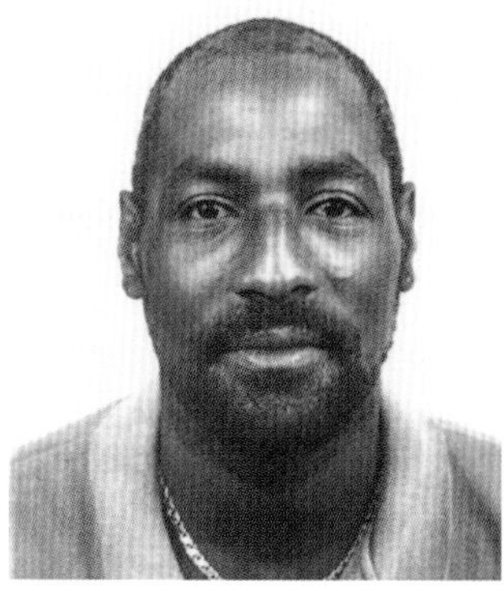

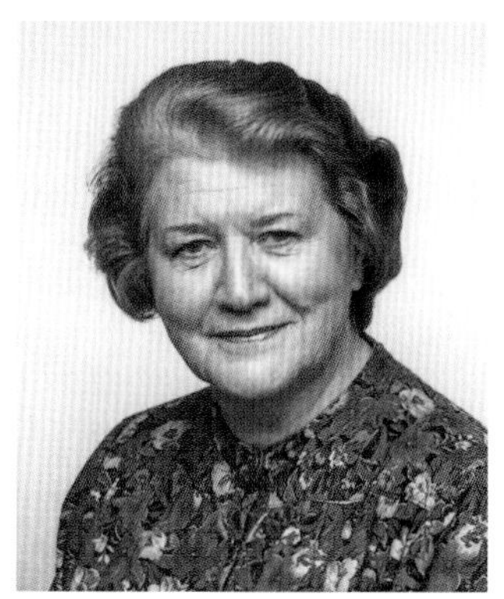

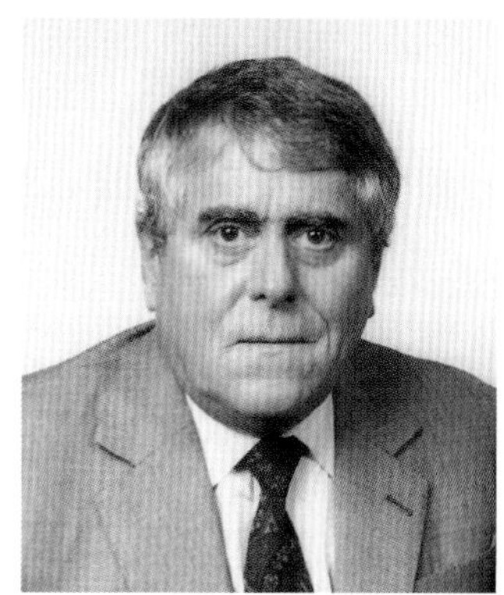

KEN RUSSELL
Director, 13 November 1989

VIV RICHARDS
Cricketer, 23 August 1994

PATRICIA ROUTLEDGE
Actor, 28 November 1995

ALBERT ROUX
Chef, 17 June 1992

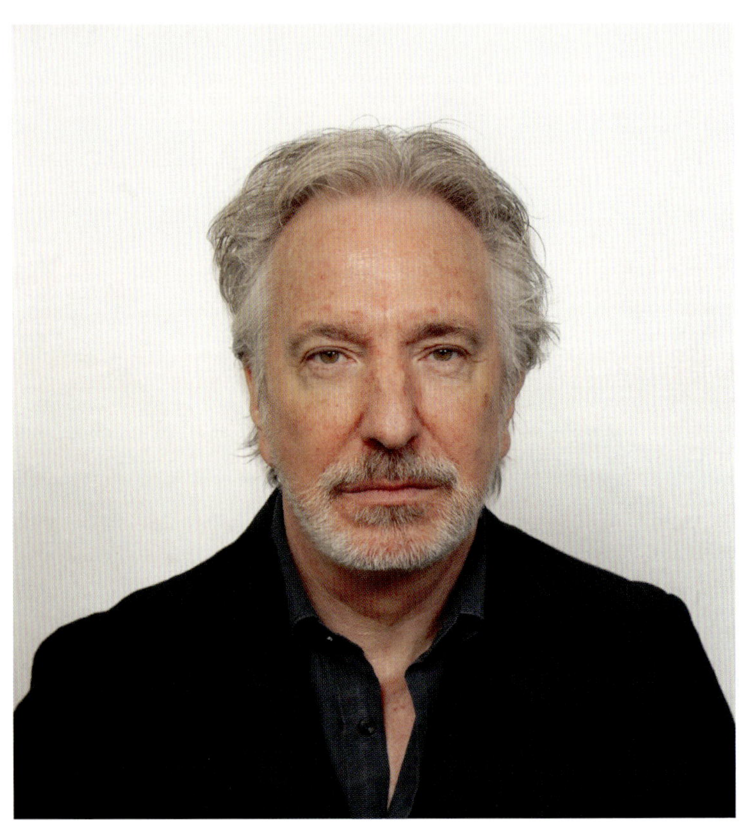

ALAN RICKMAN
Actor, 14 June 2012

No. 206

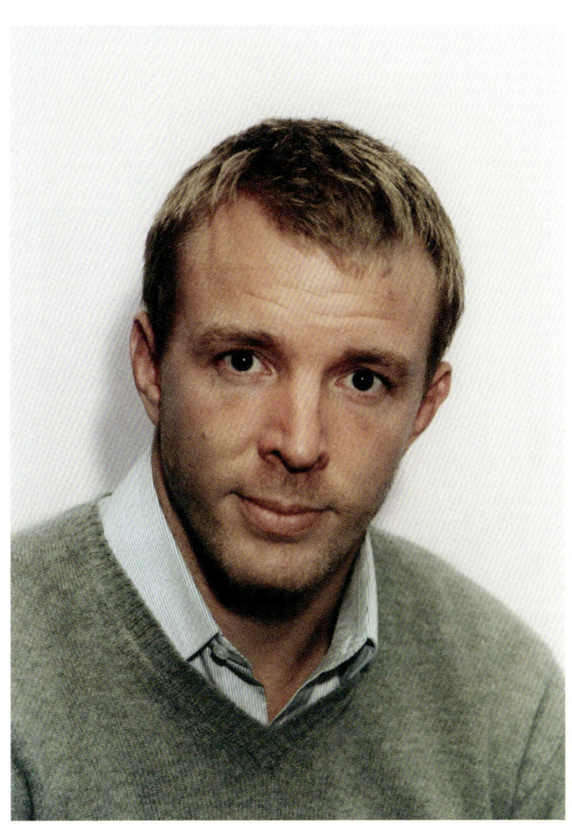

GUY RITCHIE
Director, 26 November 2001

No. 207

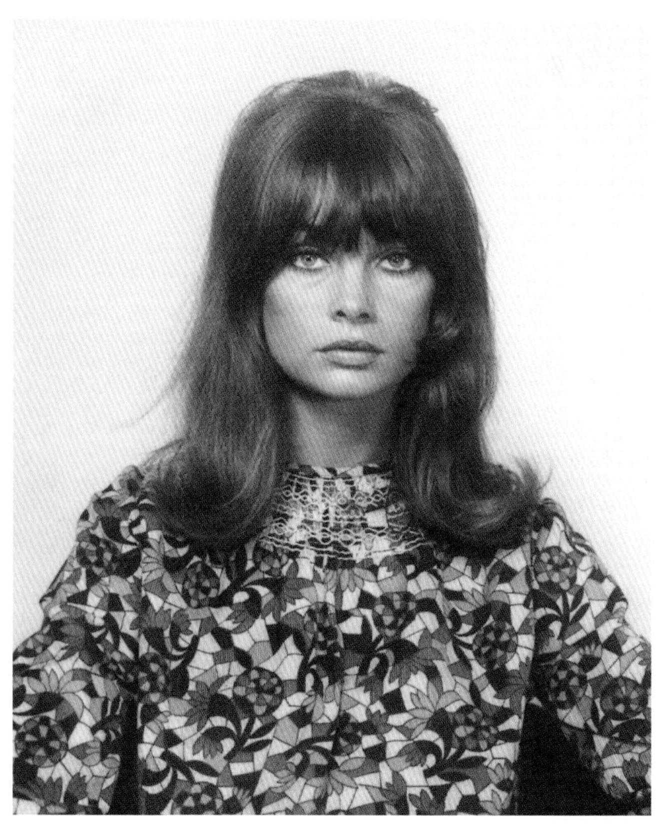

JEAN SHRIMPTON
Model, 6 October 1964

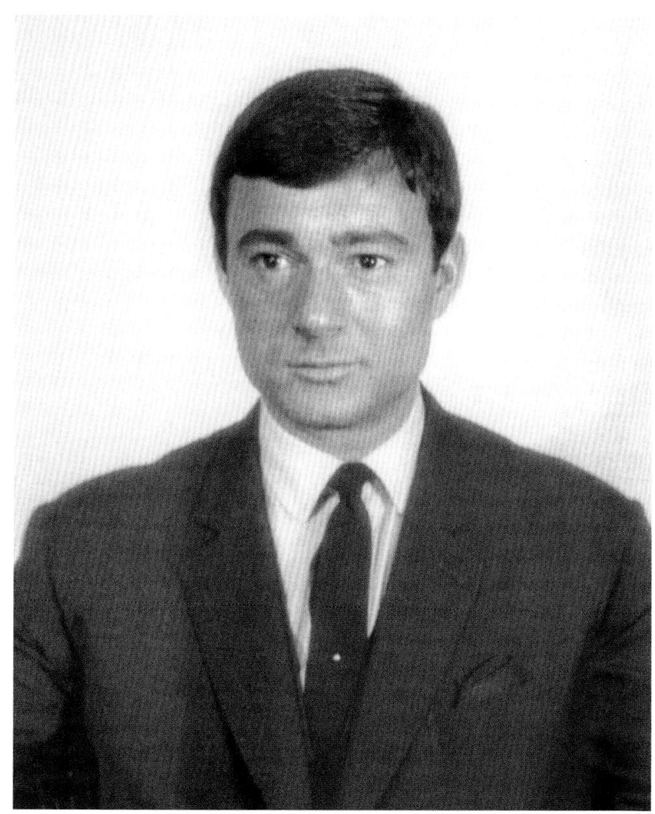

VIDAL SASSOON

Hairstylist, 6 May 1965

Just before the studio closed in June 2019, I was helping a young woman fill in her visa form with her boyfriend next to me. As I completed the travel companion details, he told me his name was London Sassoon, so I took him over to our frame of the famous and pointed out his grandfather. The father of modern hairdressing, Vidal Sassoon had popularized the geometric 'five point' cut made famous by the model Mary Quant in the Swinging Sixties.

ARNOLD SCHWARZENEGGER

Actor/Politician, 11 November 1977

Arnie had lived in London from 1966 to 1968, staying with his bodybuilding mentor Charles 'Wag' Bennett and his family in Forest Gate, east London. He went on to win many world bodybuilding titles in the United States, living and training at Gold's Gym in Santa Monica, California. Some say he had overstayed his visa, so when we photographed him for his successful US green card application, perhaps we played a small part in his future success as an actor and Governor of California. His catchphrase, made famous in the film *The Terminator* (1984), was, 'I'll be back.' We're still waiting ...

No. 210

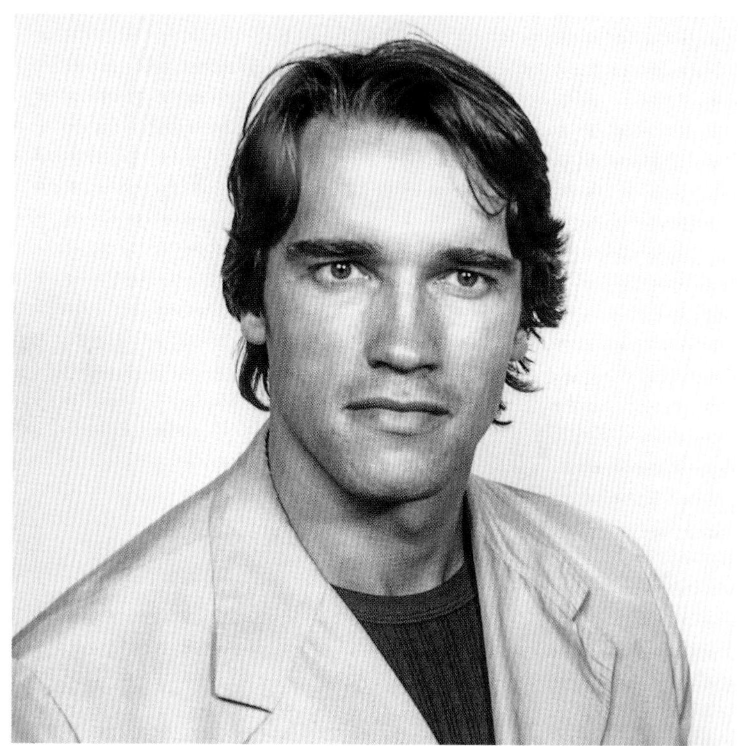

No. 211

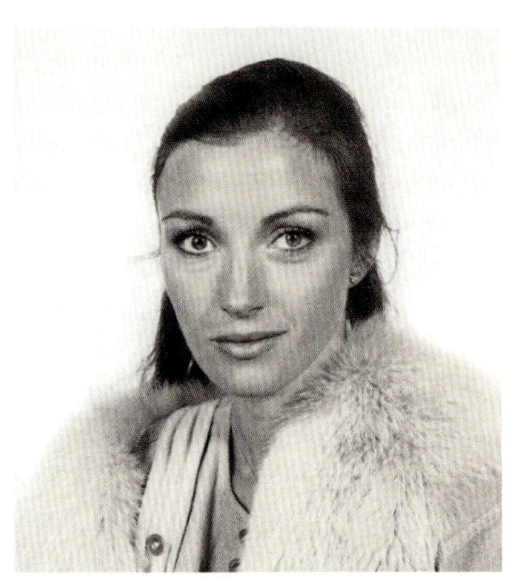

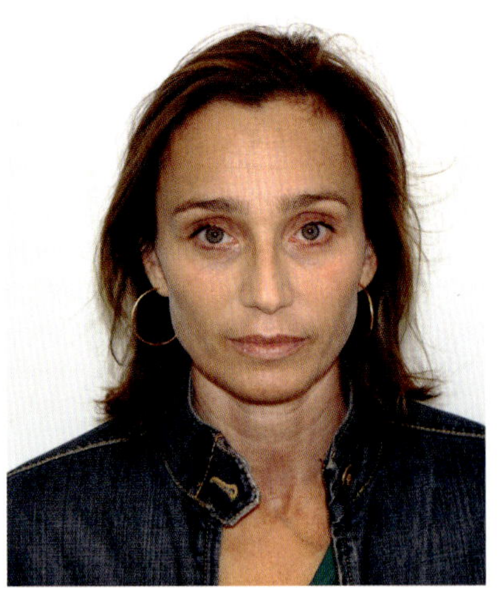

JANE SEYMOUR
Actor, 22 March 1984

KRISTIN SCOTT THOMAS
Actor, 27 August 2008

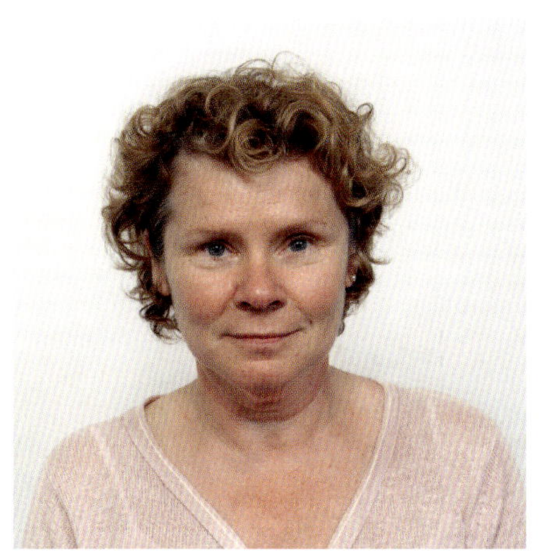

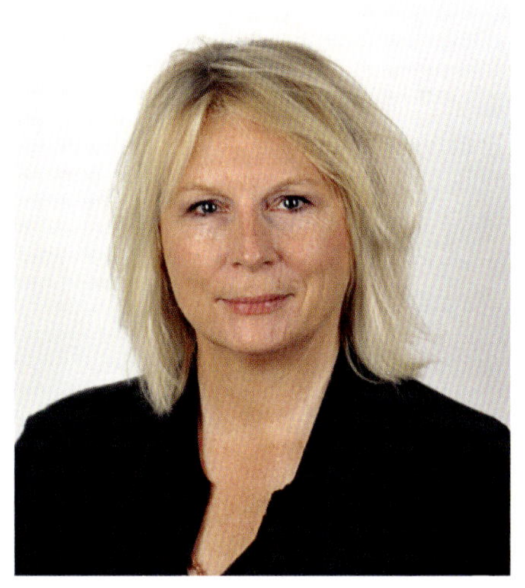

IMELDA STAUNTON
Actor, 7 August 2008

JENNIFER SAUNDERS
Actor, 3 August 2017

No. 213

MEL SMITH

Actor, 24 November 1981

Mel Smith had written a play called *The Gambler*, which my friends and I had gone to see at a pub in Kentish Town. Before the show started, he and his co-writer Bob Goody would go around the audience tossing a coin and going double or quits on the result. As luck would have it, I kept winning, and when we got to £32, all eyes were on us. A hush fell on the crowd when we both agreed to toss again. I was hoping I would lose, since this was probably going to be more than their takings for the performance, but I went 'heads' and won £64, at which point he finally said, 'No more.' When he came into the studio, I reminded him that I was the fortunate winner of our high-stakes game, and his reaction was fruity to say the least. I think he exclaimed, 'So it was you, you jammy bastard!' upon seeing me. I reckon he was only joking, but I can't be too sure!

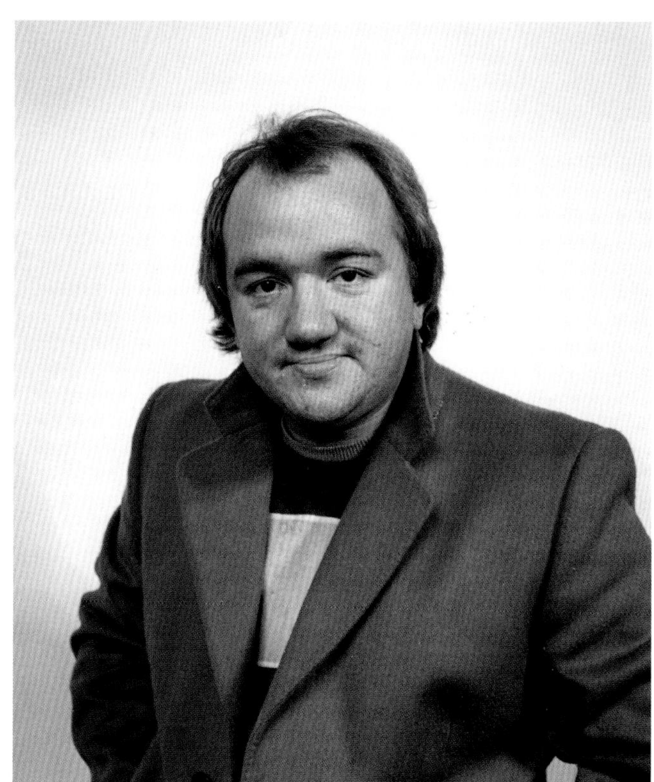

No. 215

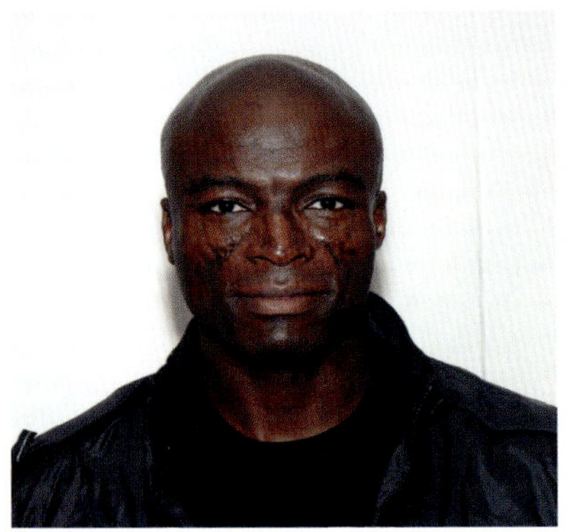

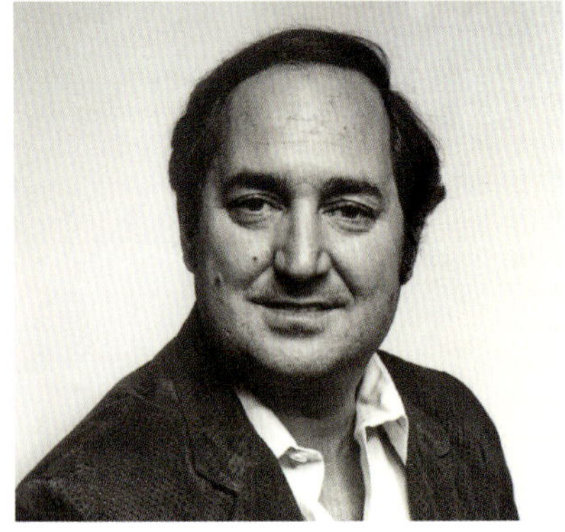

SEAL

Singer, 11 October 2010

NEIL SEDAKA

Musician, 26 April 1979

Beautifully dressed in a salmon-pink suede jacket, the singer Neil Sedaka happened to come in on my birthday and shared some cake my mother had made for me.

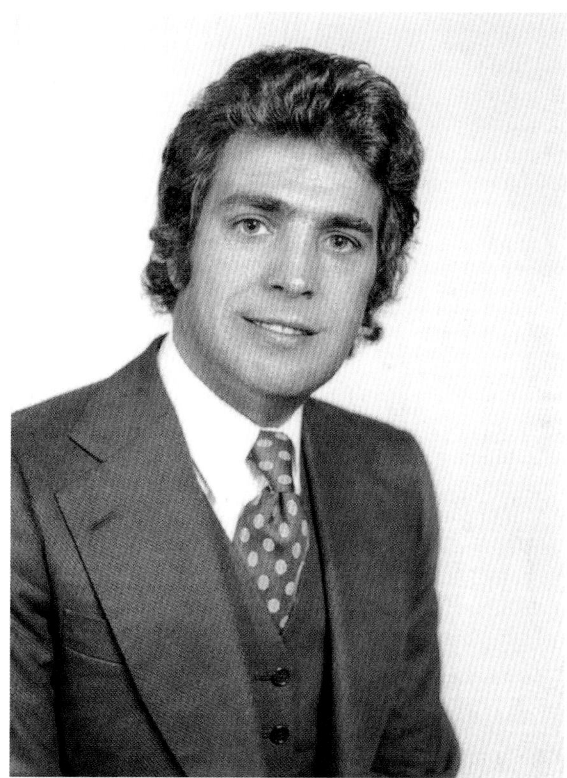

JOHN STEPHEN

Fashion designer, 18 June 1971

Known as the 'King of Carnaby Street', John Stephen is credited with making that part of Soho the world-famous fashion centre of Britain's Swinging Sixties. His hip menswear was worn by the likes of The Rolling Stones, The Kinks and The Who. We photographed him and his partner Bill Franks in 1971, and later in the 1970s he opened his eponymous shop below us at 447 Oxford Street.

No. 217

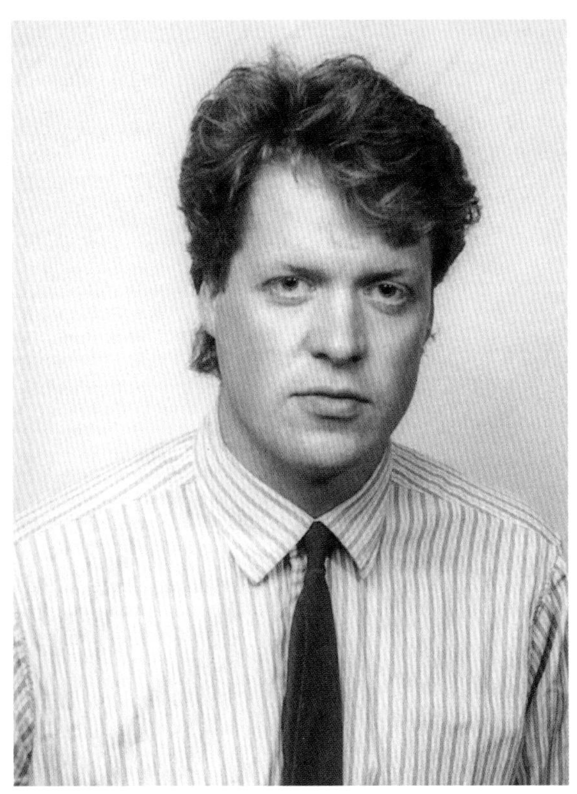

CHARLES SPENCER
9th Earl Spencer, 26 August 1987

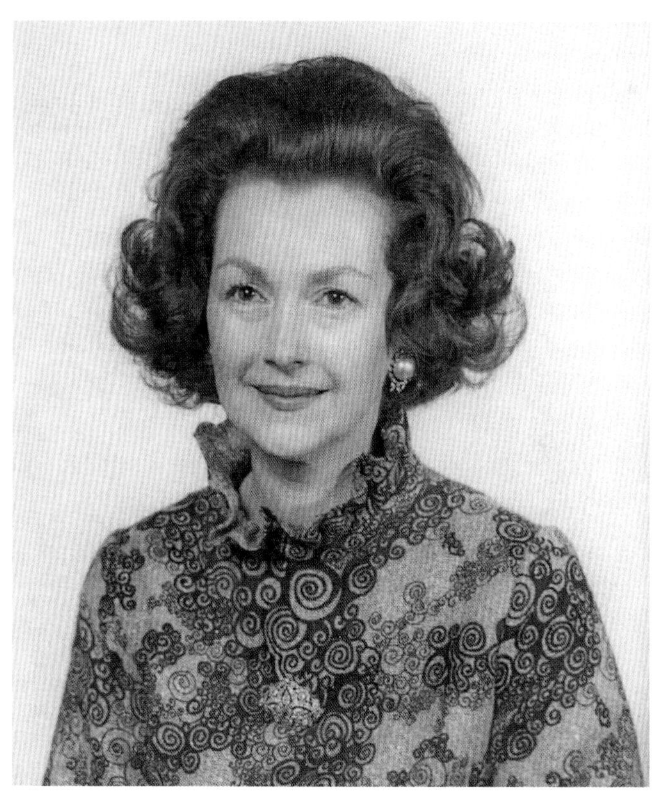

RAINE SPENCER

Countess Spencer, 2 February 1972

TOM SPRINGFIELD

Musician, 19 March 2007

A quiet private man, Tom Springfield had been in a few times for publicity pictures as well as his passport photo. Once when he was there and I was developing his photographs, the radio in the darkroom was playing 'You Don't Have to Say You Love Me', sung by his sister Dusty Springfield. I came out and told him just how much I loved Dusty's voice and what a wonderful song it is. He nodded in agreement and gave a gentle smile, saying how special and talented she was. I'm sure I could see a tear in his eye as he spoke about her.

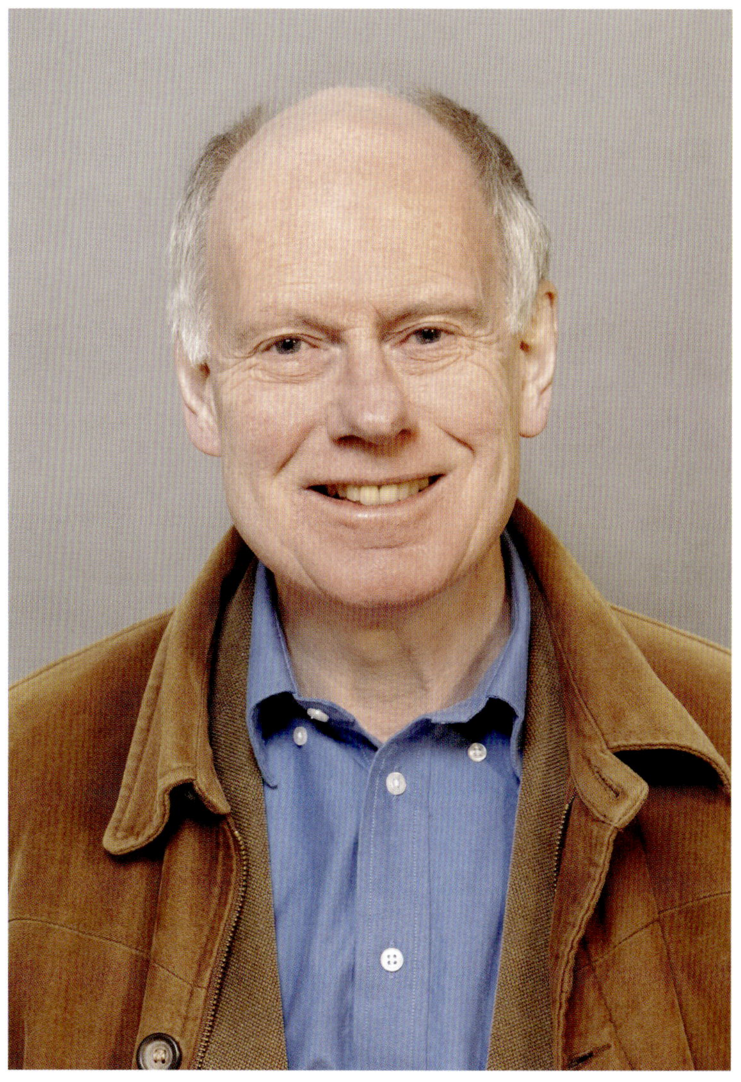

No. 221

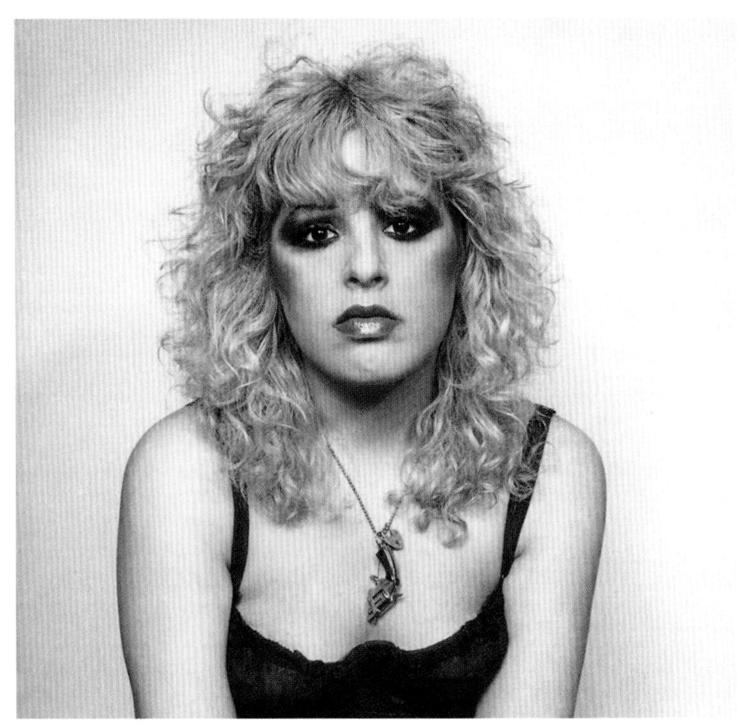

NANCY SPUNGEN

10 August 1978

Sid Vicious's girlfriend came in for what would be her last passport photo. Tragically, she was killed two months later. She was originally wearing a badge that read 'I'm a McLaren puppet', which I suggested she take off for her photo.

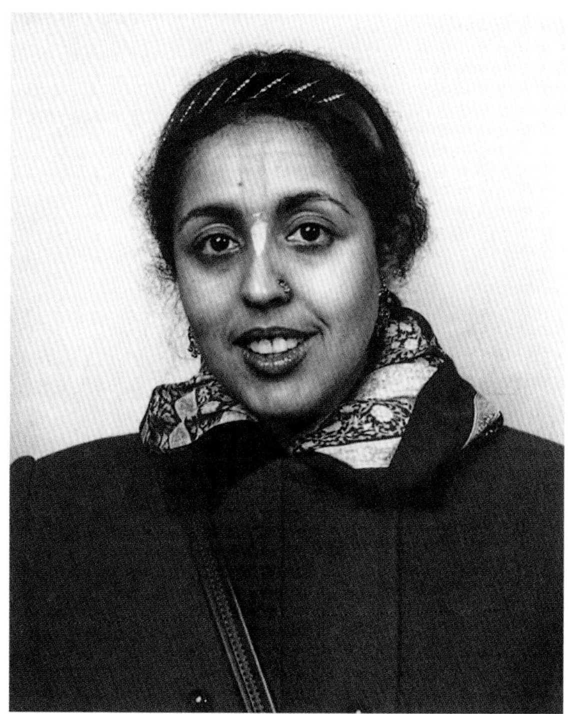

POLY STYRENE

Musician, 28 October 1997

Marianne Joan Elliott-Said, better known by her stage name Poly Styrene, was a dear friend of many years, who died too young. Graeme took a fantastic photo of her and her X-Ray Spex bandmate Lora Logic when they were both involved with the Hare Krishna movement. Marianne would visit often – usually for her India visa, since she remained interested in mysticism – and would always have time to chat about her music, her spiritual beliefs and our mutual friends.

No. 223

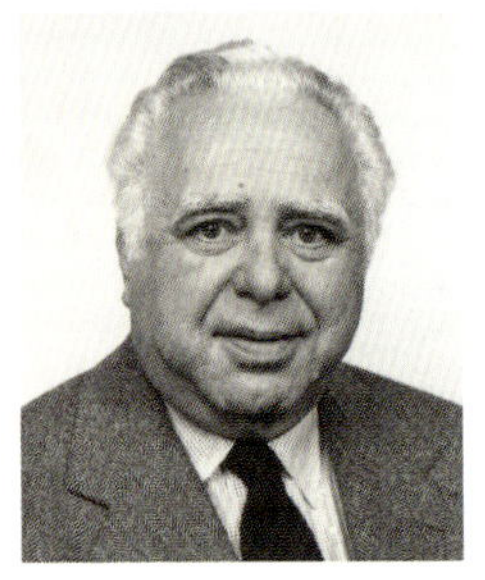

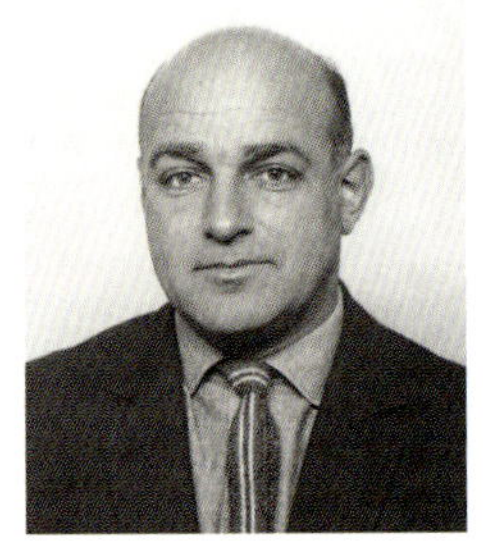

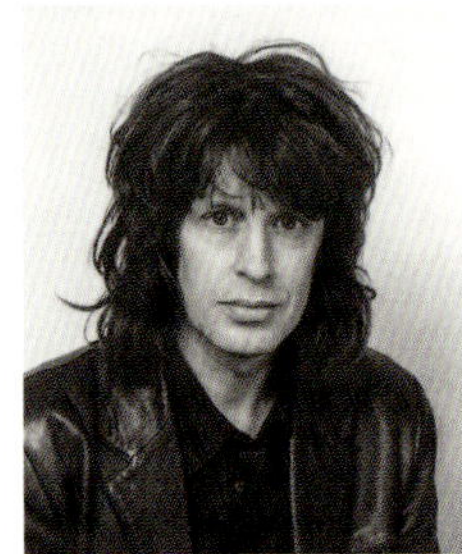

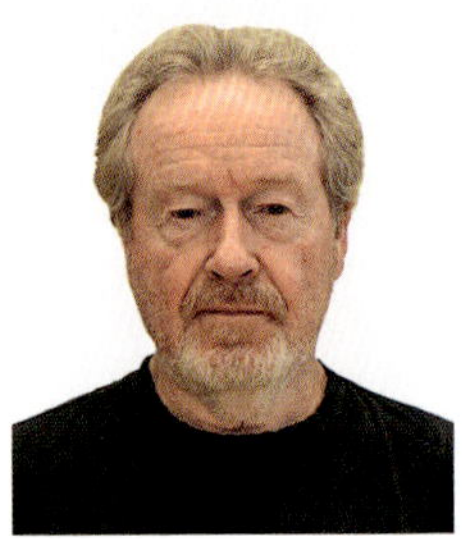

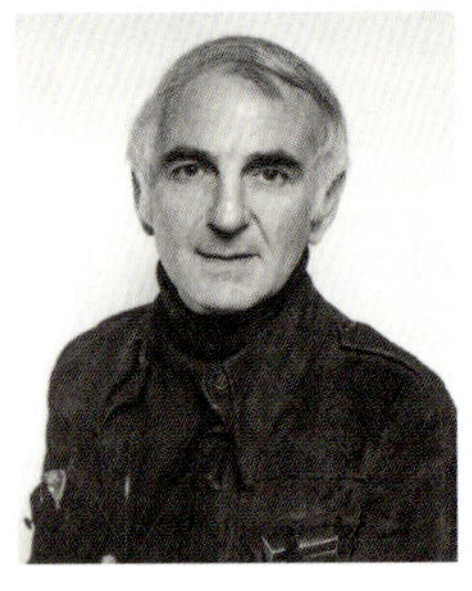

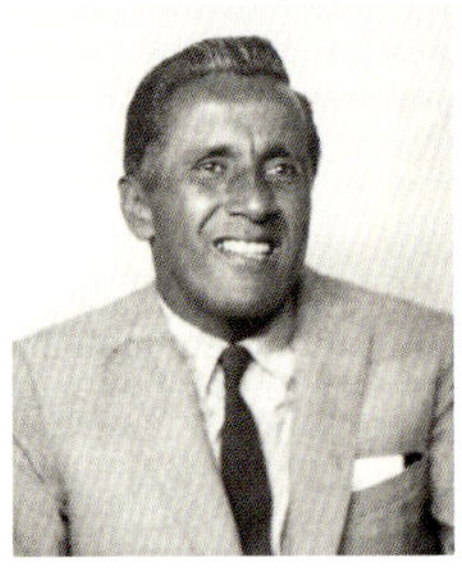

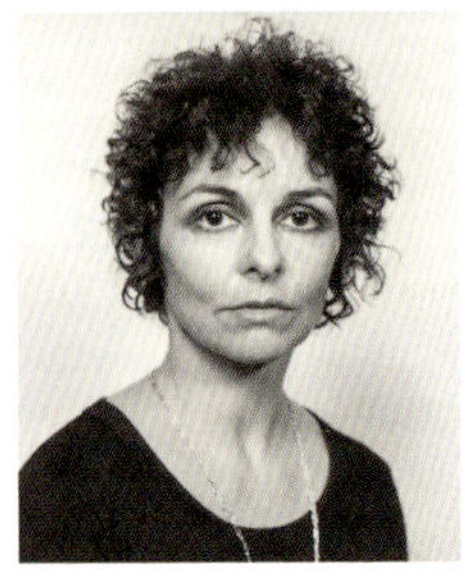

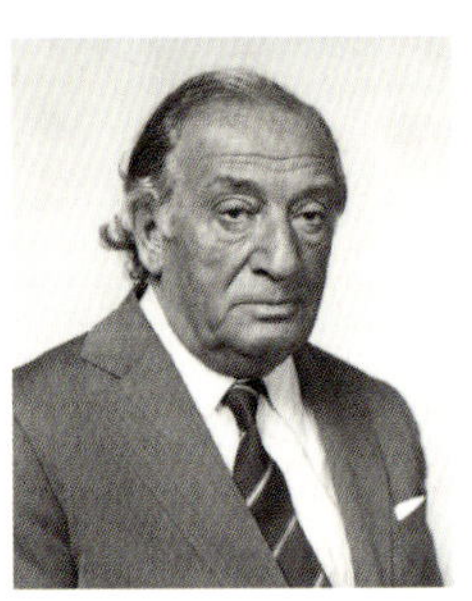

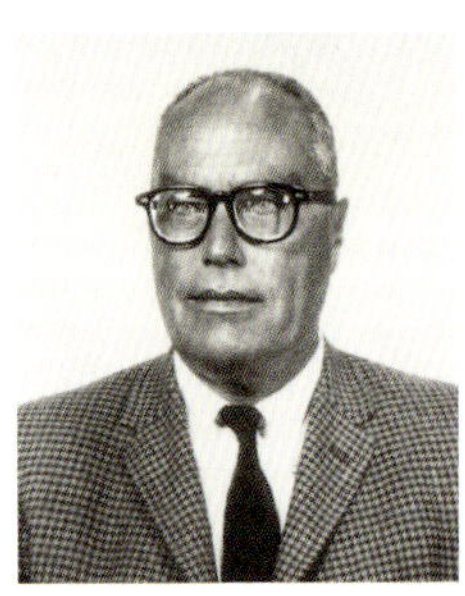

HARRY SALTZMAN
Producer, 1975

RIDLEY SCOTT
Director, 5 October 2011

LYNN SEYMOUR
Ballet dancer,
29 March 1978

JOHN SCHLESINGER
Director, 26 November 1963

RONNIE SCOTT
Musician/Club owner,
20 June 1977

SAM SPIEGEL
Producer, 18 January 1973

MIKE SCOTT
Musician, 12 April 2002

PANCHO SEGURA
Tennis player,
21 November 1960

JOHN STURGES
Director, 3 May 1966

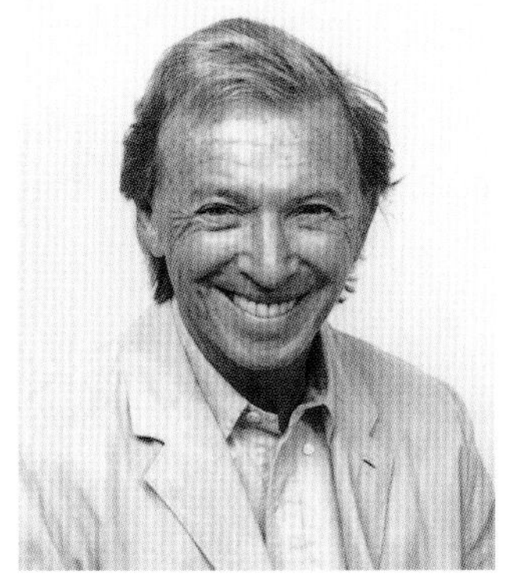

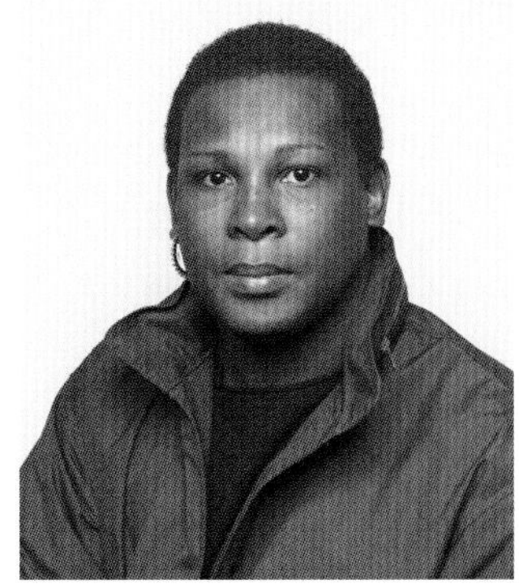

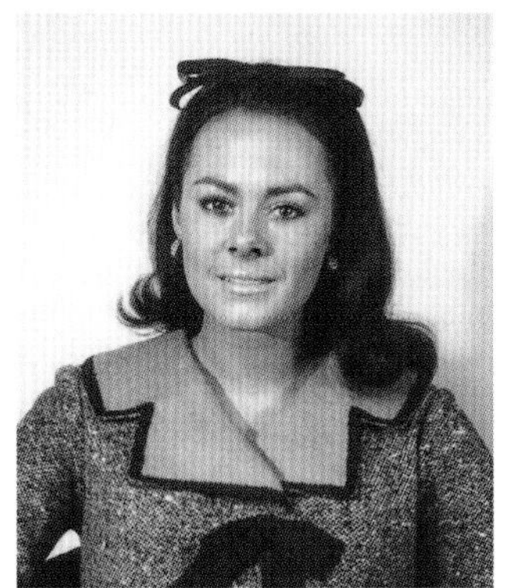

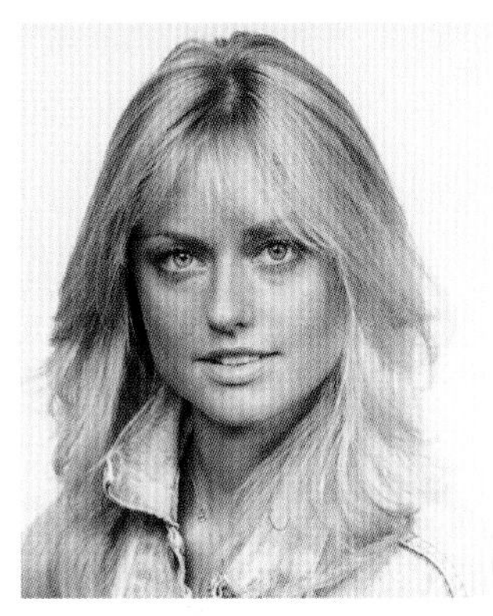

TOMMY STEELE
Actor/Singer, 24 April 2004

SYLVESTER
Musician, 11 November 1982

ANN SIDNEY
Model/Actor, 1964

MARY STÄVIN
Model/Actor, 14 June 1983

RINGO STARR

Musician, 4 August 1987

Ringo came into the studio many times. When Stephen, who was a huge Beatles fan, photographed him, Ringo jokingly advised him, 'Don't have the camera too low or it'll make me hooter look huge.' Stephen also told him that he had an obscure LP that Ringo had released in 1983 called *Old Wave*. Ringo jokingly replied, 'Ah, so you're the person who bought it!' I last photographed Ringo at his flat near the King's Road. After shooting a few frames, he ended the session with his iconic peace sign.

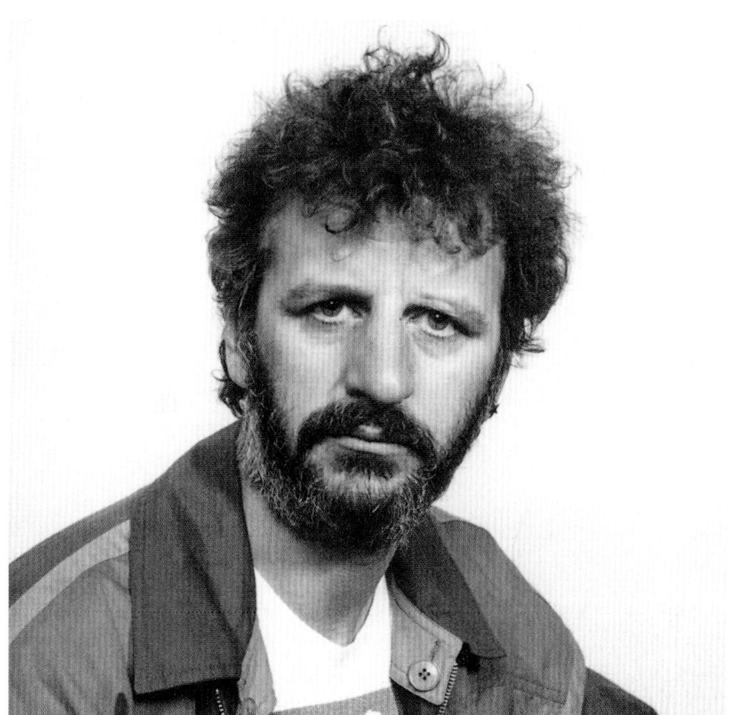

No. 227

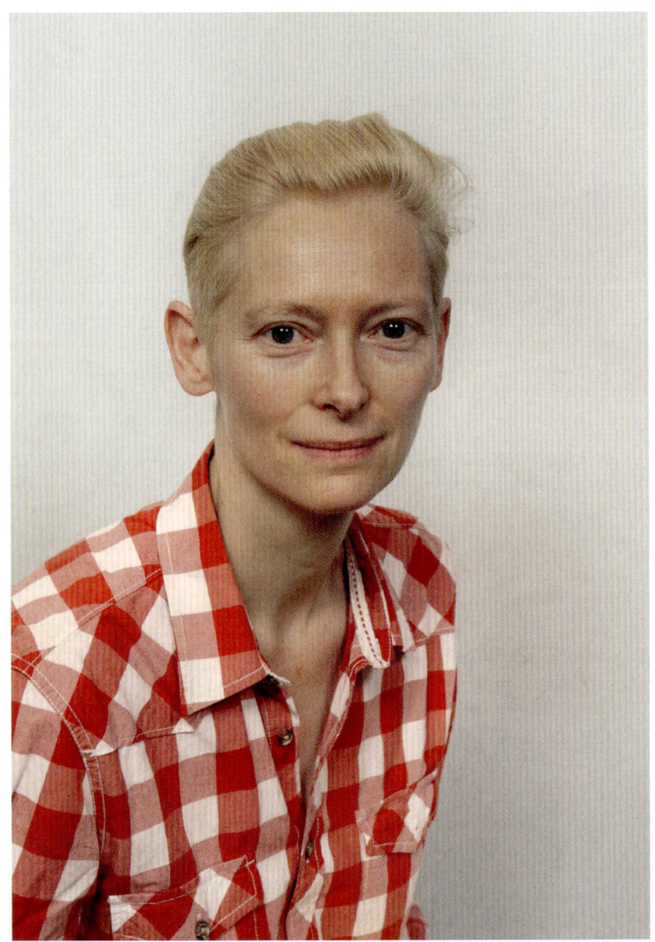

No. 228

TILDA SWINTON

Actor, 18 May 2013

It used to be that you couldn't bring any electronic devices into the US embassy, so we would store things like phones for customers. Sometimes we got lucky, and an interesting person would have to come back twice. After a quick dash in for her visa photo, Tilda Swinton came back to pick up her mobile. She was happy for me to take a nicer, more posed photo for the board. She and her partner stayed and chatted for some time, since they were interested in the storied history of the studio and the fascinating people we had photographed.

No. 229

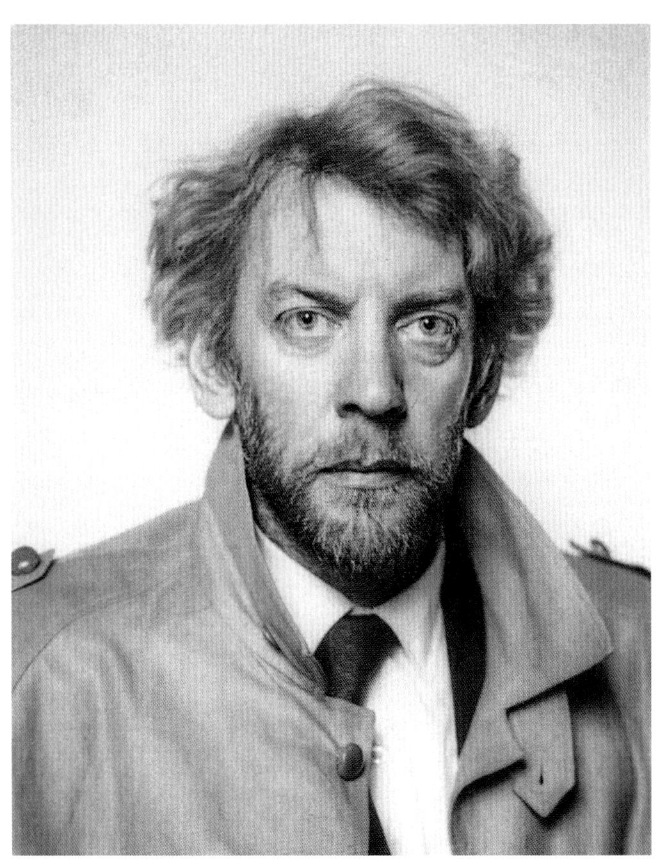

DONALD SUTHERLAND
Actor, 2 May 1977

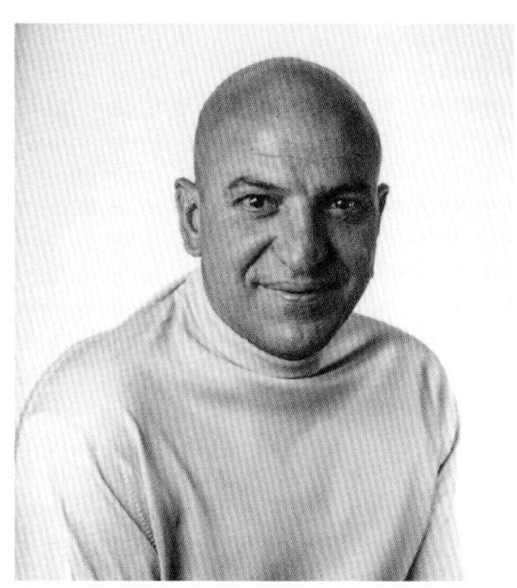

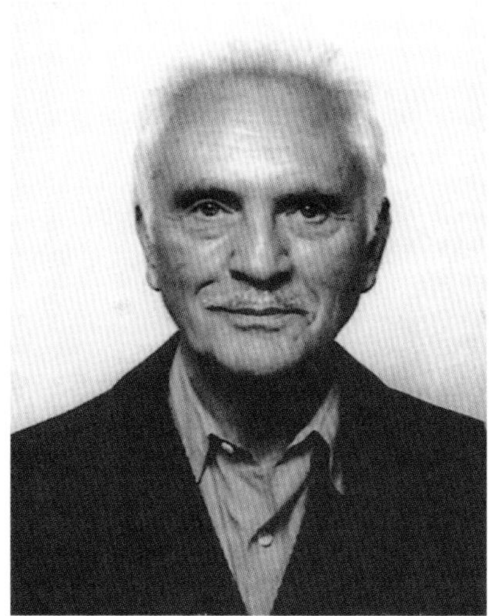

TELLY SAVALAS
Actor, 11 June 1969

TERENCE STAMP
Actor, 19 January 2006

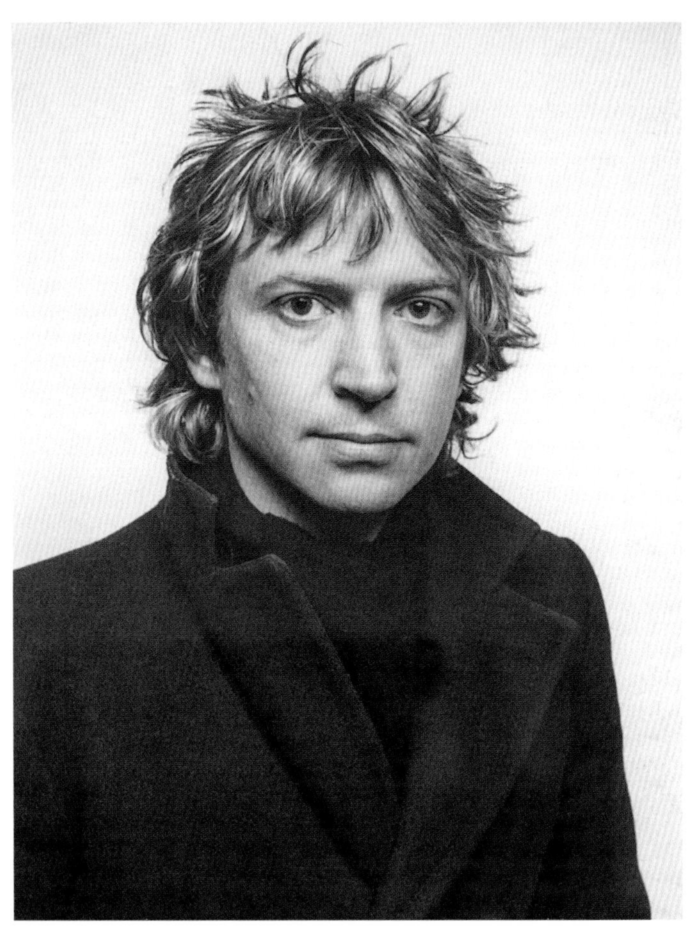

ANDY SUMMERS
Musician, 26 February 1979

No. 232

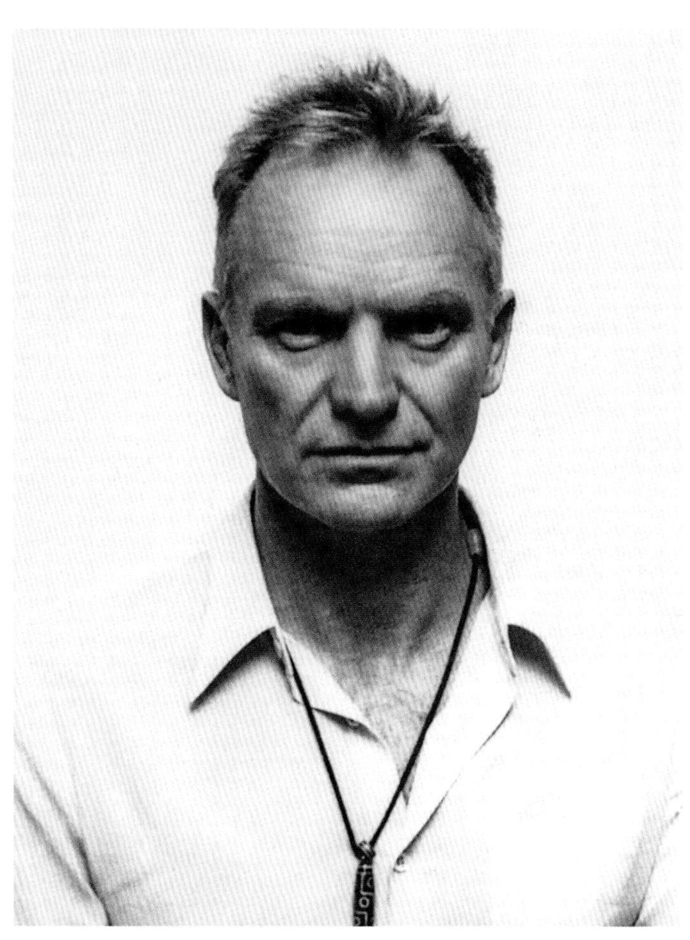

STING
Musician, 3 May 2006

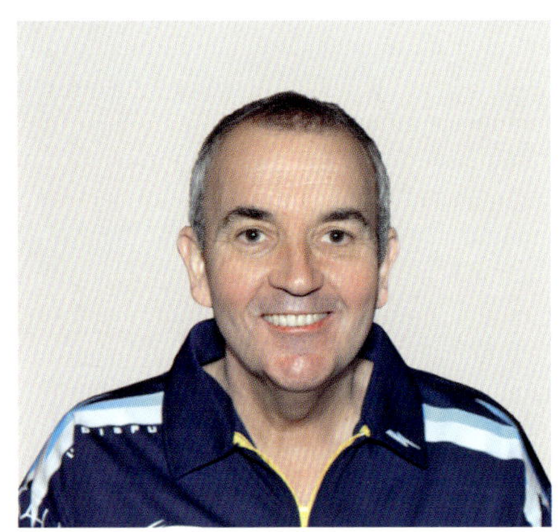

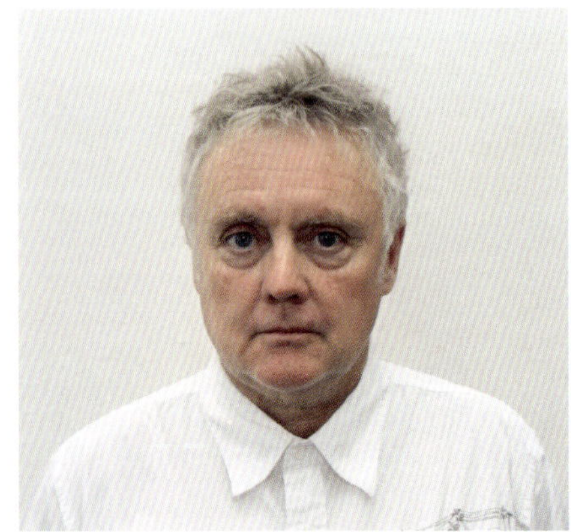

PHIL TAYLOR
Darts player, 3 February 2014

ROGER TAYLOR
Musician, 27 August 2008

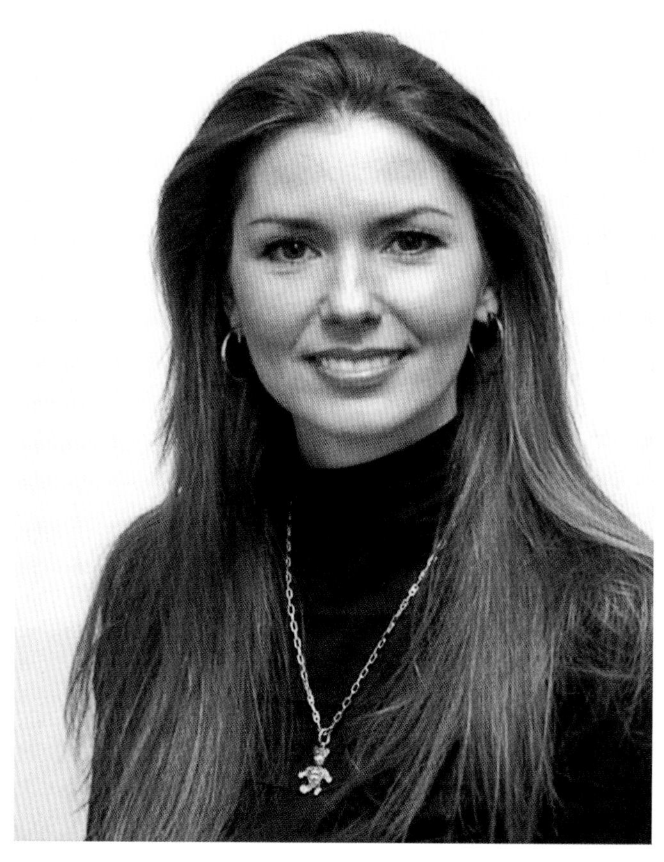

SHANIA TWAIN
Musician, 5 March 2003

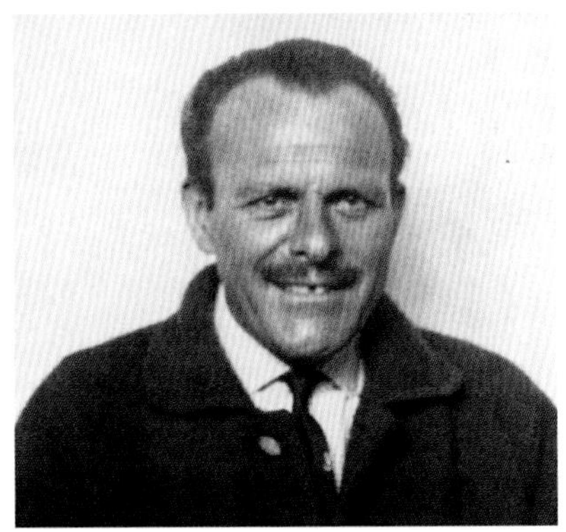

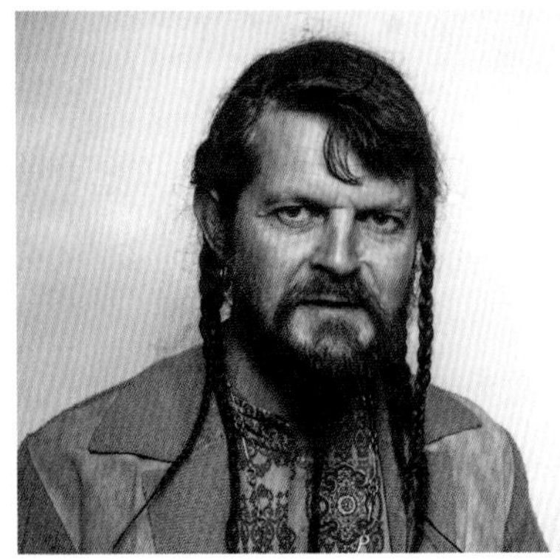

TERRY-THOMAS
Actor, 31 March 1959

ALEXANDER THYNN
7th Marquess of Bath, 1 December 1972

A regular over many years. As his hairstyle in this picture attests, Lord Bath (or Viscount Weymouth, as he was then) was always flamboyant and unconventional.

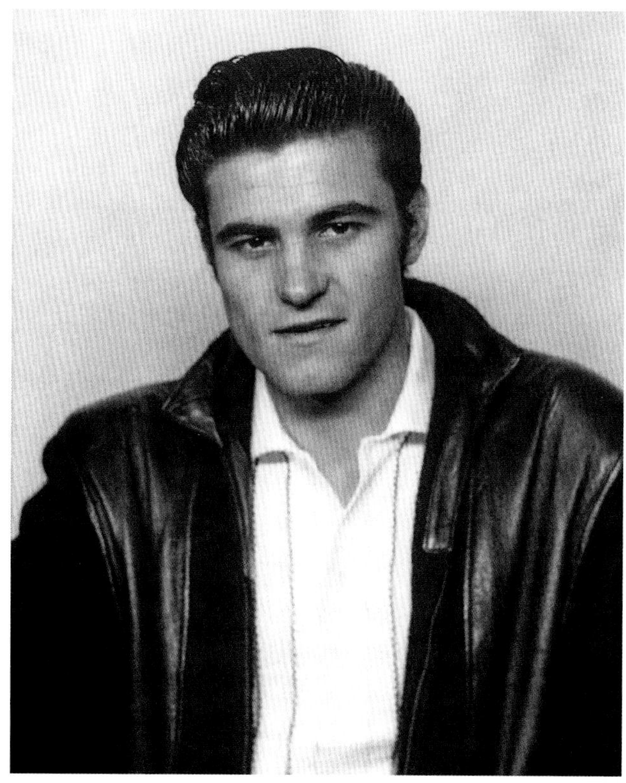

VINCE TAYLOR

Musician, 24 October 1960

Little did we know when we photographed Vince Taylor that the musician would soon become the inspiration for David Bowie's persona Ziggy Stardust. Even though Taylor had only one hit record, he seems to have become a seminal figure in rock 'n' roll history. His song 'Brand New Cadillac' was covered by The Clash on their album *London Calling* (1979), and Adam Ant, Van Morrison (see p.173) and Golden Earring namechecked him in their songs.

GAVIN TURK

Artist, 17 March 2000

The artist Gavin Turk first came into the studio in 1993. At the time, we didn't take his passport photo but instead captured close-ups of his eyes, which he used for the waxwork sculpture *Pop* that he made that year of himself as Sid Vicious posed like Elvis Presley in the famous Andy Warhol painting *Triple Elvis* (1963). He returned a few years later for a regular old passport photo and reminded us about the unorthodox way in which the previous snaps had been used.

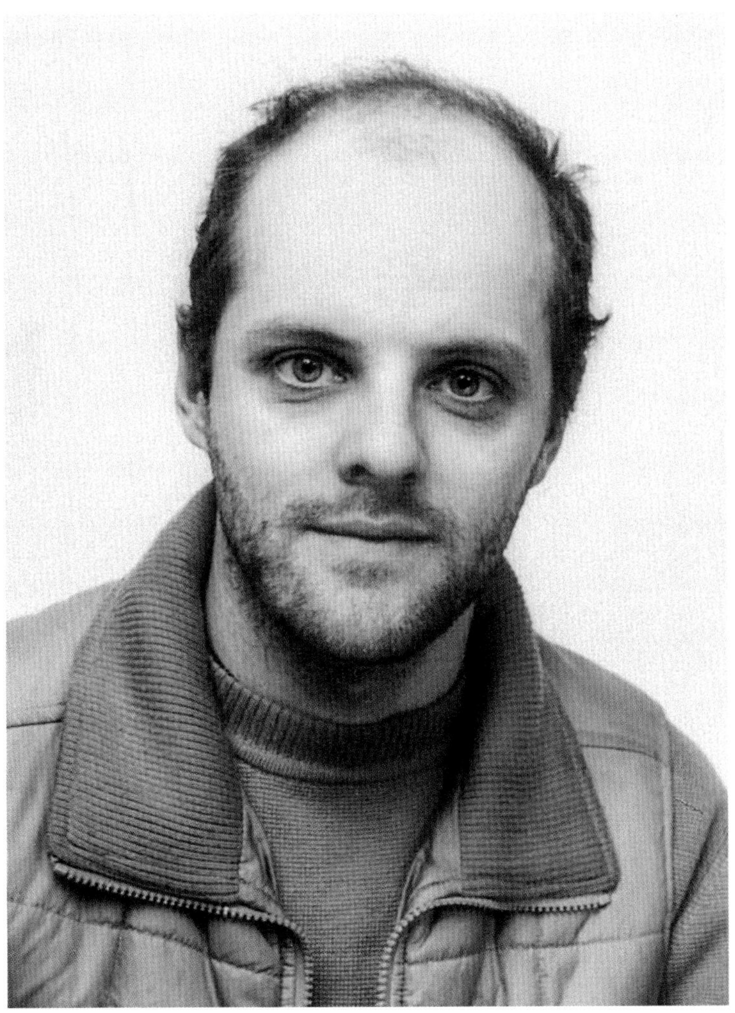

No. 239

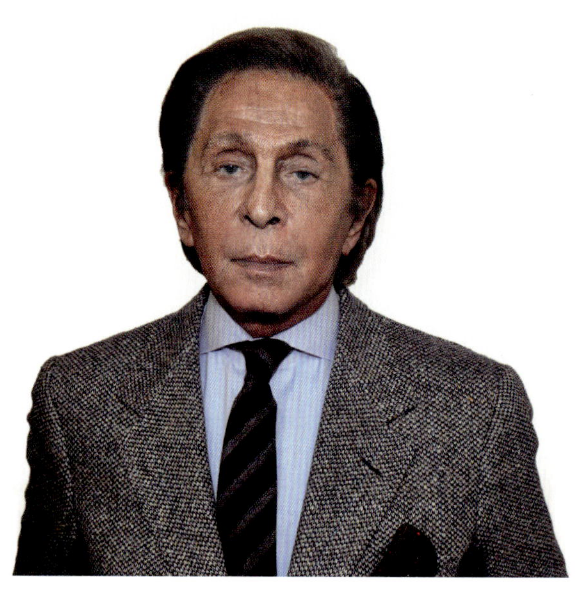

VALENTINO
Fashion designer, 3 October 2013

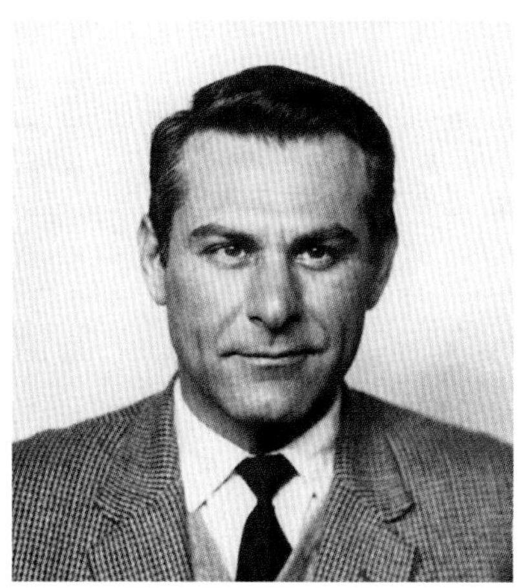

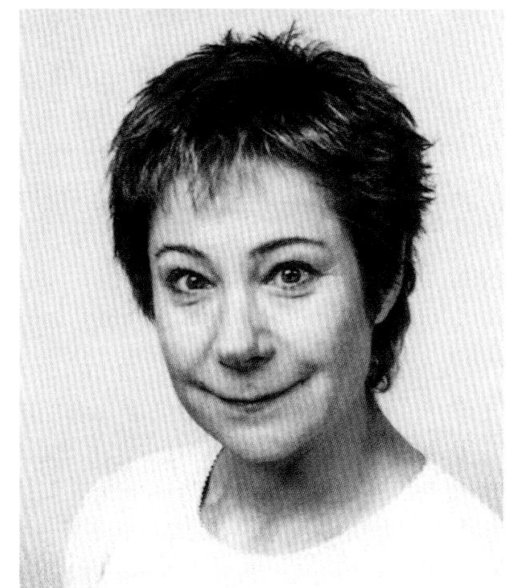

SAM WANAMAKER
Actor/Director, 21 November 1960

ZOË WANAMAKER
Actor, 11 March 1997

No. 241

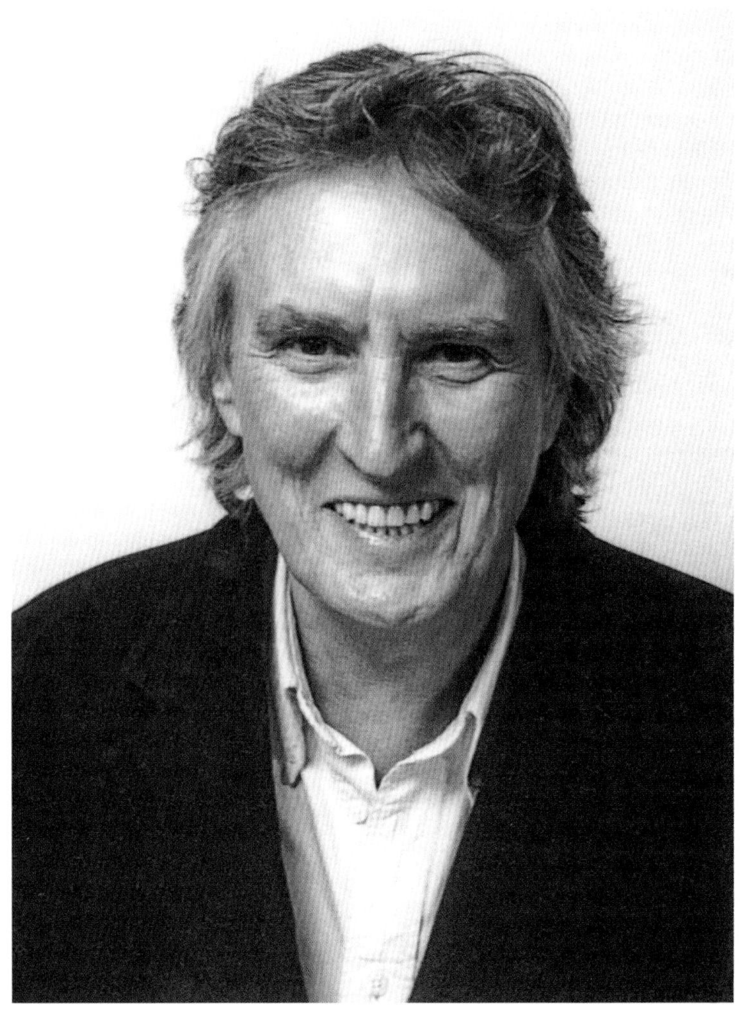

No. 242

JOHNNIE WALKER

Radio DJ, 11 February 2005

The radio DJ Johnnie Walker was another customer who had made the classic mistake of not filling in his DS-160 visa form, which I did for him. This service proved a lifesaver for many, including us, since digital technology had depleted the number of people coming in for photographs. As I was tapping away, I came to the question, 'At what address will you stay during your visit to the US?' Walker replied, 'Oh, I don't know. I'm going out to interview Barry Gibb of the Bee Gees and I'm staying at his house.' 'Well,' I said, 'as we have no way of finding his address, and he probably has the biggest house in Florida, I'll just write "Barry Gibb's House, Florida."' He came back to pick up his mobile phone with a big smile on his face, laughing that our answer had been good enough to please the interviewer.

No. 243

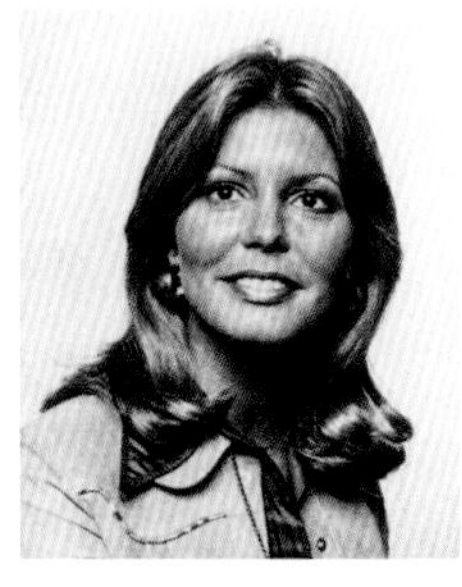
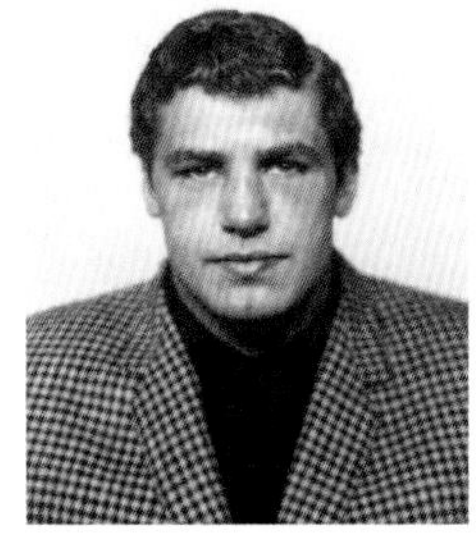
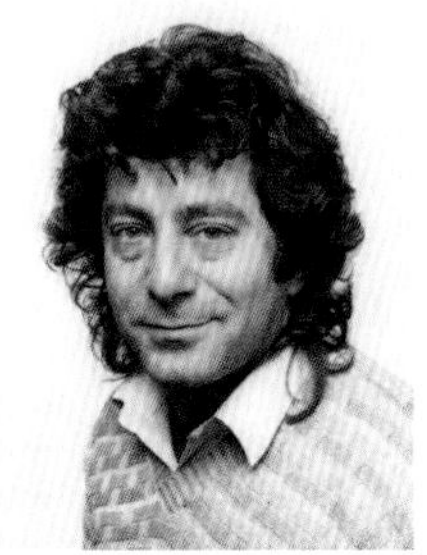
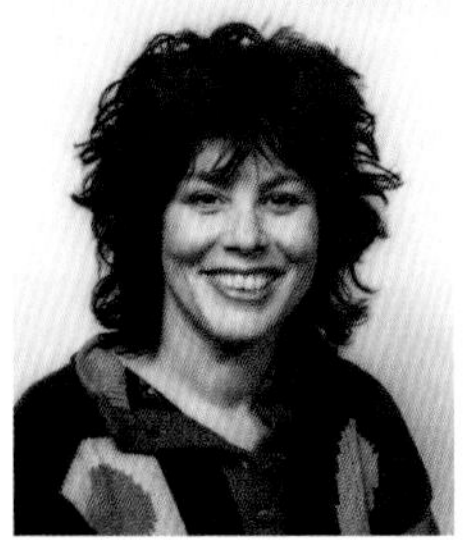
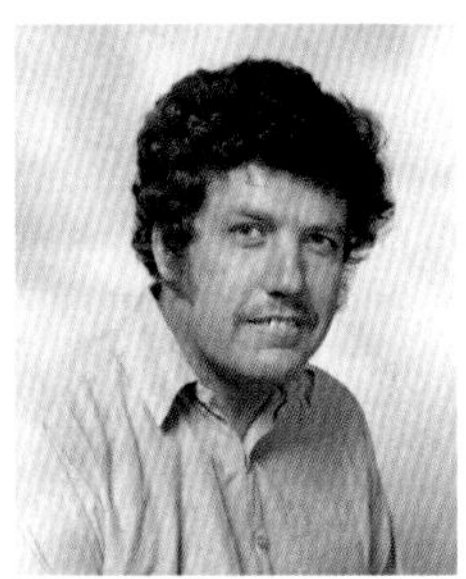
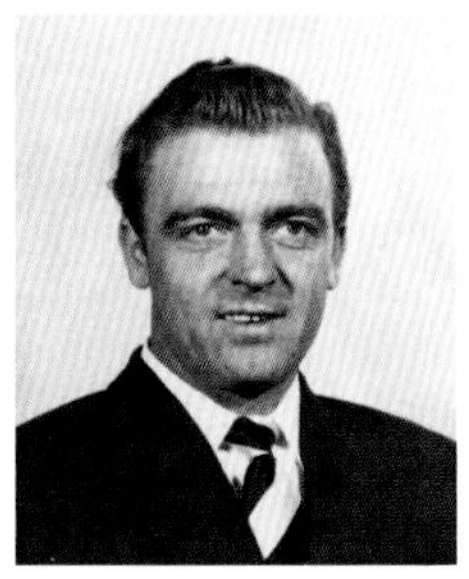
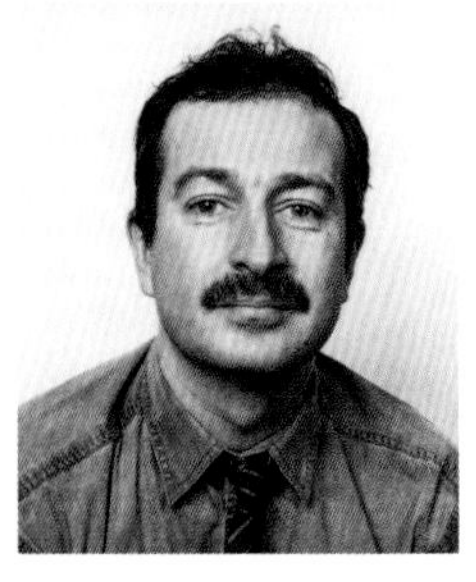
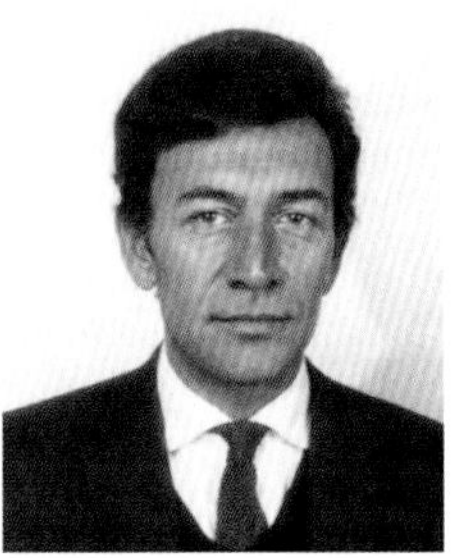
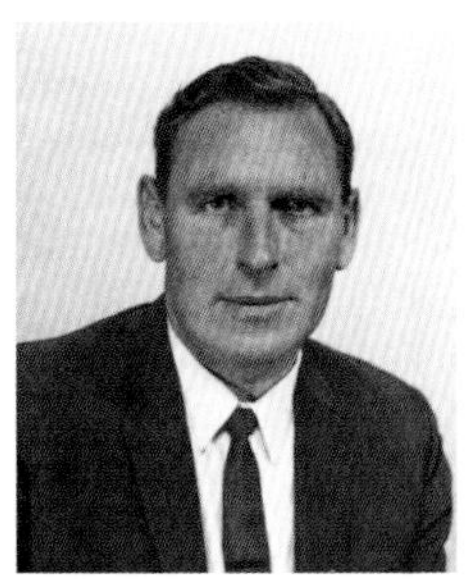

MARJORIE WALLACE
Model, 26 February 1974

RUBY WAX
Actor, 7 January 1994

STEVE WRIGHT
Radio DJ, 24 April 1991

BILLY WALKER
Boxer, 29 November 1962

COLIN WELLAND
Actor/Writer, 1960s

PETER WYNGARDE
Actor, 21 December 1964

JEFF WAYNE
Composer, 17 December 1984

DAVID WHITFIELD
Singer, 1950s

KENNETH WOLSTENHOLME
Football commentator, 1960s

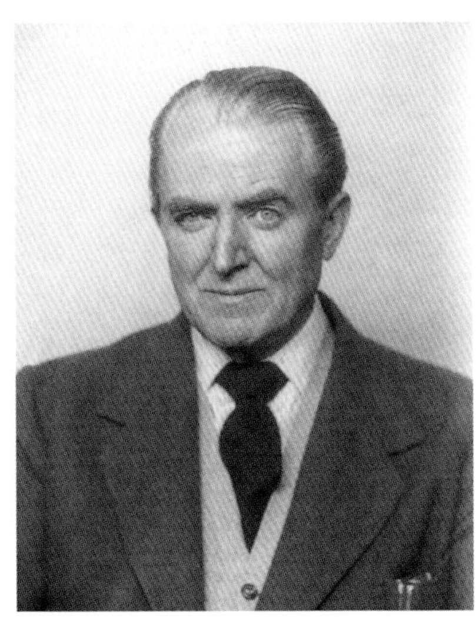

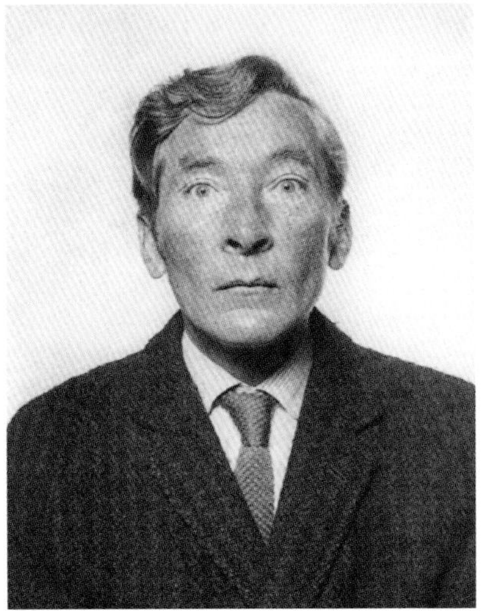

JACK WARNER

Actor, 21 May 1962

Jack Warner was one of the country's most recognizable actors, and his series *Dixon of Dock Green* was enormously popular at the time. He generously gave my father a half-crown ($12\frac{1}{2}$ pence) tip – a lot of money in 1962.

KENNETH WILLIAMS

Actor, 8 January 1975

Kenneth Williams was a challenging subject to photograph and had his own idea of how to pose, with his chin high. I had to take a few shots before he was satisfied. Thankfully, there is no mention of our encounter in his book *The Kenneth Williams Diaries* (1993).

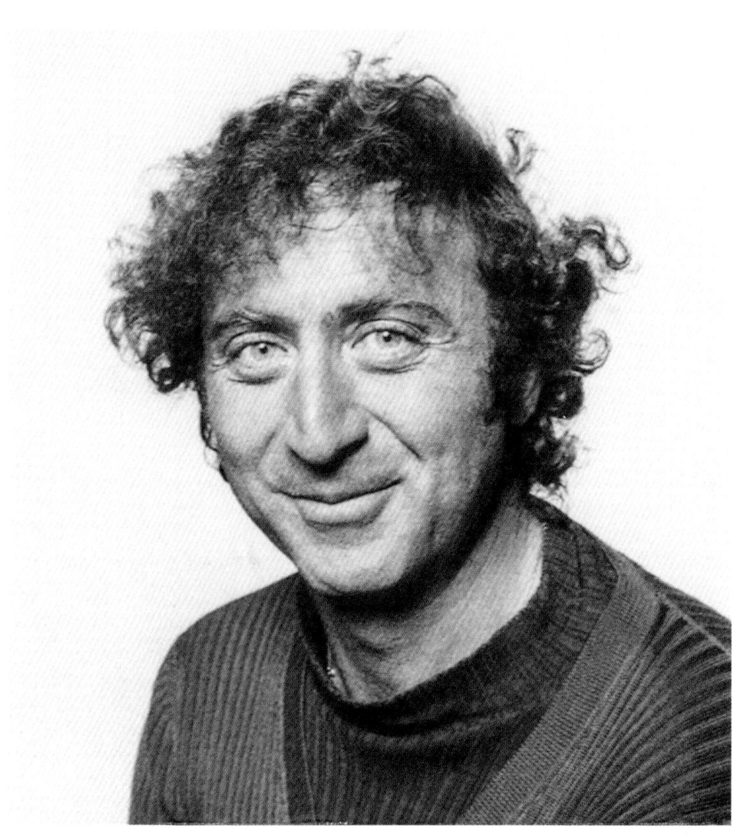

GENE WILDER
Actor, 11 January 1974

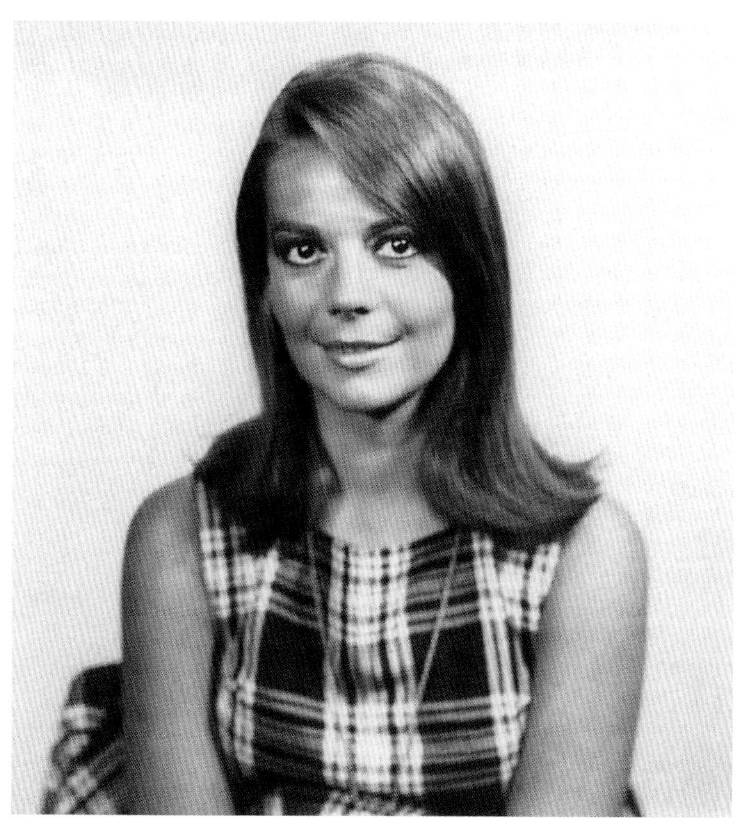

NATALIE WOOD
Actor, 19 May 1967

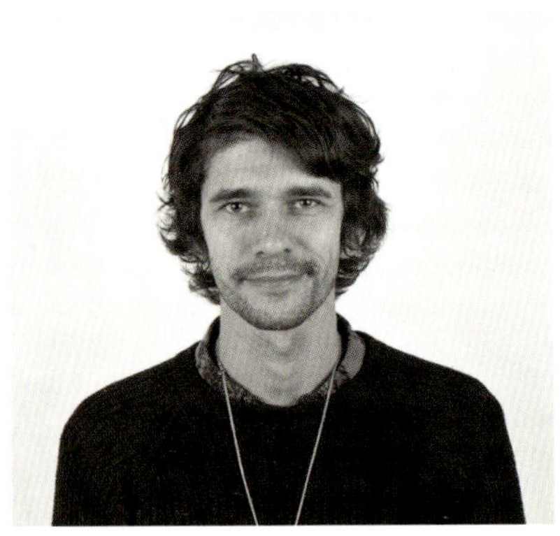

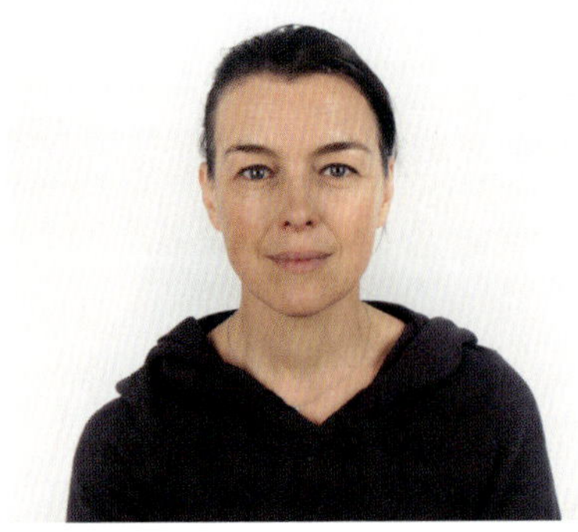

BEN WHISHAW

Actor, 14 March 2019

OLIVIA WILLIAMS

Actor, 14 September 2015

Baffled by the complexities of her US visa application, Olivia Williams thankfully found Lisa Carr, an expert in all things visa and a great friend of the studio, bringing us many celebrity clients. Ms Williams gave us a lovely mention in her *Telegraph* article about Lisa from 2012.

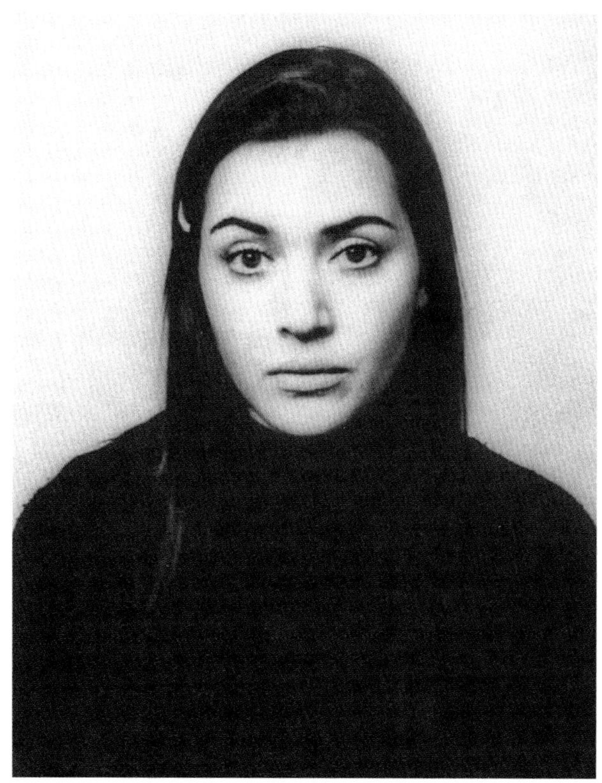

KATE WINSLET

Actor, 2 October 1997

Ms Winslet came in for a passport photo that wasn't actually for her own passport, but for her character's in the movie *Hideous Kinky*, which came out in 1998. Her stylist from the film set was on hand to dress her up and style her hair as the 1960s hippie chick she played in the film.

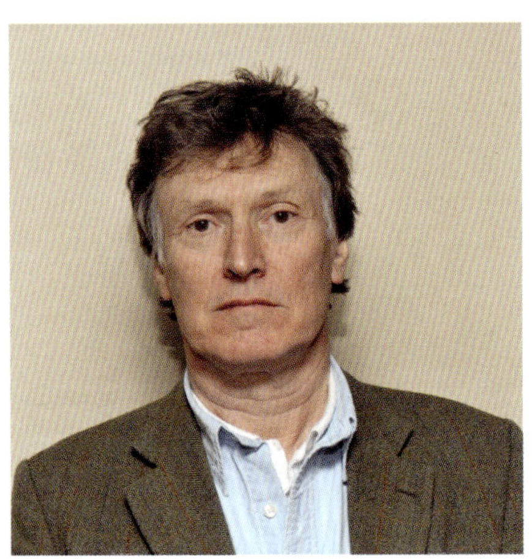

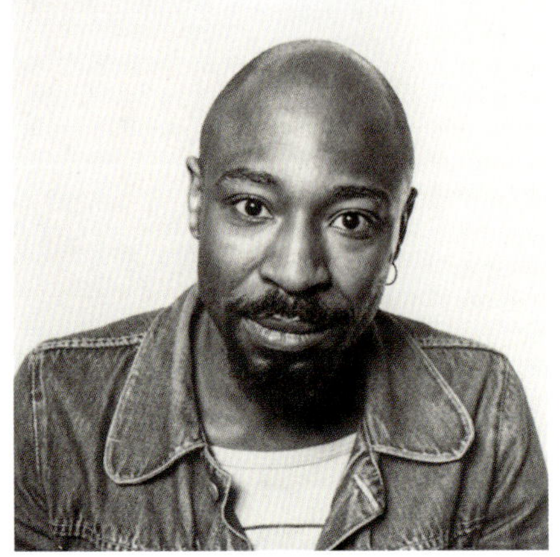

STEVE WINWOOD
Musician, 1 June 2011

GENO WASHINGTON
Musician, 1975

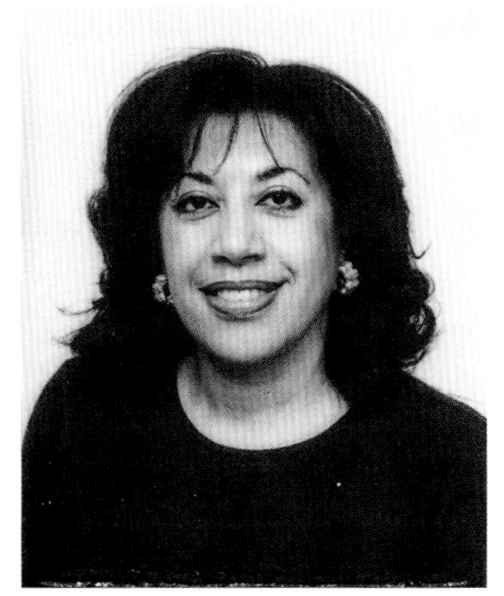

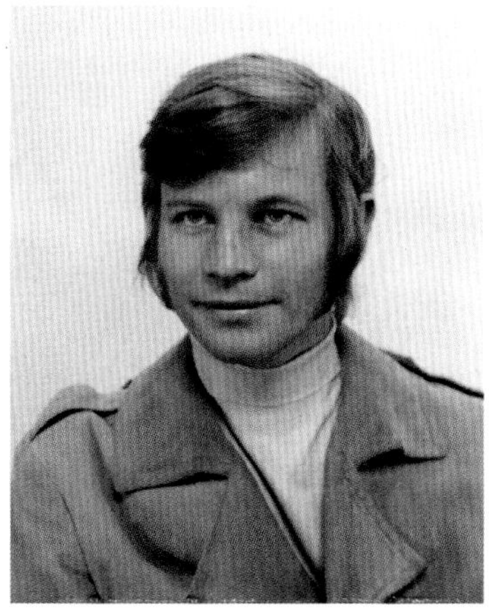

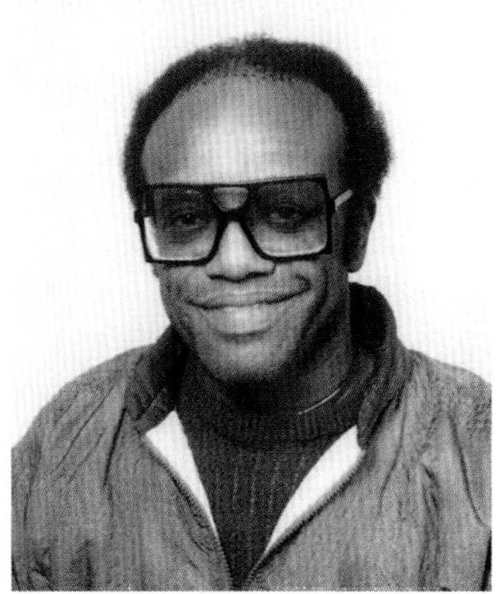

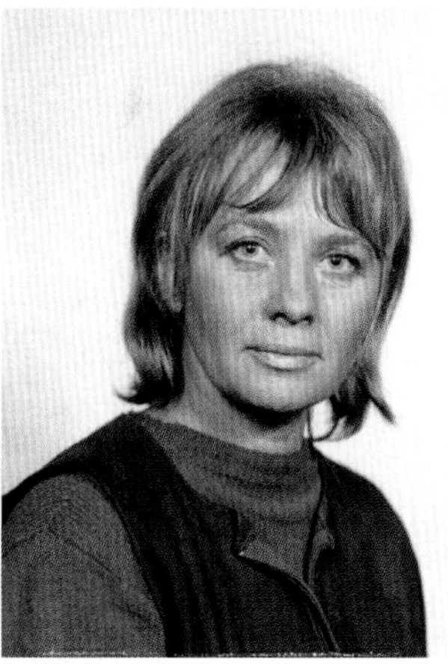

MARY WILSON
Singer, 15 February 2000

BOBBY WOMACK
Musician, 21 January 1987

MICHAEL YORK
Actor, 1968

MAI ZETTERLING
Actor/Director, 1972

INDEX

Page numbers in *italics* refer to illustrations

Phaidon Press Limited
2 Cooperage Yard
London E15 2QR

Phaidon Press Inc.
111 Broadway
New York, NY 10006

Phaidon SARL
55, rue Traversière
75012 Paris

phaidon.com

First published 2026
Reprinted 2026

ISBN 978 1 83729 122 9

A CIP catalogue record for this book is available from the British Library and the Library of Congress.

Commissioning Editor: Deborah Aaronson
Project Editor: Olivia Clark
Production Controllers: Gary Hayes and Adela Cory
Design: Associate

Printed in China